Key Concepts in
Medical
Sociology

Recent volumes include:

Key Concepts in Social Research
Geoff Payne and Judy Payne

Fifty Key Concepts in Gender Studies
Jane Pilcher and Imelda Whelahan

Forthcoming titles include:

Key Concepts in Leisure Studies
David Harris

Key Concepts in Critical Social Theory
Nick Crossley

Key Concepts in Urban Studies
Mark Gottdiener

The SAGE Key Concepts series provide students with accessible and authoritative knowledge of the essential topics in a variety of disciplines. Cross-referenced throughout, the format encourages critical evaluation through understanding. Written by experienced and respected academics, the books are indispensable study aids and guides to comprehension.

JONATHAN GABE, MIKE BURY
AND MARY ANN ELSTON

Key Concepts in
Medical
Sociology

SAGE Publications
London • Thousand Oaks • New Delhi

SAGE Publications Ltd
1 Oliver's Yard
55 City Road
London EC1Y 1SP

SAGE Publications Inc
2455 Teller Road
Thousand Oaks
California 91320

SAGE Publications India Pvt. Ltd
B–42 Panchsheel Enclave
PO Box 4109
New Delhi 110 017

British Library Cataloguing in Publication data
A catalogue record for this book is available from the British Library

ISBN-10 0-7619-7441-5   ISBN-13 978-0-7619-7441-3
ISBN-10 0-7619-7442-3 (pbk)   ISBN-13 978-0-7619-7442-0 (pbk)

Printed on paper from sustainable sources

Typeset by M Rules, Southwark, London
Printed and bound in Great Britain by
Cromwell Press Limited, Trowbridge, Wiltshire

contents

vi

contributors

AB   Antonia Bifulco, Reader in Mental Health, Department of Health and Social Care, Royal Holloway, University of London.

CN   Chris Ntau, Doctoral Candidate, Department of Social and Political Science, Royal Holloway, University of London.

CS   Clive Seale, Professor of Sociology, Department of Human Sciences, Brunel University.

DV   Denny Vågerö, Professor of Medical Sociology and Director of the Centre for Health Equity Studies, University of Stockholm.

GW   Gareth H. Williams, Professor of Sociology, School of Social Sciences, Cardiff University.

JG   Judith Green, Senior Lecturer in Sociology, Health Services Research Unit, London School of Hygiene and Tropical Medicine, University of London.

JGA   Jonathan Gabe, Reader in Sociology, Department of Social and Political Science, Royal Holloway, University of London.

JN   James Nazroo, Professsor of Medical Sociology, Department of Epidemiology and Public Heath, University College London Medical School, London.

JS   Jane Sandall, Professor of Midwifery and Women's Health, Florence Nightingale School of Nursing and Midwifery, Kings College, London.

KB   Karen Ballard, Lecturer, Department of General Practice and Primary Care, King's College, London.

KL   Karen Lowton, lecturer, Florence Nightingale School of Nursing and Midwifery, King's College, London.

LM   Liz Meerabeau, Professor and Head of School of Health and Social Care, University of Greenwich, London.

LY   Liz Young, Research Fellow, Department of Health and Human Sciences, University of Essex.

MAE	Mary Ann Elston, Reader in Medical Sociology, Department of Social and Political Science, Royal Holloway, University of London.
MB	Mike Bury, Emeritus Professor of Sociology, Department of Social and Political Science, Royal Holloway, University of London.
MBO	Mary Boulton, Professor of Sociology, School of Social Sciences and Law, Oxford Brookes University.
RF	Ray Fitzpatrick, Professor of Public Health and Primary Care, Institute of Health Sciences, University of Oxford.
SA	Sara Arber, Professor of Sociology, Department of Sociology, University of Surrey.
SC	Sarah Cant, Senior Lecturer in Applied Social Sciences, Canterbury Christchurch University College.
SM	Sally Macintyre, Professor of Medical Sociology and Director of the MRC Social and Public Heath Sciences Unit, University of Glasgow.
SN	Sarah Nettleton, Senior Lecturer in Social Policy, Department of Social Policy and Social Work, University of York.
SR	Susan Robinson, Research Associate, Department of General Practice and Primary Care, King's College, London.
SW	Simon Williams, Reader in Sociology, Department of Sociology, University of Warwick.

viii

introduction

Sociology can relate to health and illness in two different ways (Bury, 1997: 4). On the one hand, a sociological perspective can be applied to the experience and social distribution of health and health disorders and to the institutions through which care and cure are provided. In this sense, medical sociology can have an applied orientation to understanding and improving health, and can be seen as one of many disciplines that might appropriately be studied by providers of health care. On the other hand, the sociological study of health, illness and institutions of health care can stand alongside analysis of other significant social experiences and institutions, as a means of understanding the society under study. Thus, medical sociology is also a theoretically orientated field, committed to explaining large-scale social transformations and their implications, as well as interactions in everyday settings, as these are expressed in health and illness.

These two aspects of medical sociology have, in a well-worn phrase, been characterized as sociology *in* medicine and sociology *of* medicine (Straus, 1957). This double-edged character is, in our view, one of the reasons why medical sociology is such an exciting, challenging and rewarding field to work in. We hope that this book helps guide students through some of the complexities of the field, encouraging further study and equipping the reader with knowledge to understand health and illness, whether as a sociology student, a health care professional in training, or an already experienced practitioner. Many excellent medical sociology textbooks and readers have been published in English. We have chosen to add this book of 'Concepts' to the learning resources available to students in a somewhat different and unusual form: a collection of short, highly focused essays on particular topics.

The aim behind the 'key concepts' approach is to provide students with systematic, easily accessible information about the building blocks of the field of medical sociology. We have selected key concepts (defined loosely here to include substantive issues) which have preoccupied medical sociologists in the past 30 years and which have shaped the field as it exists today. For each of one of these concepts, contributors were asked to write an entry that covered the origin of the concept or the background to the issue, an account of its subsequent development and, where relevant, an assessment of its significance to the field. Each entry is preceded by a working definition. These were not always easy to write because some of the concepts are contested within the literature. The definitions serve to give an immediate orientation to readers. The text that follows elaborates on the definition, identifying controversies and variations in use. Thus, the entries go beyond the inevitable over-simplification of a dictionary, or of the passing references that many concepts receive in textbooks. By following cross-references, a picture of the relationship between different concepts can be built up. The short bibliography given at the end of each entry provides suggestions for further reading.

Before we describe the contents of the book in more detail, we present a short account of the recent development of medical sociology, which brings out its dual orientation, to sociology and to health care. We hope that this will help the reader to understand the context in which the field and its key concepts have been shaped.

THE DEVELOPMENT OF MEDICAL SOCIOLOGY

Thirty-five years ago, medical sociology was a scarcely known subfield of the then controversial but expanding discipline of sociology. Those who called themselves medical sociologists were few and far between. Moreover, they were usually working on applied projects related to public health and social aspects of medicine, often located in medical schools. In doing this, sociologists were continuing a long, diverse tradition of research into the relationship between social factors and health in Europe and North America (Bloom, 2000). However, as academic departments of sociology grew in the 1960s, and developed a strongly theoretical orientation, the study of health and illness was sometimes regarded with disdain as being 'an applied activity . . . lacking in theoretical substance' (Bird et al., 2000: 1). Yet today, medical sociology is the largest specialist professional study group within both British and North American sociology, and thrives in many other parts of the world, notably Australia and New Zealand and the Nordic countries. Sometimes, it will be found under alternative designations, such as the 'sociology of health and illness': the term 'medical' being regarded by some as evoking too strong an association with one particular health care profession and with pathology, rather than health. But, whatever the terminology (and in this volume we have chosen to retain the older title), courses which examine sociological aspects of health and disease and health care are now almost ubiquitous offerings within undergraduate sociology programmes, as marked by the number of textbooks (for example, Annandale, 1998) and readers (Albrecht et al., 2000; Bird et al., 2000).

As a result, medical sociology can no longer be regarded as an isolated and applied specialism within its parent discipline. In recent years, there has been increasing rapprochement between long-standing analytical concerns of medical sociology and new issues in sociological theory, most notably in the growing theoretical interest in sociological aspects of embodiment (for example, Nettleton and Watson, 1998; Williams and Bendelow, 1998), emotions (for example, James and Gabe, 1996) and risk (for example, Gabe, 1995; Green, 1997). At the same time, medical sociologists have been increasingly, and successfully, working across the boundaries with other sociological or interdisciplinary fields, for example, criminology (Timmermans and Gabe, 2003) and social studies of science and technology (Elston, 1997).

A further area of growing medical sociology research that crosses disciplinary borderlands has been that concerned with studying the organization of health care and health policy. The accessibility and quality of health care are significant issues for citizens of any country and, at least in affluent countries, health care (public and/or private) is a major component of the domestic economy and one of the largest employers of labour. Moreover, almost all affluent and many less affluent countries, have experienced major reforms to their health care systems since the 1970s. Sociological analysis of these changes and their significance has brought new vigour to the academic study of health policy (for example, Green and Thorogood, 1998).

So, medical sociology has now established a secure and prominent place in the social science academe. But this has not been at the expense of its applied institutional roots. In the 1960s and early 1970s, although medical sociologists were mainly to be found in medical schools, their position there was generally a marginal one. Three decades later, the place of social science is far more central in radically revised medical curricula. Sociology textbooks for medical students are now well established and undergo regular revision (for example, Armstrong, 2003; Scambler, 2003). And, with the increasing incorporation of professional education for nurses and professions allied to medicine within universities, new medical sociology courses for a wider range of health care students have been burgeoning, as have those for qualified professionals, for example through the distance learning programmes of institutions such as the Open University in the United Kingdom.[1]

Thus, at the start of a new millennium, medical sociology is a subject studied by a wide range of students: some intent on pursuing a career in one of the health professions, some, at the other end of the spectrum, with strong theoretical interests in post-modernist social theory. One of the impetuses behind this book was our concern that all such students should have the opportunity to learn about the building blocks of their chosen subject.

KEY CONCEPTS: STRUCTURE AND CONTENTS OF THE BOOK

Selecting our key concepts has inevitably involved some difficult decisions about what to omit. Other medical sociologists' final list might have looked a little different, but would differ, we believe, only a little. Most of our colleagues would agree, we think, that the topics we have chosen are ones that have significantly shaped the discipline, even if we have not been able to include all possible candidates for this accolade. In line with our commitment to giving readers a sense of how medical sociology has developed, we have probably erred (in the eyes of some) in favour of including classic concepts rather than opting only for those of obvious current (and possibly ephemeral) interest. Talking only in terms of 'concepts' is less than ideal, but in selecting topics we have recognized that, in addition to the key concepts that have been regularly used in medical sociological analysis, there are recurrent substantive issues or particular approaches which cannot easily be captured by single concepts.

The entries have been grouped into five themes that, between them, cover a substantial proportion of medical sociological research and scholarship. And there is, of course, overlap between the five themes, as reflected in the cross-references made between entries.

Part 1 is concerned with the social patterning of health, and is itself sub-divided into two sections: health inequalities and the social causation of health. In the first sub-section, entries describe the key social divisions within, and, by including an entry on health and development, between societies. The entries set out the ways in which such divisions have been shown to be associated with various measures of health status, and discuss the ways in which such concepts have been operationalized. The study of inequalities in relation to occupational social class has been particularly prominent in the United Kingdom and the Nordic countries. However, as the other entries in the section show, age, gender, ethnicity and place of residence are all associated with the distribution of life chances and with health. The entries show how research deploying these concepts has developed through collaboration with other disciplines such as epidemiology.

Understanding how this social patterning of health comes about requires moving beyond statistical correlations. The second group of entries in Part 1 outlines some of the different conceptual approaches that have been used to study the causes of health inequalities. One of the striking aspects of this section is how clearly the different approaches can be related to classic sociological debates. The relative role in health causation of ideas and values compared to material factors in shaping social change and individual behaviour, and the significance of social integration for health are concerns that would be recognizable to the discipline's founding European triumvirate, Karl Marx, Max Weber and Emile Durkheim. However, pathways linking social and biological factors in health outcomes have been the focus of new debates about lifecourse influences in recent years, and these are reflected in chapters here.

In Part 2, the sociological themes are ones that derive more directly from North American traditions of sociology, in the form of functionalism and symbolic interactionism, with the conception of illness as a form of deviance linking the two. Sociological studies of the experience and meaning of illness and of interacting with professionals have, indubitably, generated concepts that have had a profound impact on both sociology as a discipline and on the delivery of care. Arguably, the concepts of stigma, uncertainty, and quality of life have become so taken-for-granted in discussions of health care, that their origins in particular concerns and the ways in which their use may have changed can be overlooked. Few sociology students go back, for example, to Parsons' (1951) original formulation of the sick role and the doctor-patient relationship and, as a result, often fail to appreciate fully either the context in which Parsons wrote or that his concept of the sick role was a depiction of normative expectations not of actual behaviours. Other contributions to this section cover concepts that have risen to prominence more recently, such as that of illness narrative, embodiment, risk and the highly contested concept of disability (Bury, 1996). In developing and using these concepts, medical sociology has sought to move beyond uni-dimensional accounts of illness as deviance to link with more general concerns with self-identity and cultural meaning that characterize early twenty-first-century societies. The experience of illness can therefore be seen to reflect and contribute to the shaping of contemporary cultures. The emphasis on personal narratives in studies of illness has expressed this central motif, both for sociology and the wider society.

Knowledge of and practice about health are the themes of Part 3. Here the entries begin by discussing what has, at times, been regarded as not so much a useful analytical concept, but more an object to be attacked: the medical model. Underpinning this model is scientific knowledge about

xiii

the working of the human body and the next two entries examine recurrent concerns of medical sociology: the social shaping of this scientific knowledge and the relationship between it and the knowledge of, and understanding of, health and illness of lay people. In health care, scientific knowledge and technologies are combined to create forms of practice in which professionals and lay people interact. In recent years, there has been growing medical sociological interest in how this interaction is shaped, particularly in relation to innovative technologies such as those increasingly involved in the management of reproduction and in genetic medicine. Finally, reflecting the influence of the French social thinker, Michel Foucault, on medical sociology, another growing area of practice is discussed, that concerned with monitoring and promoting the health of populations. This area discusses the tension between promoting the welfare of patients and the role of health care – especially health promotion – in effecting surveillance and 'disciplinary power' over the behaviour of lay people. At the same time, modern health care is a highly developed set of social processes, involving many different forms of activity and is provided by many actors, from highly trained professionals to self-care. This complex division of labour is, therefore, the focus of Part 4.

Until relatively recently, medical sociology's preoccupation was with doctors, as members of an archetypal, autonomous profession of a particular occupational form and as the dominant occupational group in health care provision. The first entries in Part 4 cover these issues and another classic concern of medical sociology, professional socialization, outlining the initial, predominantly functionalist approach and its replacement by more critical approaches to professional power. Since the 1970s, sociological research on health care providers has developed beyond the study of doctors in three main ways. First, there has been some, albeit limited, increase in research on other health care occupations. Second, particularly since the mid-1980s, sociologists' interest in the rise of medical power and authority has been superseded by consideration of their putative decline. One possible indication of this is the apparent growth in resort to non-orthodox medicine, which has revived sociological interest in the concept of medical pluralism. Third, there has been a shift in emphasis away from specific occupations towards the division of labour itself and the character of health care work, wherever it is carried out. The symbolic interactionist concept of 'negotiated order' has been particularly influential in studies of inter-professional interactions and boundary work. This is also an area where the influence of feminism on medical sociology has been important since the 1970s. On the one hand, this has led to recognition of the value of emotional labour as a concept relevant to studying health care as a form of people-processing. On the other hand, it has led to a wider conception of the location of health and the division of labour, as including that which takes place in the home. The concept of informal care has been added to the medical sociology toolkit and is discussed in relation to health here.

The final section, Part 5, considers some of the key concepts and issues that have shaped medical sociological research on health care organization and policy. As described in the first contribution, such work can be focused on different levels, the macro, societal level, the meso level of the formal organizational structure, and the micro interactional level. However, recent medical sociological interest in health care organization has been predominantly at the first of these levels. This is reflected in our choice of topics in this section. The key concepts and issues reviewed here fall into three main, albeit overlapping, categories. First are the theoretical concepts used to analyse the major shifts that are currently occurring in health care across much of the affluent world, such as privatization, managerialism, consumerism, and the reconfiguration of citizenship in relation to health care entitlement. Second, there are sociological concepts that have been deployed in the analysis of how some issues become health policy. We have space in the book only to discuss two of these: social movements and social problems. Finally, there are concepts relating to institutional processes and organizations that are increasingly prominent in contemporary health care, such as new public health, medicines regulation, evaluation and malpractice. These latter feed back into the discussion of the possible decline of an autonomous and all-powerful medical profession.

BACKGROUND AND CONTRIBUTORS TO THIS VOLUME

In describing the development of medical sociology since the mid-1960s, we are also outlining, at least with respect to the United Kingdom, the history and contribution of one particular post-graduate course: the MSc in Medical Sociology, established by the late Professor Margot Jefferys at Bedford College over 30 years ago alongside the Social Research Unit, originally under the now somewhat archaic-sounding title of 'MSc in Sociology with Special Reference to the Sociology of Medicine'. In the early 1960s, Margot Jefferys was both convinced of the value that a sociological perspective could bring to medical care and frustrated at the lack of receptiveness to her ideas in the medical school environment in which she then worked. She found a more conducive institutional base at Bedford College, originally founded in 1848 as the first college for women's higher education in Britain, but, by the 1960s, a college of the federal University of London, in the process of becoming co-educational. Bedford's social science department had a long tradition of applied work, of training women for public service. This perhaps distinguished it from some of the more theoretically orientated sociology departments then emerging in Britain's newer universities. Thus Bedford's tradition, Margot Jefferys' commitment to reforming medical education and to training good social researchers, and the lively intellectual climate in sociology in the late 1960s and early 1970s, were brought together in the Bedford College MSc. This course was the first in the United Kingdom to combine intensive study of social aspects of health and illness and health care organization with systematic training in social research methods. Then, as subsequently, the course was intended primarily for those whose first degree was in social science, but was also taken by many health professionals, including doctors, dentists, nurses and physiotherapists, who had a strong interest and some prior background in sociology.

Margot Jefferys' early graduates were to be the pioneers among a Bedford medical sociology diaspora that gradually spread into health care professional training schools, universities and research units at home and overseas, often founding their own postgraduate programmes. Although there were other key founding individuals and institutions for medical sociology in the United Kingdom, and the field has long established its independence from this particular parentage, we consider that the Bedford College postgraduate and research programme was of key importance in medical sociology's development, particularly in the United Kingdom. Later, the programme was successfully relocated to Royal Holloway, following its merger with Bedford College in 1985. As teachers for many years on what has become known as the 'Royal Holloway' MSc, we consider ourselves privileged to have been able to carry on the work established by Margot Jefferys and her colleagues.

In conceiving this volume, we had in mind marking the contribution that those associated with medical sociology at Bedford and Royal Holloway have made to the field over the past three decades. Just over half of all the entries have been written by past or present MSc and/or PhD students, past members of the Social Research Unit or past teachers of medical sociology from the two colleges.[2] Thus, our contributors include graduates from the 1970s and 1980s who have gone on to become established names in the field, through some from the 1990s who are rapidly developing professional reputations, to those who, at least when they wrote their contributions, were still completing their PhDs.

Together, we believe they give an impressive indication of the quality of work of our alumni and, of course, these particular contributors are only a tiny proportion of all those who have studied or taught medical sociology at Bedford or Royal Holloway since the 1960s. As well as editing the volume, we ourselves have written the remaining entries. The quality of these is for others to judge. Suffice to say, we have drawn extensively on the knowledge we have gained from our students over many years and on course material. We are grateful to all our students, past and present, and, especially, to the contributors to this volume, although final responsibility for the volume as a whole, as well as for our individual entries, rests, of course, with us.

NOTES

1   Bloom (2000) gives a parallel account of the development of medical sociology in the USA.
2   Authors of individual contributions are identified by initials at the end of each entry with a key provided in the *list of contributors*.

REFERENCES

Albrecht, G.L., Fitzpatrick, R. and Scrimshaw, S.C. (eds) (2000) *Handbook of Social Studies in Health and Medicine*. London and Thousand Oaks, CA: Sage.
Annandale, E. (1998) *The Sociology of Health and Medicine*. Cambridge: Policy Press.
Armstrong, D. (2003) *Outline of Sociology as Applied to Medicine*, 5th edn. London: Arnold.
Bird, C.E., Conrad, P. and Fremont, A.M. (2000) 'Medical sociology at the millennium', in C.E. Bird, P. Conrad and A.M. Fremont (eds), *Handbook of Medical Sociology*, 5th edn. Upper Saddle River, NJ: Prentice Hall, pp. 1–10.
Bloom. S. (2000) 'The institutionalization of medical sociology in the United States, 1920–1980', in C.E. Bird, P. Conrad and A.M. Fremont (eds), *Handbook of Medical Sociology*, 5th edn. Upper Saddle River, NJ: Prentice Hall, pp. 11–31.
Bury, M. (1996) 'Defining and researching disability: challenges and responses,' in C. Barnes and C. Mercer (eds), *Exploring the Divide: Illness and Disability*. Leeds: The Disability Press, pp. 17–38.
Bury, M. (1997) *Health and Illness in a Changing Society*. London: Routledge.
Elston, M.A. (ed.) (1997) *The Sociology of Medical Science and Technology*. Oxford: Blackwell.
Gabe, J. (ed.) (1995) *Medicine, Health and Risk*. Oxford: Blackwell.
Green, J. (1997) *Risk and Misfortune*. London: UCL Press.
Green, J. and Thorogood, N. (1998) *Analysing Health Policy: A Sociological Approach*. London: Longman.
James, V. and Gabe, J. (eds) (1996) *Health and the Sociology of Emotions*. Oxford: Blackwell.
Nettleton, S. and Watson, J. (1998) *The Body in Everyday Life*. London: Routledge.
Parsons, T. (1951) *The Social System*. New York: Free Press.

xvii

Scambler, G. (2003) *Sociology as Applied to Medicine*, 5th edn. London: Saunders.

Straus, R. (1957) 'The nature and status of medical sociology', *American Sociological Review*, 22: 200–4.

Timmermans, S. and Gabe, J. (eds) (2003) *Partners in Health, Partners in Crime*. Oxford: Blackwell.

Williams, S.J. and Bendelow, G. (1998) *The Lived Body: Sociological Themes, Embodied Issues*. London: Routledge.

introduction

PART 1

Social Patterning of Health

social class

Definition: *A social class is a segment of the population, distinguished from others by similarities in labour market position and property relations.*

The concept of social class is tied to theories of social stratification. All societies are socially stratified and their members therefore occupy different positions in the social structure. Class stratification theory is one way of trying to explain the principles of social stratification today, how it emerged historically and the consequences it has for members of society. Stratification in society, for instance by social class or by gender, is always linked to power relations between groups in society and to differences in access to resources. Many theories of social stratification identify property as a source of power and privilege. Labour market position, indicated by type of job and decision latitude within the job, is another source of power, income and control. A social class could be defined as a segment of the population that shares a similar position in these respects; the constraints they experience in daily life may be of a similar kind.

Among the consequences of belonging to a specific social class, certain aspects are more commonly studied, such as social mobility, educational career and income. Often these are referred to as 'life chances'. We should add here that the concept of 'life chances' must include health, survival and mortality also. The latter point is well taken in medical sociology but often ignored in general sociological works. Health, survival and mortality differ systematically by social class at any stage of life, an important aspect of health inequalities. Health inequalities are reproduced in each new generation, even in the most advanced welfare states, and even where all children have food and shelter and access to comprehensive medical care. This persistence of health inequalities is quite remarkable and their understanding therefore is a major challenge to sociology.

If people live in similar circumstances, they will tend to react similarly to what is going on around them; thus there will be an element of collective response and action based on social class. The experience and behaviour of a social class, therefore, are not just an aggregate of individual

3

experiences and behaviours. Similarly, the level of health enjoyed by a social class is not only a result of what the individual members of that class do and experience as individuals; it is also a result of their collective responses and bargaining powers, both in matters of health and other matters. A specific social class, such as the manual workers of a country, has a certain history which can be more or less known by its members. Thus, a social class can be more or less class conscious; it is probably usually the case that the upper classes are more conscious than the lower ones about their own power and influence and therefore more often tend to act as a collective agent. Class interests are only one aspect of modern political conflict, but they are nevertheless visible, for instance, when tobacco companies form lobbying groups to influence legislation, or when workers form trade unions to be able to negotiate from a position of strength to improve their work environment and protect their health.

A modern interpretation of social class, such as that of Erikson and Goldthorpe (1992), distinguishes between uni-dimensional concepts of social hierarchy and multi-dimensional concepts of social class. The latter are defined by several criteria and cannot easily be ranked along one dimension. The former can be based on the status or social prestige of occupations and thus can in principle be ranked. The modern discussion about class continues the old discussion about whether social class primarily represents the objective distribution of resources and constraints, or rather the perceived prestige and ranking that are linked to certain social positions or occupations. The predictive power of social class is probably best explained by its objective aspects. Thus, the life expectancy of manual workers was always considerably lower that that of non-manual workers in Communist Europe in spite of the claim that these societies were 'worker states'.

Older discussions of social class were often based on Marx. For Marx, classes were born out of the production of goods and commodities, in which the worker was at the same time exploited economically and alienated from himself. Through alienated labour the worker 'mortifies his flesh and ruins his mind' (Marx, 1975: 326). Marx, like Engels, often quoted the English Public Health Reports of the day to demonstrate how work ruined health. If exploitation created contradictory class interests, then social classes by necessity became locked into mortal battle ('the history of all hitherto societies is the history of class struggles'). Marx was primarily concerned with explaining history; therefore, he discussed the rather broad and sweeping formulations.

Sorokin, who had first-hand experience of Marxism translated into state ideology, pointed out that 'there has not been and does not exist any

4

permanent social group which is "flat" and in which all members are "equal"' (1959). Thus, social classes are heterogenous and their members may differ both in rank and many other aspects, for instance, gender and ethnicity. These aspects are also linked to health and therefore contribute to a large variation in health within social classes.

Weber, whose writings were also heavily influenced by contemporary events, wrote in 1920:

> we can speak about class when 1) a number of people have in common a specific causal component of their life chances, insofar as 2) this component is represented exclusively by economic interests in the possession of goods and opportunities for income and 3) is represented under the conditions of the commodity or labour markets. (Weber, 1968)

This rather awkward translation from German nevertheless reveals the predominance of economic market opportunity and of labour market position in Weber's definition. According to Weber, there could be very many economic classes but in any historical situation economic classes combine into social classes, characterized by relatively easy social mobility within classes and restricted mobility between. Those who do move between social classes tend to differ from their peers in certain ways; if moving upwards, they tend to be of better health and, if moving downwards, of poorer.

The National Statistics' Socio-economic Classes now used in Britain is a classification of occupations. It is based on characteristics of the job itself, as well as on its position in the labour market. Important considerations are whether or not the job is of a routine nature and whether it requires skills or professional qualifications. Also important is whether or not it involves power over employees. Occupations are classified by such criteria into distinct groups, independently of how these criteria are perceived by those working in the occupations. This appears to be close to the Erikson–Goldthorpe social class schema (Erikson and Goldthorpe, 1992: 35–47). It is certainly a stricter classification than the previous Registrar General Social Class (RGSC) classification, which was based on the ranking of occupations by appointed referees, who were supposed to judge by 'general standing in the community'. This procedure was widely criticized as open to arbitrary judgement. In spite of its shortcomings the application of RGSC to British mortality statistics has clearly demonstrated the persistence of social class differences in mortality throughout the twentieth century.

The National Statistics' Socio-economic Classes, like their predecessor

5

the RGSC, differ with regard to mortality for both men and women. In the comparative European study on health inequalities the Erikson-Goldthorpe Scheme was successfully applied to a large number of (West) European countries. This scheme seems to be both authoritative and at the same time has been applied to the greatest number of countries in modern studies of health and mortality. The choice of any of these occupationally based stratification schemes did not lead researchers to conclude that class differences in health were due to work or to direct employment relations (Mackenbach et al., 1997). Occupations and their aggregates differ in many other respects, income being the most obvious one. Income is strongly linked to health. Occupations may also form 'occupational cultures', in which smoking and drinking habits may vary systematically. Aggregates of occupations, i.e social classes, may have distinct cultural characteristics and health attitudes. Therefore, the assumption that social class differences in mortality primarily are caused by work, because measuring of social class may be based on occupations, is not justified. It is only one of several equally plausible propositions.

The so-called Cambridge Scale of Occupations, in contrast to the above measures, is based on estimates of the 'social distance' between occupations. If two friends have different occupations, this is taken as an indication that the social distance between those occupations is short. The distances between occupations are seen as providing a continuous rank order of occupations, measured by Cambridge scores. Prandy explains that this is a rank order that reflects 'differences in generalised advantage and disadvantage and hence in life style' (1990: 635). Application of this scheme also reveals substantial differences in mortality, but again the suggestion that this is based on lifestyle or any other specific aspect is just a hypothesis.

Which of the above stratification schemes is the better one? Most sociologists would agree that such a question must be answered with reference to general sociological problems, rather than to problems of health inequalities. One consideration is that theories of social stratification can hardly be limited to one gender, one country or to one point in history. On the other hand, it is obviously important to know how health, mortality and life expectancy are linked to different concepts of social class or of general standing in the community. Such knowledge could add a great deal to the discussion of which sociological principles are sound and fruitful.

Thus, the choice of a particular scheme of social class cannot primarily be based on a hypothesis of its relevance for health. Nor does it presuppose a definite answer to the question of what causes social class

6

differences in health. How to understand the causal pathway between social position and health is a further, and different, issue.

Women are often excluded or ignored in studies of socio-economic mortality differences. The justification given for this practice is often the lack of data, but it is also true that contributing to this habit is the belief that social class differences in health are smaller among women than among men. The important study of socio-economic mortality differences by Koskinen and Martelin (1994) suggested that the smaller differences among women arose entirely from the subpopulation of married women; for single, divorced or widowed women mortality differences were of the same size as in men. It follows that a more effective way of classifying married women is a key methodological problem.

A long theoretical controversy within sociology reveals that this is a difficult issue, reflected in a number of recent papers struggling to come to grips with the issue of health inequalities among women. Consider two possibilities: one can restrict oneself to data on the occupation of the woman herself (if they exist) or one can use the household-based 'dominance' method. The latter involves a comparison of the two spouses' occupations and assigning the highest of these to the woman as well as to the man (and the children). Swedish data comparing the first method, based on one's own occupation, with the household-based method showed greater social differences among women when the latter method was applied (Vågerö and Lundberg, 1998). This was true both for cardiovascular disease and total mortality. British data on self-assessed health (but not on long-standing illness) gave the same results; the household-based measures of social position demonstrate greater social differences than individual-based methods. What this means is that the knowledge that a nurse is married to a doctor, rather than to a bus driver, is allowed to influence our classification of her/his social position; and further that we expect to see greater social differences by this method than if we only take into account the occupation of the women/man her/himself.

Koskinen and Martelin also suggested the gender difference in cause-of-death structure as the other major explanation for the reporting of smaller differences in women. They demonstrated that, when looking at specific causes-of-death, socio-economic mortality differences in women were not generally smaller than in men. It would therefore not be surprising to find socio-economic mortality differences in women to be as large as, or even larger than in men when one studies specific causes-of-death using a household-based indicator of social position. For a major

7

cause of death, such as cardiovascular disease, the latter may indeed be the case.

There is a fundamental inequality in all societies; in part, this takes the form of stratification by social class. All human beings are not born equal. Some have better life chances than others. Regardless of how social class is measured, there are clear social class differences in health, survival and mortality in all countries, among men, women and children.

See also: *material and cultural factors.*

REFERENCES

Erikson, R. and Goldthorpe, J. (1992) *The Constant Flux: A Study of Class Mobility in Industrial Countries.* Oxford: Clarendon Press.

Koskinen, S. and Martelin, T. (1994) 'Why are socioeconomic mortality differences smaller among women than among men?', *Social Science and Medicine*, 38: 1385–96.

Mackenbach, J., Kunst, A., Cavelaars, A., Groenhof, F., Geurts, J. and the EU Working Group on Socio-Economic Inequalities in Health (1997) 'Socioeconomic inequalities in morbidity and mortality in Western Europe: a comparative study', *The Lancet*, 349: 1655–9.

Marx, K. (1975) *Early Writings: Economical and Philosophical Manuscripts.* Harmondsworth: Pelican.

Prandy, K. (1990) 'The revised Cambridge Scale of Occupations', *Sociology*, 24: 629–55.

Sorokin, P. ([1927]1959) *Social Mobility.* Glencoe, IL: Free Press.

Vågerö, D. and Lundberg, O. (1995) 'Socio-economic mortality differentials among adults in Sweden', in A. Lopez, T. Valkonen and G. Casselli (eds) *Premature Adult Mortality in Developed Countries.* Oxford: Oxford University Press.

Weber, M. ([1922]1968) *Economy and Society: An Outline of Interpretative Sociology.* New York: Bedminster.

DV

gender

> **Definition: Gender relates to culturally appropriate behaviour of men and women, whereas sex refers to biological differences.**

Gender roles and relationships are socially constructed and therefore change over time and across societies. Over recent years the simple dichotomy of biological sex has been questioned, as has the cultural gender dichotomy of male/female. The distinction between masculinity and femininity is increasingly recognized as a continuous dimension, with each individual having both masculine and feminine attributes in varying degrees.

A gender-informed analysis of the social patterning of health needs to consider the wider context of social and economic relations between women and men, and recognize the impact of gender inequalities of power and economic resources on the health of both women and men. It is also essential to take account of the importance of diversity (or inequality) among each gender.

Since the 1970s, it has become accepted wisdom that 'women get sicker but men die quicker'. Women in most Western societies live longer than men, but have higher morbidity rates. This was discussed by Nathanson (1975) as a 'contradiction' which required explanation. Several of her explanations related to gender roles, for example, that women tend to over-report morbidity more often than men, and that women are more predisposed than men to rate their health as poor.

Differences in men's and women's reported illness rates may also arise from diagnostic behaviour and treatment by doctors, as well as gender differences in the process of seeking care – 'illness behaviour'. Reported gender differences in coronary heart disease have been found to partly reflect doctors' behaviour. Thus, gender differences in rates of recorded illness may differ from the 'true' prevalence in systematic and gender related ways. Health professionals play a key role in defining presented symptoms as 'sickness', sanctioning entry into the 'sick role', and making decisions about treatment, all of which may be influenced by gendered norms and assumptions.

In most Western countries women outlive men on average by 5–7 years. This is largely the product of women's biological advantage and men's greater mortality from occupational hazards and risky behaviours, such as smoking, drinking, dangerous sports, fast driving, and violence. As women in Western countries have entered the workforce in greater numbers and there is no longer a male excess in smoking, there has been a reduction in the gender disparity of mortality. This trend is expected to continue, as lifestyles of women and men converge and women undertake more risky behaviours.

In some developing countries there is little gender difference in mortality or men outlive women, for example in Bangladesh, Pakistan and India. In these countries women's social status is very low, and women are more likely to have poor nutrition, less access to health care, more

10

frequent births, and high maternal mortality (Doyal, 1995). In a few countries women outlive men by eight or more years, for example, in the former Soviet Union and among blacks in the USA. Here there has been a deterioration in men's life expectancy since 1980, partly associated with threats to the economic and psychosocial well-being of men in these societies, many of whom have lost a secure 'breadwinning' role.

The legacy of Parsons' functionalist conception of gender roles underpinned much early research on the social patterning of health. Men were seen primarily in terms of their occupational role as 'main breadwinners', and women in terms of their family roles. Research on women's health focused primarily on their roles, examining to what extent additional roles, such as marriage, parenthood and paid employment, had beneficial or adverse consequences for their health (e.g. Verbrugge, 1983). Research on marital status and health consistently showed that the divorced and separated had poorer health than the married, and that single men but not single women reported poorer health.

In the quarter of a century since Nathanson (1975) published her article on 'the contradiction' between sex differences in mortality and morbidity rates, there have been far-reaching structural changes in gender roles, leading to the expectation that the previous sex differences in morbidity will also have changed (Annandale and Hunt, 2000). Women have entered the paid labour force in increasing numbers and many women only remain in the role of full-time housewife for a few years when their children are young. Although women have gained greater financial independence, women and men still occupy different structural locations within society, occupational sex segregation has persisted, and women are more likely to have low incomes. Another major change has been the growth in divorce and the proportion of women bringing up children as single parents. In parallel, there have been changes in men's lives, with a higher proportion not in paid employment than in the past, because of longer periods of education, increased levels of unemployment and earlier age of exit from the labour market (Arber, 1997). Because of these gender role changes, it may be unsurprising that the orthodoxy of women being 'sicker' than men is increasingly questioned.

Recent research has suggested that gender differences in health are now much more modest than was hitherto assumed. Macintyre et al. (1996) found no consistent female excess of morbidity on a range of health measures. However, gender differences in mental health remain substantial. Although women are more likely to report neurotic disorders, e.g. anxiety and depressive disorders, when men's higher rates of alcohol and drug dependence are included, there is a much smaller gender difference in the prevalence of psychiatric disorders. Older women are more likely than older men to suffer from physical conditions which are non-fatal but result in chronic and disabling conditions (Annandale and Hunt, 2000). The gender difference in 'healthy life expectancy', that is the period of life without disability or chronic ill-health, is smaller than the gender difference in life expectancy, because of women's higher level of disability.

Women are more likely than men to be unpaid carers for family members, providing both domestic labour and health care for partners, children and parents when required. Women also provide the majority of care for chronically sick children and for older, frail or disabled relatives. Intensive care-giving places a major burden on carers, with consequences for their physical and mental health. Policies that reduce state-provided domiciliary care and the availablity of residential care for older people will therefore have gendered effects with a greater adverse impact on women, who form the majority of carers.

Many women perform the 'double shift' of household work and paid labour, so it is important to assess how combining paid and unpaid work affects their health (Doyal, 1995), while men's health may benefit from the unpaid labour of their wife in providing domestic services and health care. Bartley et al. (1992) argued that researchers should consider how the conditions of domestic work impact on health in the same way as for paid work, that is in terms of the quality of the work (home) environment, repetition of the work process, latitude of control and work status. Thus it is important to analyse the adverse health consequences of women's unpaid labour.

The previous orthodoxy that married women have poorer health than single women no longer holds in Britain, possibly reflecting changes in the nature of marriage and career opportunities for married women which 30 years ago only existed for single women (Annandale and Hunt, 2000). Single mothers have particularly poor health, which largely reflects their disadvantaged socio-economic circumstances.

Within the tradition of research on inequalities in health, social class has been the prominent factor related to the health of men, whereas for women, a role framework, relating to women's marital and parental role, as well as their participation in paid employment, has been dominant. It is important to integrate these two approaches, and consider how the impact of multiple roles on women's health varies according to women's class position and their financial and material resources (Arber, 1997). There have been extensive debates over whether additional roles for women result in role enrichment and health benefits or in role strain and stress. The growing consensus is that the health effects of occupying

11

multiple roles depend largely on women's material circumstances and the nature of their paid job. Thus, a particular concern should be how poverty and disadvantaged paid work combined with unpaid caring roles adversely influence women's health.

Recent research compares gender differences in the nature and extent of inequalities in health, analysing men and women separately, and considering the same range of social factors. Occupational class may be a less discriminating indicator of health inequalities for women than men because of women's more fragmented employment career, while educational qualifications may capture comparable or greater inequalities for women than men (Arber, 1997). Financial and material resources of the household are closely tied to success in the labour market of both partners (among couples). Such resources are influenced by state policies, with the nature of welfare policies being particularly important for the financial well-being of women with children, for example, the availability of subsidized day care, after-school care and the extent of maternity benefits, especially for single mothers.

Another ongoing debate has been whether a woman's class should be measured by her own occupation irrespective of her marital status – 'the individualistic' approach, or her husband's occupation if she is married, and her own occupation if she is not – the 'conventional' approach (Arber, 1997). The individualistic approach provides the advantage of conceptual clarity, as well as capturing the recent growth in women's employment and the greater fluidity in marital status, but does not reflect as closely the household's material circumstances.

The nature of inequalities in health among women and men, as well as gender differences in health, are likely to vary across the life course, therefore it is necessary to examine different age groups, rather than assume that the same relationships remain constant irrespective of age. Looking across the life course, there is little gender difference in health in childhood, and comparable patterns of health inequalities for boys and girls. However, among young adults (age 15–34), the mortality rate for men is over twice as high as for women, largely because of the higher rate of suicides, traffic accidents and other risk-taking behaviours of young men. Thus, policies to reduce gender differences in mortality in youth and early adulthood need to address the social and cultural roles, and risk-taking behaviour of men.

During the working ages, gender differences in the pattern of health inequalities indicate that family structure has a greater effect on women's than men's health. In particular, single mothers report very poor health as do divorced/separated women and men. Married men and women

12

report the best health, irrespective of whether they have children (Annandale and Hunt, 2000). Class continues to be a major determinant of the health of working-age men and women. Whether a person is in paid employment is now a key marker of health status, and educational qualifications increasingly differentiate health, especially among women. In later life, an individual's own class, based on their last occupation, as well as their material resources, continues to be strongly associated with the health of both older men and women.

In conclusion, gender inequalities in health, and the nature of health inequalities among women and men, are likely to differ over time and between societies reflecting variations in gender roles and relationships.

See also: *social class* and *lifecourse.*

REFERENCES

Annandale, E. and Hunt, K. (eds) (2000) *Gender Inequalities in Health*. Buckingham: Open University Press.

Arber, S. (1997) 'Comparing inequalities in women's and men's health: Britain in the 1990s', *Social Science and Medicine*, 44: 773–87.

Bartley, M., Popay, J. and Plewis, I. (1992) 'Domestic conditions, paid employment and women's experiences of ill-health', *Sociology of Health and Illness*, 14 (3): 313–43.

Doyal, L. (1995) *What Makes Women Sick: Gender and the Political Economy of Health*. London: Macmillan.

Macintyre, S., Hunt, K. and Sweeting, H. (1996) 'Gender differences in health: are things really as simple as they seem?', *Social Science and Medicine*, 42: 617–24.

Nathanson, C. (1975) 'Illness and the feminine role: a theoretical review', *Social Science and Medicine*, 9: 57–62.

Verbrugge, L. (1983) 'Multiple roles and physical health of women and men', *Journal of Health and Social Behaviour*, 24: 16–30.

SA

13

ethnicity

> **Definition:** *Ethnicity refers to the identification with a social group – membership of a collectivity – on the basis of shared values, beliefs, customs, traditions, language and lifestyles.*

A consideration of what is meant by the term ethnicity, and the more contentious term 'race', is, of course, central to any discussion of ethnic inequalities in health. There is a wide sociological literature on ethnicity and 'race', which can be broadly defined as concerned with understanding how ethnic and racial groups become social realities, the relationships between them and the causes and extent of social inequalities between them. Within this work there is agreement that the concept of 'race', reflecting genetically distinct groupings, does not have scientific validity – that people cannot be divided into races on the basis of genetic differences – hence the almost universal use of quotation marks around the term 'race'.

In contrast, most commentators give credence to a notion of ethnicity that reflects identification with cultural traditions that provide (fluid) boundaries between groups. Ethnic groups are: 'real collectivities, [with] common and distinctive forms of thinking and behaviour, of language, custom, religion and so on; not just modes of oppression but modes of being' (Modood, 1996: 95). However, it is important to consider how these cultural traditions are historically located and context dependent, that is, how they change over time and place. In addition, ethnicity is only one element of social identity. For example, gender and class are also important and in certain situations may be more important than an ethnic identity. Central to this 'instability' of cultural identity is the way in which geographical boundaries have become less fixed over time, both in terms of the movement of populations across them and the globalization of media. This has brought differing cultural traditions into close contact and, inevitably, led to the transformation of these traditions, though not necessarily in a straightforward way. For example, Hall (1992) argues that globalization can lead to a strengthening of cultural traditions, on the one hand, and their transformation and the formation of new, hybrid, traditions, on the other.

Some elements of these discussions of ethnicity and 'race' have been adopted by research on ethnicity and health. For example, within the UK, 'race' is never explicitly measured and ethnicity is clearly the favoured term. However, the quantitative nature of much health (rather than social) research, with a need for easily used and repeatable measures, often results in the concepts of ethnicity and 'race' not being clearly distinguished and the dynamic and contextual nature of ethnicity being ignored. So, the term 'ethnic' is frequently used to refer to supposed genetic and cultural features of the population under investigation that are considered to be stable and to mark them out as different.

The fact that even at a descriptive level ethnic inequalities in health are

14

complex aggravates this situation. Differences in health across ethnic groups, in terms of both morbidity and mortality, have been repeatedly documented in both the USA (Rogers, 1992) and the UK (Marmot et al.,1984; Nazroo, 2001). When looking at these data, the initial picture is one of uniform disadvantage for ethnic minority groups, with higher mortality (death) and morbidity (illness) rates. However, closer examination of the data suggests great diversity, with the extent of any health disadvantage varying across ethnic groups and by condition. For example, survey evidence from the UK suggests that within the ethnic minority group that is broadly described as South Asian, Pakistani and Bangladeshi people have very poor health, while Indian people have levels of health that are comparable to the general population (ibid.). And while Pakistani and Bangladeshi people have very poor health generally, their respiratory health is better than that of the general population (Nazroo, 2001). Mortality data also show the contrast by condition and ethnic group. For conditions affecting the cardiovascular system, for example, in the UK those who were born in South Asia have markedly higher death rates from ischaemic heart disease, while those born in the Caribbean have average or low death rates from ischaemic heart disease, but high death rates from strokes and other diseases related to hypertension (Marmot et al., 1984).

Rather than complex explanations for such diversity in the patterning of ethnic inequalities in health, the dominant set of explanations has been straightforwardly based on the premise of genetic and cultural differences between ethnic groups. This is at least partly a consequence of the ease with which such meanings are imposed on ethnic categorizations – ethnic difference, no matter how complex, is easily equated with fixed genetic or cultural difference, despite the obvious problems that have been outlined above. The central problem with such an approach is not that genetic or cultural explanations should be rejected out of hand, but that they are universally invoked with little supporting empirical evidence. In particular, they become explanations by exclusion, they remain once other explanations are ruled out, but are not formally tested themselves. This lack of supporting evidence is, of course, partly a consequence of the difficulty in identifying contributing genes and behaviours and subsequently measuring them in population samples. But it is also a consequence of the assumption that other, competing, explanations are either irrelevant or have been adequately accounted for in data, so all that remains must be genetic or cultural difference.

There are, in fact, several alternative explanations for ethnic inequalities in health. The most frequently considered is the possibility

15

that they are a consequence of socio-economic differences between ethnic groups. There has been considerable interest generally in socio-economic inequalities in health, which has coincided with the extensive interest in ethnic inequalities in health, but with most commentators placing emphasis on differences in material well-being for socio-economic inequalities. Given the large socio-economic inequalities faced by most ethnic minority groups in the UK and the USA (Modood et al., 1997), such an explanation for ethnic inequalities in health is clearly worth exploring. Although initial studies in the UK suggested that socio-economic differences did not contribute to ethnic inequalities in health (Marmot et al., 1984), work in the USA (Rogers, 1992) and recent work in the UK (Nazroo, 2001) have suggested that material factors make the key contribution to differences in health between different ethnic groups. Across a variety of outcomes, and for all ethnic minority groups in the UK, careful adjustment for socio-economic differences reduces the health disadvantage in comparison with the general population (ibid.).

Such careful adjustment for socio-economic indicators is not straightforward, however. For example, occupational class is commonly taken as an indicator of socio-economic position but, within an occupational class, ethnic minority people are more likely to be found in lower or less prestigious occupational grades, to have poorer job security, to endure more stressful working conditions and to be more likely to work unsocial hours. Data from a national survey in the UK have shown that for the poorest ethnic groupings – Pakistani and Bangladeshi people – the average household income is half that of white people within each occupational class, and that the average income in the highest class group for Pakistani and Bangladeshi people is equivalent to that for the lowest class group for white people (Nazroo, 2001). Indeed, even careful adjustment for socio-economic position still does not account for the numerous other forms of social disadvantage that ethnic minority people face, such as geographical concentration in poor and poorly serviced areas, discrimination and racial harassment. And there is growing evidence to suggest that such forms of disadvantage are related to poor health. For example, Karlsen and Nazroo (2002) have shown that both the experience of racial harassment and the perception of the UK as a racist society are strongly related to poor health.

So, evidence from studies that have used adequate indicators of socio-economic position suggest that socio-economic factors make a large contribution to ethnic inequalities in health. And studies exploring the relationship between racial discrimination and harassment and health suggest that these experiences are also related to poor health for ethnic minority people. However, as described earlier, the ethnic patterning of health is not one of uniform disadvantage across minority groups and outcomes. There are important differences between ethnic minority groups, the patterns are different for particular outcomes, and these cannot be easily explained by a crude 'ethnic disadvantage' hypothesis. Of course, the social patterning of ethnic disadvantage is complex also (Modood et al., 1997) and it is likely that both other factors may also be important and that the relative importance of particular factors in determining ethnic inequalities in health might vary according to the type of illness actually being considered.

There remains the possibility that cultural and biological differences contribute to ethnic inequalities in health and it is tempting to consider such explanations when ethnic disadvantage does not easily fit the pattern of inequality for a particular illness or ethnic group. However, when doing this, it is important to recognize that neither cultural practices nor biology are static. Over time, environmental factors become reflected in current biological measures, so biological differences may be a consequence of both genetic and environmental determinants. Also ethnic identity changes over time and is dependent on social context; and other elements of identity also contribute to cultural practices. The marked ethnic differences in the prevalence of smoking in the UK provide a good illustration of this point (Nazroo, 2001). Among those people broadly classified as South Asian, there are low rates of smoking among Indian people, and relatively high rates among Pakistani and Bangladeshi people. And for Indian people, smoking is strongly related to religion, with Sikhs having very low rates and Muslims having high rates. Smoking is also strongly related to gender for South Asian people, with women having very low rates regardless of country of origin or religion. And, as for the general population, it is also strongly related to class for South Asian people, with those in manual classes having higher rates than those in non-manual class. But, perhaps most importantly, smoking rates are strongly related to age on migration to UK, with those migrating at younger ages, or born in the UK, having higher rates of smoking than those migrating at older ages.

Overall, then, a more complex approach to the factors underlying ethnic differences in health is required than simply considering them to be socio-economic, or cultural, or genetic – such factors are unlikely to operate in isolation. Racism is of central importance here. First, ethnic identity and ethnic boundaries are assigned as well as adopted, and assigned on the basis of power relations. Second, the socio-economic differences between ethnic groups should not be considered as somehow autonomous. Rather, the socio-economic disadvantage of ethnic minority people is the outcome of a long history of institutional racism and discrimination that has produced the current levels of disadvantage.

See also: *material and cultural factors.*

REFERENCES

Hall, S. (1992) 'The question of cultural identity', in S. Hall, D. Held and T. McGrew (eds), *Modernity and its Futures*. Cambridge: Polity Press.

Karlsen, S. and Nazroo, J.Y. (2002) 'The relationship between racial discrimination, social class and health among ethnic minority groups', *American Journal of Public Health*, 92 (4): 624–31.

Marmot, M.G., Adelstein, A.M., Bulusu, L. and OPCS (1984) *Immigrant Mortality in England and Wales 1970–78: Causes of Death by Country of Birth*. London: HMSO.

Modood, T. (1996) 'If races don't exist, then what does? Racial categorisation and ethnic realities', in R. Barot (ed.), *The Racism Problematic: Contemporary Sociological Debates on Race and Ethnicity*. Lewiston: The Edwin Mellen Press.

Modood, T., Berthoud, R., Lakey, J., Nazroo, J., Smith, P., Virdee, S. and Beishon, S. (1997) *Ethnic Minorities in Britain: Diversity and Disadvantage*. London: Policy Studies Institute.

Nazroo, J.Y. (2001) *Ethnicity, Class and Health*. London: Policy Studies Institute.

Rogers, R.G. (1992) 'Living and dying in the USA: socio-demographic determinants of death among blacks and whites', *Demography*, 29: 287–303.

JN

18

age

> **Definition:** *In the context of health and medicine, age is a property of human individuals and groups that denotes the duration of the life span since birth and the membership of a specific cohort or generation.*

For many years, age has been a neglected variable in sociological analysis. Yet, arguably, age is just as important to the formation and maintenance of personal identity and social status as gender and ethnicity are. Age can act a positive source of self-esteem (not only for the young) but it can also act as a source of social division and discrimination. The relationship of age to health and medicine is, therefore, a complex one. While studying age is often treated as being synonymous with studying the elderly (as gender is often taken to mean the study of women), it should be remembered that age refers to many stages of the lifecourse.

The simplest starting point concerns variations in the experience of disease and illness. Mortality rates vary considerably with age. In Western countries in the past (and in many poorer countries today) infant mortality has been dominant. High rates of mortality in infants and the young depress the average life expectancy of human groups. This largely accounts for the fact that at the beginning of the twentieth century in Britain, for example, life expectancy at birth for men was 46 and 50 for women (ONS, 2000). The figures for 1998 were 75 and 80 respectively.

However, this does not mean, as is sometimes believed, that long life was impossible in the past. Average life expectancy is exactly what it says – an average, influenced by mortality rates among infants and the young, and the various risks encountered in adult life. However, survival promotes survival, and not all of those living in harsher contexts die young. Indeed, Thane (2000: 20) points out that in the past once adulthood was achieved, people could often grow into old age. Thane estimates that in seventeenth-century England those age 60 and over comprised 9 per cent of the English population, falling to 7 per cent in the eighteenth and nineteenth centuries. In the Victorian period the proportion of the population that was elderly fell as the result of a rise in fertility and thus in the numbers of young people. In the last century the figure comprising the elderly rose steadily and today stands at about 18 per cent (ibid.). Though the current situation may present particular problems for society and for individuals, the presence of elderly people is not historically unique.

What is historically true is that, today, the majority of those who achieve adulthood can expect to live into their sixties, seventies and beyond. This is associated with a major change in the pattern of mortality, as most deaths now occur in old age. Thus, death is 'postponed' and is psychologically as well as socially 'hidden away' from most humans (Elias, 1985). There are, of course exceptions. The very high mortality in young people suffering from HIV/AIDS in the 1980s (and now in lesser numbers from CJD) has been a reminder that infectious diseases and other causes of death can strike at any age, given the right conditions. But in most settled societies, the relationship between age and survival seems almost irreversible. Old age is now the prospect for the majority.

Associated with these changes in mortality and survival are those concerned with morbidity, that is, illness and disability. Age is closely related to particular forms of illness, with some being characteristic of the

19

young (cystic fibrosis, meningitis) and some of older age groups (stroke, dementia). The rise in the prevalence of many chronic disabling conditions with age is well established and is sometimes seen as a major problem for families and health care systems alike. There can be little doubt about the figures. Quoting recent data from the (then) UK Office of Population, Censuses and Surveys (now the Office of National Statistics) Tinker states that long-standing illness was reported by 56 per cent of men and 57 per cent of women aged 64–74 and 62 per cent and 64 per cent for men and women respectively aged 75 and over (Tinker, 1997: 71–2). Higher rates of self-reported poor health were also found among the older age group. Most surveys show that poor health and disability are found in older women (partly accounted for by the higher rates of conditions such as arthritis among older women) but this relationship is not always straightforward. Stroke, for example, is more common in older men. The relationship between disability and gender has been thoroughly explored by Arber and Ginn (1991), among others.

Apart from disability, another reason why old age is also emphasized in the context of health and illness is the costs of care, both to informal carers and to the health care system. Again, the figures seem to be reasonably clear on this point. Those aged 75 and over see their GPs more frequently, attend outpatient clinics more often and spend more nights as inpatients, compared with the rates for all ages (Tinker, 1997: 75). The financial costs of care, especially long-term care, have become major political issues in many countries, including Britain.

Though the relationship between age (or, more properly, growing old), health status and the use of health care is important – there are clearly major problems for individuals, families and health care systems associated with an ageing population – it is important to approach this relationship with caution.

In the first place, not all health expenditures are weighted towards the elderly. It is the case, for example, that the first weeks and the last weeks of life absorb a 'disproportionate' amount of health care expenditure. Early life is an expensive time. In 1998–99, those aged 0–4 cost the hospital and community health services £1000 per head, while those aged 65 and over cost just over £1200 per head (ONS, 2000: 147). Yet, as frequent appeals for funds testify, children in need (especially those in need of for specialist health care) are not treated as a 'problem' or 'burden'. Popular sentiments towards children can be seen to express a commitment to health care expenditure, even for the very sick. And lifetime expenditures for the young disabled and chronically sick are capable of being very high.

A similar commitment to older age groups is less in evidence, leading some to allege that 'age discrimination' or 'ageism' pervades both thought and practice in the health and medical fields. Recent debates in Britain have centred on plans to introduce a 'National Service Framework for Older People' which accepts that the health care system has discriminated against the elderly and sets out to tackle it. However, at the same time, the framework is concerned with the supposed high costs of hospital care for older age groups, and the problem of 'blocked beds'. Yet it is arguable that alternative 'cheap ill resourced' accommodation can lead to 'prolonged lengths of stay' when hospital care is found to be necessary and, just as importantly, a rise in 'human misery' (Evans and Tallis, 2001: 807).

It is also important to note that conflating the concept of age with the supposed 'problems' of the elderly can lead to inappropriate images of the ageing process itself. Today, despite the figures given here, the vast majority of older people are independent and in good health. Even taking the figures given, nearly half of people aged 64–74 do not have long-standing health problems. Substantial proportions of people at all ages do not suffer from major health difficulties, and even those that have long-standing illness can retain a picture of themselves as basically healthy. Many health disorders may be relatively mild in character, or can be adapted to in a number of ways. Bury and Holme (1991) found that even among the very old, self-reported health could be high even in the presence of considerable levels of disability. It is important to avoid assuming that growing older inevitably means poor health.

In part, this issue arises as the result of methodological biases. If the questions asked focus continually on poor health among the elderly, then those are the data that will be produced. If the questions relate to good health or those aspects of life that give or have given pleasure, then the angle of vision changes. Moreover, the nature of age and ageing is not fully captured by 'snapshot', cross-sectional data which fail to show trends over time. There is considerable debate about whether rates of illness are now changing, as healthier younger cohorts enter later life. It is possible that in the future morbidity may be 'compressed' into the last years of life for an increasing number of people, producing a healthier old age overall. This argument has recently been summarized by Phil Mullan (2000). In his book, Mullan challenges the idea that an ageing population must inevitably be seen as a social problem, including one characterized by poor health.

It is possible to connect this more positive approach to age and ageing with 'postmodern' sociological writings on the subject. Here the emphasis

21

is on the changing character of age and ageing and the breakdown in barriers to behaviours and lifestyles that were once thought to be the province only of the young. A healthier lifestyle (older age groups tend in any event to engage in less health risk behaviours than the young) and widespread consumerism in a postmodern culture have affected people at all ages. The use of computer technology, adopting 'body maintenance' regimens and generally avoiding a 'disengaged' and passive form of life can all be cultivated. Featherstone and Hepworth (1991), for example, have argued that there will be both a 'blurring' of behaviours associated with different ages, and increasingly a view of ageing as a 'mask', concealing an identity which may be associated with a younger (or older) age group. In this vision, you are, so to speak, as young as you feel. Subjective feelings about health will clearly play a major role in such sentiments, and expectations about health care may well rise among older age groups in the future.

One other feature of age and health needs to be noted, and that concerns the possibility of inter-generational conflict. Part of the argument concerning resources is about the rights and obligations different age groups have towards each other. Mention has already been made of varying sentiments attached to different age groups. Mullan points out that the effects of negative views of poor health status among the elderly and of health expenditure can erode 'inter-generational trust' (2000: 216). Equally, the divisions caused by age can lead to resentment of the old towards the young, and link with fears concerning safety, risk and social change.

Age, then, like other features of social differentiation can lead to conflict and division as well as to feelings of solidarity and identification – as in the feelings associated with belonging to a specific generation. Medical sociology needs, therefore, to approach the concept of age and its relationship to health in both a realistic and critical spirit.

See also: *lifecourse*

REFERENCES

Arber, S. and Ginn, J. (1991) *Gender and Later Life: A Sociological Analysis of Resources and Constraints*. London: Sage.

Bury, M. and Holme, A. (1991) *Life After Ninety*. London: Routledge.

Elias, N. (1985) *The Loneliness of the Dying*. Oxford: Blackwell.

Evans, G.J. and Tallis, R.C. (2001) 'A new beginning for care for elderly people?', *British Medical Journal*, 322: 807–8.

Featherstone, M. and Hepworth, M. (1991) 'The mask of ageing and the postmodern life course', in M. Featherstone, M. Hepworth and B.S. Turner (eds) *The Body: Social Process and Cultural Theory*. London, Sage.

Mullan, P. (2000) *The Imaginary Time Bomb: Why an Ageing Population is Not a Social Problem*. London: I.B. Tauris.

Office of National Statistics (2000) *Social Trends 31*. London: HMSO.

Thane, P. (2000) *Old Age in English History: Past Experiences, Present Issues*. Oxford, Oxford University Press.

Tinker, A. (1997) *Older People in Modern Society*, 4th edn. London: Longman.

MB

place

> **Definition: *Place refers to a socially significant or socially constructed location in geographical space.***

While there has been some discussion about the definition of place within medical geography, there has been little within sociology (for example there is no entry under 'place' in the 1998 *Oxford Dictionary of Sociology*). There is no single definition within medical geography, but geographers have tended to define space as being a natural and physical construct relating to geometric location, and places as being socio-culturally constructed locations in space. According to Gesler: 'place is studied with an eye to its meaning for people; space is analysed in terms of its quantifiable attributes and patterns' or, in other words, place is 'a space filled with people acting out their lives' (quoted in Kearns and Joseph, 1993). Place can also be used in a metaphorical or purely social sense, as relating to one's position in life, in a social hierarchy, or a family, or as in 'I know my place'. Here, however, the focus will be on place as having a physical, locational element, and particularly on place of residence.

An early text on the influence of place on health was Hippocrates' *Airs, Waters, Places*, written in the fifth century BC. The three elements in the title referred to features of climate and topography which were believed to influence the prevalence and types of disease likely to be found in different places. In Britain social regularities in death rates were first studied systematically in the seventeenth century by John Graunt, whose 'Natural and political observations upon the Bills of Mortality' was published in 1662. Graunt was interested not only in the direct effects of the environment on physical health, but on mental health and human

23

behaviour; for example, he believed that adultery and fornication, and anxieties resulting from concerns with business, were more prevalent in London than in the country. The health effects of industrialization in the nineteenth century prompted a considerable amount of interest in the UK and the USA in social and geographical patterning of disease. In Britain, for example, William Farr examined the social patterning of mortality by comparing the death rates of different localities. He drew up life tables for 'healthy districts', which could be used as a gold standard against which the rates for other districts could be compared, and as a basis for inferring that much premature mortality was due to environmental conditions and therefore preventable.

Following the decline in infectious diseases and improvements to the environment in the nineteenth and twentieth centuries, interest in the direct effects of the local environment on physical health decreased. In the latter half of the twentieth century much epidemiology which used geographical data mainly did so as a proxy or surrogate for individual data. Individual exposures to some pathogen in the environment, or individual levels of material disadvantage, were inferred from information about someone's place of residence. Because individual level data on socio-economic status or income are frequently not available on a large scale, material advantage or disadvantage is often measured indirectly from some-one's address, in the UK using deprivation indices based on postcode sectors, and in the USA by measures such as aggregate income in a census tract. Thus although there have been many epidemiological studies of area variations in morbidity and mortality, most have used place of residence as a vehicle for exploring hypotheses about the role of individual physical exposures or material deprivation as determinants of health. Until recently few have looked directly at the role of place itself (Macintyre et al., 1993)

Exceptions could be found in early work on mental health. Classic studies, such as those in the 1930s of the spatial patterning of schizophrenia in Chicago, generated competing hypotheses about the relative importance of the 'breeder' and 'drift' hypotheses for the concentration of high rates of schizophrenia in disorganized urban communities. The 'breeder' hypothesis suggests that such areas generate illness in their residents, while the 'drift' hypothesis suggests that ill individuals gravitate towards such areas.

During the period from the end of the Second World War to the early 1990s, epidemiology, medical geography and medical sociology tended not to study directly the impact of the local social or physical environment on human health, despite there being many community studies exploring life and health or health-related experiences in

24

particular localities. One reason for the relative neglect of the role of place in medical sociology during that period was fear of the ecological fallacy. This fallacy involves inferring individual level relationships from relationships observed at the aggregate level, and a number of influential sociological papers in the 1950s warned that this could lead to entirely incorrect inferences being made, because ecological and individual correlations between the same variables can differ markedly, and can even have different signs. As a result, ecological approaches were shunned in sociology and epidemiology (Macintyre and Ellaway, 2000)

Another reason was the dominance of methodological, conceptual and political individualism in many industrialized countries from the mid-1950s. This individualism emerged partly from analyses of the epidemiological transition, which emphasized the role in chronic disease of individual lifestyle choices (particularly the 'big four' of smoking, drinking, diet, and exercise), rather than the structural and environmental conditions which were believed to influence patterns of infectious disease or diseases of extreme want. With the rediscovery of health inequalities in the 1980s in the UK, and in the 1990s in North America and Australasia, attention initially tended to focus on properties of individuals and families such as low income or unemployment, rather than on the environments (physical or social) to which individuals or families are exposed. Debates about the relative important of health selection versus social causation echoed earlier discussions about the drift and breeder hypotheses but rarely cited this earlier literature.

Since the early 1990s there has been a resurgence of interest in the role of place in shaping people's health experiences, and a new debate has developed about the relative importance of people or place character-istics. A distinction is often made between compositional and contextual explanations for observed associations between place of residence and health. A compositional explanation is that characteristics of individuals resident in a particular area (for example, their age, sex and socio-economic status) explain area differences in health; a contextual explanation is that characteristics of the area, over and above those of resident individuals, help to explain area differences. Compositional explanations would suggest that individuals with particular characteristics would have the same levels of health wherever they live; the contextual explanation would suggest the health experiences of individuals will depend partly on characteristics of the area in which she or he lives (Curtis and Rees Jones, 1998).

Compositional explanations have usually been preferred, partly because of the above-mentioned fears about the ecological fallacy. However, a number of studies in the UK and the USA, often using multilevel statistical methods, have found residual effects of area of residence over and above the predictive value of individual or household characteristics. For example, the Alameda County Study found that residents in a poverty area experienced higher mortality over a follow-up period than residents in non-poverty areas. This increased risk of death persisted with multivariate adjustment for age, sex, baseline health status, race, income, employment status, education, access to medical care, health insurance coverage, and a whole range of behavioural factors. This and other subsequent studies (reviewed in Macintyre et al., 2000) show that one's health is not only predicted by who one is, but also by where one lives (or, in the case of studies taking migration into account, where one once lived). Another useful distinction has since been made, between derived or aggregate area variables, which summarize the characteristics of individual residents, such as the percentage unemployed, and integral or global variables, which describe features not reducible to characteristics of the group, such as de-industrialization (Diez-Roux, 1998).

Although there is now some empirical evidence for the role of place of residence in influencing health, the pathways by which place might influence health have been somewhat under-theorized. Place effects have often been treated as a black box, of residual variation in statistical models left over when one has controlled for every conceivable individual variable. However, there are now some attempts to improve the conceptualization of place and its effects. One suggestion has been to develop a model of what residents need in the local residential environment in order to lead healthy lives, ranging along a hierarchy of human needs from air, water, food, shelter, etc., to facilities for religious expression, collective activities, and play, and then to try to operationalize and measure these and explore how these features of the local environment might individually or collectively relate to different aspects of health (Macintyre et al., 2002). An influence on recent theorizing on how place might influence health has been a debate within the broader field of inequalities in health about the relative importance of psychosocial as compared to material influences on health, and in the case of the income inequalities debate, the role of psychosocial factors such as social comparison, social capital and social cohesion as compared to the role of investments in public and private services and amenities (Lynch et al., 2000)

While this entry has focused on place of residence, it should be noted that the concept of place has been widely applied to number of other settings (including health care settings, therapeutic environments including landscapes, schools, workplaces and churches); to a number of other health-related outcome variables (such as preventive health behaviours, health risk behaviours, access and use of health care); and to more abstract concepts such as 'a sense of place'. If places are socially constructed and have social significance, then medical sociologists should be interested in them as social contexts within which people's lives and health-related experiences are played out. Whereas sociologists conducted many of the early health-related community studies, sociology and sociological theory have been less apparent in the recent literature on the role of place and health, which has been dominated by epidemiologists and medical geographers.

See also: *material and cultural factors.*

REFERENCES

Curtis, S. and Rees Jones, I. (1998) 'Is there a place for geography in the analysis of health inequality?', *Sociology of Health and Illness*, 20 (5): 645–72.

Diez-Roux, A. (1998) 'Bringing context back into epidemiology: variables and fallacies in multilevel analysis', *American Journal of Public Health*, 88 (2): 216–22.

Kearns, R. and Joseph, A. (1993) 'Space in its place; developing the link in medical geography', *Social Science and Medicine*, 37 (6): 711–17.

Lynch, J., Davey Smith, G., Kaplan, G. and House, J. (2000) 'Income inequality and mortality: importance to health of individual income, psychosocial environment, or material conditions', *British Medical Journal*, 320: 1200–4.

Macintyre, S. and Ellaway, A. (2000) 'Eclogical approaches: redisovering the role of the physical and social environment', in L. Berkman and I. Kawachi (eds), *Social Epidemiology*. Oxford: Oxford University Press, pp. 332–48.

Macintyre, S., Ellaway, A. and Cummins, S. (2002) 'Place effects on health; how can we conceptualise, operationalise and measure them?', *Social Science and Medicine*, 55: 125–39.

Macintyre, S., Maciver, S. and Sooman, A. (1993) 'Area, class and health; should we be focusing on places or people?', *Journal of Social Policy*, 22: 213–34.

SM

27

health and development

Definition: Health and development refers to the linkages between the level of economic and social life and health outcomes. It focuses attention on the need for a comparative approach to health.

Health and development are concepts which are elusive and defy simply categorization and precise definitions. Health, seen through the medical model, and emphasized in medical school training, is considered in terms of diagnosing and combating disease. During the era of the germ theory, emphasis was placed on isolating germs and viruses. As Kannan and colleagues put it, '[the] environmental influence on health, in the biomedical context, is often conceptualized in terms of the organism's interaction with other macro or micro organisms, toxins, pollutants, temperature, trauma, and such other physical, chemical or biological agents' (Kannan et al., 1991: 1). Based on this disease orientation, rather than a focus on the patient as a person, the physician was expected to return the sick person to normality (see discussion on the sick role).

The biomedical conception of health, however, changed in the 1970s following the Alma Ata Conference in 1978. The conference, jointly organized by World Health Organization (WHO) and United Nations International Children's Fund (UNICEF), focused attention on primary health care, that came to be associated with essential health care made accessible at a cost that the country and community could afford. Five principles were identified as pivotal to primary health care strategy, namely equity, community participation, appropriate technology, prevention and inter-sectoral collaboration (Phillips and Verhasselt, 1994a; Streefland and Chabot, 1990).

The perception of health shifted, then, from the earlier view which emphasized the eradication of disease by biomedical means, to a new emphasis on the social and economic determinants of health. The biomedical model had ignored the broader but vital influence of social and economic influence on the health of populations (Kannan et al., 1991). As the germ theory failed sufficiently to account for the many illnesses that arose, such as psychiatric disorders, it became clear that the solution to health problems affecting the population could not only be sought by way of isolating germs and viruses. Instead, the solution was sought within the social environment. The post-germ theory therefore witnessed the emergence of a renewed social epidemiology (defined as the study of the origin, distribution, and means of transmission of disease in populations) which located the origin of disease in its social context (Jones, 1991: 15). The environment within which people lived or work could be seen to give rise to particular illnesses. For example, specific diseases were associated with specific occupations (asbestos workers and some forms of cancer). Lifestyle too became linked with stress-related disease such as hypertension and mental illness (ibid.: 15).

With the shift in the conception of health came new concepts such as 'health development' and 'investment in man', which primarily placed 'the person' and the socio-political and cultural environment at the centre stage. In other words, people's social behaviour, nutritional preferences and consumption habits, together with their social location, were considered important. As Walt and Rafkin (1990: 13) put it '[the] call for social justice and equity permeated all the sphere of political and social life in both developing and developed countries'. Health was seen as 'a state of complete physical, mental and social well-being and not merely the absence of disease or infirmity' (Phillips and Verhasselt, 1994a: 3; Walt and Rifkin, 1990). This view, and its precise wording, formed part of the WHO constitution. Accordingly, health was understood as a consequence of and a contribution to political and social order, and not solely the result of the availability of medical services.

With regard to the concept of development, it has generally been understood to entail 'change and often important alterations to people's environments' (Phillips and Verhasselt, 1994a: 3). Some researchers prefer to look at development in terms of measurable indictors notably increasing income per capita, gross national product (GNP) and infrastructural development. The quantifiable fiscal elements notwithstanding, development in broad terms encompasses aspects of human dignity such as access to basic necessities of life; food, housing and education. Generally understood, therefore development means a 'process of improving the quality of all aspects of human life' (ibid.: 3).

Heath and development are inextricably linked. Economic development has contributed to improving the quality of life and health status of the population, through indicators such as increased life expectancy, declining infant, child and maternal mortality rates and enhanced access to services (ibid.: 5). However, it is crucial to note that economic development does not always lead to improvement to populations' health status equitably. Inequalities in health exist within individual countries and across nations based on gender, age, place and the resource capacity of individual countries. Studies have shown that inequalities in resource distribution aggravate poor health. Even in Western industrialized societies, social class has a direct contributory role in determining his health status. The Black Report highlighted the differential mortality between classes in Britain. The disparity in health status has grown with increasing disparity in incomes (Townsend and Davidson, 1982).

The United Nations Development Program (UNDP) Human Development Report 2001 divides countries into three categories: 'high human development', 'medium human development' and 'low human development'. Countries are then ranked by various health and economic indicators to show how they fare compared with others. Unsurprisingly, high in the ranking order were the rich Western countries, with high income per capita. Industrialized countries dominating the 'high human development' category had high life expectancy (Japan recorded the highest at 80.5 years). Figures for infant mortality rate, under-5 mortality rate and maternal mortality ratios were generally lower in the 'high human development' countries than in 'medium' and 'low human development' countries (UNDP, 2001). However, it is important to note that some countries such as Cuba (not included in the UNDP report), although less resource endowed, recorded impressive results in most health indicators. The possible explanation could be the political will of the ruling elite in such countries being instrumental in improving the quality of life of citizen/population.

It is important to recognize that many development policies designed to improve living standards and economic conditions of communities can have unexpected or unintended effects on health (Phillips and Verhasselt, 1994a). Environmental change and its effect on health are of major concern especially in developed countries. Much concern has centred on the consequences of the depletion of the ozone layer and increased exposure of people to ultraviolet radiation which could lead to skin cancers and eye disorders. Further, as Phillip and Verhasselt (1994b: 302) have argued, above-normal temperatures associated with global warming could lead to loss of food-producing areas and threats from flooding in low-lying areas. 'Global warming may also considerably extend the areas in which certain vectors of infection diseases will be able to survive.'

Urban residents have also been affected by the environmental change. They have often been exposed to higher levels of potentially toxic substances, radiation, traffic pollution and industrial noise and waste in the environment. However, it has been difficult to know the extent to which people have been exposed and for what duration, due to the constant movement of people.

Other concerns in recent years, affecting populations in both developed and developing countries, have been the reduction on many forms of public provisions. Cutbacks in public expenditure on health and welfare, and in public subsidies for services have been occurring in developed countries. Developing countries have not been left behind, with numerous instructions coded as 'technical advice' passed onto them to introduce austerity measures to cut their budgets on social services.

Some have been handed 'structural adjustment programs' to be implemented without fail, by the World Bank and the International Monetary Fund (IMF). In the United States, during the Clinton administration, cutbacks on social services were accompanied by increases in taxes to cut financial deficit (Phillips and Verhasselt, 1994b). It became the responsibility of individuals to access health care through private insurance schemes, and governments encouraged policies which advocated cost sharing. These policies had an adverse impact on the health of the population, especially the needy (elderly, chronically ill and the poor).

With technological and economic developments, new health challenges have arisen, affecting groups of people regarded as 'vulnerable, often rendered so by social change and by development conditions' (ibid.: 308). The vulnerable include the elderly, women, children and the poor. As observed above, in recent years, child survival rates have been improving, birth rates and total fertility rates have been reducing, and people generally have been living longer in developed countries. Even in developing countries, life expectancy has been steadily increasing, although this situation is likely to be reversed by the advent of HIV/AIDS in some countries, especially those in Sub-Saharan Africa.

As the population ages, it places new and different demands on health care services, which require strategic planning. For European and North American countries, vast research efforts have been conducted, looking at the demographic causes of population ageing and their economic consequences (Phillips and Verhasselt, 1994b) and it seems more research efforts could focus on the social support mechanisms for older people.

The developing countries, on the other hand, in addition to the steady increase in numbers of the elderly, face threats from infectious diseases such as cholera, malaria, hepatitis and AIDS, and an ever increasing tide of chronic conditions; heart disease, cancers and cerbrosvascular disorders. They have to deal with these conditions with depleted resources (ibid.: 307). Children, especially in poor countries, continue to be vulnerable and to die from infectious diseases and malnutrition, to live in poverty and are often without schooling.

Most critically, an increasing number of women, especially in developing countries, are being affected by HIV/AIDS, often at a higher rate than men. According to Phillips and Verhasselt (1994b) in some cities in Africa, but alos in North America and Europe, AIDS is now the largest cause of death among women aged 20–40. Women almost invariably are the main caretakers for the sick; as such, they will carry the burden if someone close develops AIDS (ibid.: 308). Women's health, as well as

31

issues dealing with health effects of population ageing, alongside children's health, are likely to continue to dominate health discussion in the twenty-first century.

See also: *social class.*

REFERENCES

Jones, K. (1991) *The Sociology of Health and Illness.* Cape Town: Juta and Co. Ltd.
Kannan, K.P., Thankappan, K.K., Kutty, V.R. and Aravindan, K.F. (1991) *Health and Development in Rural Kerala.* Kerala: Kerala Sahityn Parished.
Phillips, D.R. and Verhasselt, Y. (1994a) 'Introduction', in D.R. Phillips and Y. Verhasselt (eds), *Health and Development.* London: Routledge.
Phillips, D.R. and Verhasselt, Y. (1994b) 'Health and development: retrospect and prospect', in D.R. Phillips and Y. Verhasselt (eds), *Health and Development.* London: Routledge.
Streefland, P. and Chabot, J. (eds) (1990) *Implementing Primary Health Care: Experiences Since Alma-Ata.* Amsterdam: Royal Tropical Institute.
Townsend, P. and Davidson, N. (eds) (1982) *Inequalities in Health: The Black Report.* Harmondsworth: Penguin.
UNDP (2001) *Human Development Report 2001: Making New Technologies Work for Human Development.* New York: United Nations Development Program.
Walt, G. and Rifkin, S. (1990) 'The political context of primary health care', in P. Streefland and J. Chabot (eds), *Implementing Primary Health Care: Experiences Since Alma-Ata.* Amsterdam: Royal Tropical Institute.

CN

material and cultural factors

32

> **Definition:** *The concept of 'material factors' refers to those aspects of the physical world, natural or man-made, that affect individual human beings in their thinking, behaviour or health. The concept of 'cultural factors' refers to those aspects of culture that affect individual human beings in their thinking, behaviour or health.*

The distinction between the material and the cultural is part of an age-old discussion within sociology and anthropology. The distinction is linked to an equally old philosophical conflict between materialism and idealism. The question is whether or not the structure of human society and the way it determines human action is primarily material or cultural. These unresolved issues are the basis for considerable confusion and conflict. This is true also in also in medical sociology, when determinants of human health are in focus.

A good example is the Black Report (Townsend and Davidson, 1982) and its ambitious efforts to explain social differences in health within populations. Here the material factors were seen as those of the social structure, and culture was linked to, or even equated with, individual behaviour. Hence the opposing explanations of material/structural factors versus cultural/behavioural factors. Making this kind of distinction can be likened to the Marxist distinction between the 'economic base' and the 'ideological superstructure'. In this theory, the first ultimately determines the second. The primacy of 'the material' seems to be common to Marxism and classic economic theory, where human drive is primarily based on collective self-interest (Marxism), or individual self-interest in the form of maximization of utilities (economic man).

Materialist explanations, whether old or new, make certain assumptions, which could and should and be scrutinized. Cultural constraints can certainly be as forceful and imposing as can material constraints, as evidenced for instance by the strict rules for male and female behaviour in all societies.

Thus, it is true that a certain tradition in the social sciences derives the social structure from the production of material goods and commodities, but it is equally true that other social science traditions, influenced by anthropology, claim the primacy of 'culture'. Between sociology and anthropology this was always a very controversial issue. In 1958, an attempt to settle it by a robust compromise was outlined in a joint paper by Talcott Parsons and A.L Kroeber, chairpersons of the American Sociological and Anthropological Associations, respectively.

Sociologists tend to see all cultural systems as a sort of outgrowth or spontaneous development, derivative from social systems. Anthropologists are more given to being holistic and therefore begin with total systems of culture and then proceed to subsume social structure as merely a part of culture . . . Our objective in the present joint statement is to point out, so far as methodological primacy is concerned, that, neither of these assumptions is preferential a priori and cannot be validated in today's state of knowledge . . . In sum we feel that the analytical discrimination should be consistently maintained without prejudice to the question which is more 'important', 'correct' or 'fundamental', if indeed such questions turn out to be meaningful at all. (Kroeber and Parsons, 1958: 582–3)

Culture, for those authors, was defined as: 'the transmitted and created content and patterns of values, ideas, and other symbolic-meaningful systems as factors in the shaping of human behavior and in the artefacts produced through behavior' (ibid: 583).

Culture, evidently, cannot be reduced to an agglomerate of individual behaviours or lifestyles. It refers to relatively deep-rooted patterns of ideas and values which are often transmitted from one generation to the next, and as such represent long-term influences on human behaviour (and its material artefacts). Cultural explanations of human health, consequently, are no more or no less individual, no more and no less structural, than so-called material (materialist) explanations. In referring to specific cultural and material factors, we should not assume any of them to have primacy, or to be more fundamental than others.

By talking generally about cultural and material factors we are able to include most aspects of human existence. In health-related studies the term material factors is often used more narrowly to mean poverty, material deprivation or material inequality. However, poverty, deprivation and material inequality are not equivalent concepts. Material inequality, for instance, would seem to refer not only to the poverty end of the income (or other material wealth) distribution, but to the full range of it. Richard Wilkinson's (1996) proposal that a society's material inequality as such, perhaps through a 'culture of inequality', can cause poor health is a much discussed hypothesis today.

The definition of poverty is also at issue. Poverty has often been defined in income terms, but as Amartya Sen has pointed out, this is a conceptual weakness in this field. Sen's concept of poverty has an 'irreducible absolute core', in that it refers to capability to meet human needs of food, shelter and social esteem (1984: 332). In discussing hunger in rich countries Sen stresses that its persistence in America cannot be fully understood with reference to the size of income only (Sen, 1992: 114). Presumably cultural factors are important in its transmission from one generation to the next.

An absolute definition of poverty was used also by Seebohm Rowntree, who referred to 'the minimum necessities of merely physical efficiency', in his classic definition (1901). At the other end stands Peter Townsend, who advocates a relative definition of poverty or deprivation. Townsend's (1987: 125) definition is extremely wide-ranging: 'deprivation may be defined as a state of observable and demonstrable disadvantage relative to local community or the wider society or nation to which an individual family or group belongs'.

Rowntree is close to an absolute definition, but included in these necessities was tea, which can only be regarded as necessary out of social convention in England. Sen, similarly, includes lack of social esteem as one core aspect of poverty, thereby introducing a cultural element to it. In practice, an absolute poverty concept is never strictly applied; we always compare concepts, which are more or less relative. Poverty in an absolute sense, and poverty in a relative sense, will obviously not have the same effect on the human body and the human mind (Vågerö and Illsley, 1995). Absolute poverty may work through poor nutrition, decreased physical and mental resistance, retarded growth, and impaired immune competence. Relative poverty, in contrast, may not carry any of those risks, if the level of resources of those living in relative poverty is sufficiently high. The relatively poor of the developed world are in general much better off than the absolutely poor of developing countries. Therefore, this distinction may be especially crucial in studies of health.

In health, as in virtually all other areas of human activity, people make choices under constraints; hence health outcomes are a product of both individual choice and the constraints under which people make these choices. The notion of control seems important as it combines structural constraints, both material and cultural. Having cultural resources (such as education) or material resources (such as income) represents being under fewer constraints. On the whole we would expect good health to be more common in life situations over which a person can exercise more control and in which he/she suffers fewer constraints. Constraints could be material or cultural, neither group of factors being, *a priori*, more important than the other.

See also: *social class* and *lifecourse*.

REFERENCES

Kroeber, A.L. and Parsons, T. (1958) 'The concepts of culture and of social system', *American Sociological Review*, 23: 582–3.

Rowntree, S. (1901) *Poverty: A Study of Town Life*. London: Macmillan.

Sen, A. (1984) 'Poor, relatively speaking', in A. Sen (ed.), *Resources, Values and Development*. Oxford: Basil Blackwell.

Sen, A. (1992) *Inequality Re-examined*. Oxford: Clarendon Press.

Townsend, P. (1987) 'Deprivation', *Journal of Social Policy*, 16: 125–46.

Townsend, P. and Davidson, N. (1982) *Inequalities in Health: The Black Report*. Harmondsworth: Penguin Books.

35

Vågerö, D. and Illsley, R. (1995) 'Explaining health inequalities: beyond Black and Barker', *European Sociological Review*, 11: 219–41.

Wilkinson, R. (1996) *Unhealthy Societies: The Affliction of Inequality*. London: Routledge.

DV

—psycho-social factors—

> *Definition:* **A summary label to characterize relevant socio-environmental and personal conditions that elicit recurrent stressful experience and increase risk of illness.**

Stressful experience is conceptualized as a mismatch between environmental demands put on an individual in challenging situations and his/her ability to meet the situation with adequate response. Such mismatch affects health adversely by triggering physiological dysfunction. Stressors involving socio-environmental and psychological factors over extended periods of time constitute 'psycho-social risks'.

The study of psycho-social factors has a long history emerging from sociological, psychological and medical disciplines. Farr, in the mid-1800s, noticed different mortality rates in marital groups while Freud some decades later examined the role of early life experiences in the genesis of adult psychopathology. Cannon in the late 1920s laid the groundwork for psycho-physiological research by studying bodily changes related to emotional arousal, with Selye in the 1950s responsible for identifying the physiological correlates of stress.

Medical sociology and medical psychology have studied a variety of factors in the social causation of diseases. There has been some polarization with medical sociology emphasizing the role of socio-environmental factors and medical psychology stressing the importance of personality and cognitive factors, but with somewhat less exploration of the interaction between the two. Sociological studies have explored adverse effects on health produced by socio-cultural instability, rapid social change, high level of social anomie or socio-economic status. Such effects can be direct, for example, where poor living conditions increase risk of respiratory infections or transmission of infectious agents. Others

36

are less direct, for example, in migrant populations who are at increased health risk through a number of factors including social separation, socio-economic status, social exclusion and changes in dietary habits.

Psychological studies have focused on personal characteristics influencing disorder. Thus, low self-esteem, aggression, external locus of control/helplessness and 'Type A' behaviour are all identified as personal traits associated with poor health outcomes (Steptoe and Appels, 1989). Health risk behaviours have been studied by both groups. These include smoking (risk for cardio-vascular and lung disease), alcohol consumption (risk for diseases of liver, stomach and central nervous system as well as traffic accidents and suicide), obesity (risk for diabetes mellitus, cardio-vascular disease) and physical activity (risk for cardio-vascular disease). Causes of these have been sought in both socio-environmental (for example, social class, marital status, dietary habits) and psychological (for example, antisocial disorders personality, 'Type A' personality type) domains.

The two lines of enquiry have also been linked by common interest in the investigation of adverse childhood experience as a precursor to worse adult health status. Socio-environmental factors such as loss of parent, neglect and abuse have been associated with a range of poor health outcomes. These are also associated with subsequent adult psycho-social risks, for example lower socio-economic status, single parent status and domestic violence, worse education and poorer employment record, as well as lower self-esteem and higher aggressive behaviour. This has led to the development of lifetime models risk tracing psycho-social risk pathways for disorder (Bifulco and Moran, 1998).

Determining a *causal* role for psycho-social factors requires ascertaining the direction of causality and timing of risk to health outcome, the degree to which the risk factors can be manipulated and an understanding of the likely disease mechanisms involved. In terms of timing, psycho-social risk factors can act as antecedent, perpetuating or residual factors of ill-health. For example, in the work domain, loss of job can trigger mental or physical health problems, lack of employment can aggravate disorders and chronic unemployment is often a residue of long-term ill health. Similar distinctions can be made in marital status where health differences between marital groups can result from both an effect of health on marital status (through selection of health in partners) and an effect of marital status on health (stress induced by unhappy relationships leads to health problems).

A causal factor is one which when manipulated can be shown to change risk of outcome. In the study of psycho-social factors adequate distinction is rarely made between fixed and varying risks. A fixed marker is unchangeable, and encompasses aspects such as race, gender and year of birth. Although these might be distally associated with health outcomes, they are unlikely to account for the timing of disorder, nor can they be manipulated to change health outcome. Variable risk factors can either change spontaneously within a subject (such as age or weight) or be changed by intervention (for example, self-esteem and marital status). The change potential for psycho-social risks are important not only in understanding causal agency for disorder but also for devising interventions. The degree to which psycho-social risks vary is under-estimated in many health studies, due to single-time point measurement.

Although substantial investigation has been made of a range of psycho-social risks and their association with different health outcomes, relatively little is currently known about the process of risk mediation. It is important to note that the origins and mode of mediation of a risk factor on health are not synonymous. Thus, psycho-social risks may be responsible for bringing about certain health outcomes but the mediator of risk is likely to be in the physiological domain. For example, reasons for smoking include a number of factors including personality, cultural factors and access to cigarettes. But risk processes linking smoking with cardio-vascular disease and lung cancer concern the physical influences of carbon monoxide and carcinogenic tars on the body. The origin of the risk factor is important but on its own is uninformative about the process of risk mediation.

The psycho-social risks associated with poor health outcome will be illustrated in three arenas: marital status; work status and childhood experience. In each the influence of both socio-environmental and psychological factors will be outlined.

It is clear that marital status affects health. Married people have lowest health problems, followed by those never married and widowed, and divorced people have the most health problems. This is generally interpreted by the fact that married persons are more socially integrated, and the quality and quantity of social relationships are directly related to health. Marital status also has psychological correlates. Conflict, lack of support and single-parent status may relate to low self-esteem and poor coping and contribute to psychological disorders, particularly depression (Brown and Moran, 1997).

Poor health is linked to employment experience. This can be through stress at work, and lack of control over such stress, or through unemployment and resulting loss of self-identity and social contact. Clear social class gradients in health have been found for coronary heart disease, chronic bronchitis and diabetes millitus (Marmot et al., 1997). Thus a study of civil servants showed those in the lowest grades had lower control and variety at work, poorer social support and more life events

38

than those in higher grades. The gradient between lowest to highest employment grades held for both psycho-social risk factors and for ill health and provided an explanation for the social gradient in coronary heart disease. Similarly, lack of employment relates to poor health outcomes, particularly mental health, and a study in young people has shown social causation rather than merely selection being present (West and Sweeting, 1996). Employment has been found to have a protective effect on depressive disorders in women, but only when level of work-strain and role conflict between work and domestic arenas is low. Thus for single mothers with young children, part-time work has been shown to be more beneficial that full-time work (Brown and Bifulco, 1990).

Early loss of mother and poor parenting in terms of neglect, physical and sexual abuse increase risk of a wide range of mental disorders. The long-term effects of such experiences relate to marital difficulties, worse parenting, work problems, socio-economic disadvantage, lower self-esteem and poorer coping (Bifulco and Moran, 1998). Thus early life experiences are antecedent to many of the other psycho-social risks associated with ill health.

A major new influence on the study of psycho-social stress in childhood has emerged from the field of behavioural genetics. Here socio-environmental factors are categorized in terms of whether they are 'shared' or 'non-shared' by family members (Plommin, 1994). The effect of shared or non-shared environment on mental health and development is inferred from the degree to which twins reared together are more similar to one another than would be predicted on genetic grounds alone. While early formulations gave greatest weight to 'non-shared' environment or personal experience over that 'shared', emphasis on genetic interpretations of experience has gained greater weight. Some investigators have concluded not only that there is an important genetic component in almost all environmental measures, but that psycho-social research should be rejected as a meaningful way to study health and development in favour of gene–environment interaction (Rutter, 2000).

Despite ingenuity of design, large sample sizes and sophisticated statistical analysis, behavioural genetic studies have suffered from poor measurement and narrow sample selection. Thus, twin studies have lacked depth and scope of measurement and tend to under-represent those socially deprived. Little of the environment is directly measured in detail in large twin studies – much is inferred from the similarity of outcome in twin pairs whose genetic similarity is known. This means that the 'shared' and 'non-shared' labels are applied crudely with 'equalizing' effects assumed whereby shared experiences are assumed to influence family members in the same way. However, effects can be independent and

39

focused on just one member, or polarize with the experience of living together differentiating family members in different directions. Such studies have rarely tackled more extreme environments in terms of social deprivation and experiences such as neglect or abuse, despite evidence that such factors can over-ride genetic susceptibilities.

Challenges for future investigation include improved measurement adapted for use in the large samples required for investigating multiple factors, identification of causes of time trends in changes in psycho-social risks and their effects, delineation of lifetime liability to poorer health outcomes and understanding individual susceptibility to illness including genetic influences.

Rutter describes the current point in the study of psycho-social factors and health and development as a 'crossroads'. He states:

> We have moved from an era of 'epidemic environmentalism' where strong assump-
> tions were made about the overwhelming importance of psycho-social
> experiences . . . through a biological revolution (in which some of the proponents of
> biological research expressed profound scepticism about any substantial influence
> from psycho-social experiences), to an appreciation that there is good evidence of
> the importance of environmental influences (including psycho-social effects) . . . but
> also to an appreciation that we know much less about the specific risk and protective
> mechanisms involved than we may have thought a few years ago. (Rutter, 2000: 398)

See also: *life events* and *social support.*

REFERENCES

Bifulco, A. and Moran, P. (1998) *Wednesday's Child.* London: Routledge.

Brown, G.W. and Bifulco, A. (1990) 'Motherhood, employment and the development of depression: a replication of a finding?', *British Journal of Psychiatry*, 156: 169–79.

Brown, G.W. and Moran, P.M. (1997) 'Single mothers, poverty and depression', *Psychological Medicine*, 27: 21–33.

Marmot, M., Bosma, H., Hemingway, H. et al. (1997) 'Contribution of job control and other risk factors to social variations in coronary heart disease incidence', *The Lancet*, 350: 235–9.

Plomin, R. (1994) *Genetics and Experience: The Developmental Interplay between Nature and Nurture.* Newbury Park, CA: Sage.

Rutter, M. (2000) 'Psychosocial influences: critiques, findings and research needs', *Development and Psychopathology*, 12: 375–405.

Steptoe, A. and Appels, A. (eds) (1989) *Stress, Personal Control and Health.* Chichester: Wiley.

West and Sweeting, (1996) 'Nae job, nae future: young people and health in the context of unemployment', *Health and Social Care in the Community*, 41: 50–62.

TB

social support

> **Definition:** *Social support refers to those aspects of social relationships that provide a sense of self-worth and offer resources in tackling life's troubles.*

When exploring the links between social processes and health, it is often useful to distinguish between cause and context. As other concepts in this book show, a host of social factors can be associated with health and illness – marriage, social class, gender, ethnicity and age, to name but a few – but whether such variables can be shown to play a *causal* role in the occurrence of health and illness, or whether they act as important *contexts* in which health and illness can be better understood is not always clear. This problem is particularly acute with a concept such as social support. It is worth, therefore, distinguishing between the two approaches.

In a wide-ranging review of social relationships and health, Berkman et al. (2000) argue that social support acts as a powerful mediating factor in a range of physical and mental health problems. Social support, in this account, is a 'micro' level process, or set of processes, that mediate a causal sequence that takes us from the structural position and social networks people inhabit, to resulting health-related outcomes. These outcomes might be psychological, physiological or behavioural in character. The origin of the concept, these authors note, comes partly from Durkheim's emphasis on the role of social integration (or the lack of it) in his study of suicide. Social integration can operate at a number of levels, from whole societies to local communities. Berkman et al. also locate the concept of social support in Bowlby's work on 'attachment theory', developed in the 1960s and 1970s and in the many studies carried out in the past 40 years or more on social networks, kinship and community, and their links with health.

In the context of current research, social support is defined by Berkman et al. as having four dimensions. First, there are *instrumental* forms of support involving practical help in solving life's daily problems, from helping with domestic chores to financial matters. Clearly, financial support may involve issues that are tied to the material conditions in which people live. Second, *informational* support relates to the 'provision of advice or information in the service of particular needs' (Berkman et al., 2000: 848). Such needs, again, may be practical or of a more significant existential kind.

Third, *appraisal* support is often likely to flow from the provision or sharing of information, and refers to the way in which decision-making is carried out and courses of action agreed upon. Finally, and perhaps most importantly, there is *emotional* support. Berkman et al. argue that sources of self-esteem, through love and understanding, are essential to health outcomes. Such support is likely to be the result of an intimate relationship, though it may also come from wider circles of confidants and friends. Of course, it is important to remember that not all forms of support all equally positive; some support received might carry a heavy cost for the individual in terms of expectations of reciprocity or unwanted and difficult obligations.

Evidence for the causal influence of social support on promoting good health has been adduced in a number of studies. Wilkinson (1996: 182) for example, argues that 'various forms of social support and social contact are now generally accepted as having an important beneficial effect on health'. In particular, such support may help to protect people against adverse life events, and by the same token its absence may expose them to increased stress. Wilkinson, like Berkman, links social support to other aspects of social networks, and to aspects of social cohesion and the degree of social inequality. The absence of social cohesion, especially when combined with the experience of personal isolation, has been linked with an increase in mortality from a variety of causes (ibid.). Good social support appears to be positively associated with a lower risk of developing heart disease, to take just one example (Wadsworth, 1996: 159).

As the above makes clear, a core component of social support involves being valued and loved. Berkman et al. and many other commentators have drawn on the work of John Bowlby in emphasizing the importance of attachment and separation, especially in the early years of life. Indeed, attachment theory can offer a powerful means for understanding psychological needs and their causal impact on health, and also the need for social cohesion and solidarity. Social networks can be examined in terms of day-to-day support, or in terms of wider community participation or 'inclusion'.

Studies of the causal role of social support also make a distinction between the *availability* of social support, *perceived* support and the *delivery* of support when it is most needed, for example, following a major life event. Such support can act as a direct and positive influence in promoting good health, and its opposite, social isolation, can lead to poor health. But social support can also operate *indirectly* by protecting (acting as a 'buffer') in the presence of stress. Considerable work is currently under way to understand the biological mechanisms (through the immune system, hormonal pathways or neurotransmitters) that might explain the connections between social and psychological experiences, and their impact on the body and health.

One of the difficulties in establishing causal connections stems from the wide variations in meaning that different cultures, or sub-cultures, may attach to social support. It is important to note that research on social support and 'health causation' runs the risk of examining 'support elicited as a result of ill health rather than support, or the lack of it, leading to ill health' (Stansfield, 1999: 157). After all, the onset of illness can itself be a life event. Thus, the temporal order of events and other aspects of causal analysis becomes crucial to understanding the pathways being examined.

In the mental health field, considerable work has been undertaken to tackle these problems. Bifulco and Moran (1998), for example, have summarized several prospective studies which have established links between social conditions and the onset of depression. In particular, Bifulco and Moran examine the lasting influence of early adversity on adult illness. Where a child has faced poor social support in their early years and where their world was 'either bare or hostile, and there was no source of comfort, respect or belonging needed for growth' (ibid.: 145), the risk of adult depression was significantly increased. This was particularly true where safety and self-esteem were compromized. In adult life, Bifulco and Moran show that the most important factors that made women in their studies vulnerable to depression were low self-esteem and 'difficulties in relationships entailing poor support' (ibid.: 147). Those circumstances that, in adult life, mirror adversity in childhood (involving particularly neglect and abuse) are most likely to lead to depression.

As far as the *contextual* character of support is concerned, it is clear that support is vital to the quality of life of people in many different situations, including where illness or health disorder is already present. Studies of later life in particular have shown how vital social support is in promoting well-being. Much discussion has been given to the distinction between *instrumental* and *emotional* support in informal care among older people and those with chronic disorders. In a national study of people aged 90 and over, Bury and Holme (1991) found that informal care (usually provided by daughters) could involve anything between six and eight hours of work each day (ibid.: 142). Many of the tasks involved were of an immediate practical nature, such as cooking, washing and shopping but were often perceived as forms of care going beyond the merely instrumental, indicating that in everyday life, the line between practical and emotional support may often be feint.

In such studies the issues of reciprocity and dependence involved in social support become particularly salient. Fear of becoming dependent among the very old, for example, may well be matched by resentment, as well as commitment, by those offering such care, especially in the face of physical frailty or illness of the person being cared for. Indeed, carers themselves may be in need of support in order to avoid the physical and psychological costs in caring. It is in these circumstances that the more intimate and emotional aspects of support are difficult to separate out, especially when practical support is given over long periods of time, and requires considerable emotional investment by the carer. Even the carrying out of simple practical tasks for an elderly relative may compromise other relationships with a partner or immediate family members.

In a major study of chronic illness and disability in south London, Morgan (1989) has reported on various aspects of social support on the course of disabling illness. Social support was examined along four dimensions in the study: (1) the degree and extent of social contact; (2) emotional support; (3) feelings of loneliness; and (4) whether the person had a confiding relationship on which they could rely (ibid.: 166). Of particular interest is the fact that disabled people who were not born in Britain were more likely to have a larger network of contacts they could confide in – reflecting the existence of large kin networks among the foreign-born respondents. This study also examined the interaction between support and health status by showing that those with higher levels of support were less likely to be suffering from severe disability and that those who were married were least likely to feel lonely (ibid.: 169). Over time those whose condition deteriorated most were those who had experienced adverse life events and had low levels of social support. In this context the interaction between cause and context becomes complex as the course of a disorder unfolds.

The issues of social support throw into relief some of the most important features of the interaction between social circumstances and health. Studying social support can throw important light on the processes leading to the onset of illness, and on the contexts in which its course unfolds. However, the difficulties of establishing the causal role of social support on health have been noted. The strength of the concept may lie more in its ability to help us contextualize the experience of illness.

See also: *psycho-social factors* and *life events*.

social support

Berkman, L.F., Glass, T., Brissette, I. and Seeman, T.E. (2000) 'From social integration to health: Durkheim in the new millennium', *Social Science and Medicine*, 51: 843–57.

Bifulco, A. and Moran, P. (1998) *Wednesday's Child*. London: Routledge.

Bury, M. and Holme, A. (1991) *Life After Ninety*. London: Routledge.

Morgan, M. (1989) 'Socialities, support and well-being', in D.L. Patrick and H. Peach (eds), *Disablement in the Community*. Oxford: Oxford University Press.

Stansfield, S.A. (1999) 'Social support and social cohesion', in M. Marmot and R.G. Wilkinson (eds), *Social Determinants of Health*. Oxford: Oxford University Press.

Wadsworth, M. (1996) 'Family and education as determinants of health', in D. Blane, E. Brunner and R. Wilkinson (eds), *Health and Social Organisation: Towards a Health Policy for the 21st Century*. London: Routledge.

Wilkinson, R.G. (1996) *Unhealthy Societies: The Afflictions of Inequality*. London: Routledge.

MB

life events

> **Definition:** *An environmental circumstance indicating change, that has an identifiable onset and ending, and carries a potential for altering an individual's present state of mental or physical well-being.*

There is a long history of the links made between life events and poor health outcomes. As early as the seventeenth century Robert Burton described how melancholia was precipitated by environmental adversity, including inter-personal loss. Such observations began to be more systematically documented in the last century, especially in the 1950s. Clusters of life events were noted to occur prior to the onset of physical and mental illness. Adolf Meyer was the first modern practitioner to suggest that life events might relate to psychopathology and develop a chart system for recording the temporal association of life experiences and disorder. A substantial amount of research in the 1970s and 1980s examined the full potential of life events as social causes of disease. The initial conceptualization of the event–illness link emphasized *changes* in life circumstance producing stress on the *physical* system to affect its dynamic steady state and increasing likelihood of ill health. Subsequent

45

investigation emphasized the *stressfulness* or threat of the events in terms of the social and psychological meanings attached to them on the *cognitive* states mediating between event, physiological impact and ill health.

The following aspects have been examined in determining the role of life events in disease processes: (1) the characteristics of events which might have particular potency for different types of illness identified; (2) their independence from individual agency and timing in relation to onset, recovery and relapse; (3) a disease model highlighting the provoking role of life events, in interacting with an individual's prior vulnerability and subsequent coping behaviour to bring about disorder developed; and (4) the role of life events throughout the lifecourse, particularly those in early life increasing risk for event production and illness in later life.

The study of life events has made most progress in the field of mental health, their role first identified in schizophrenic relapse, but then explored in more detail in relation to depression and anxiety states. The research by George Brown and colleagues into social factors in mental health was responsible for many of the developments in measurement and conceptualization that have ensued (Brown and Harris, 1978). This was subsequently extended to examine the role of life events in physical conditions (Brown and Harris, 1989).

An important observation concerning life events is that although disorder (particularly mental disorder) frequently occurs shortly after the experience of a severe life event, the majority of individuals who suffer severe life events do not become ill. That is, life events may be a necessary but not sufficient cause of ill health. This has led to three inter-related lines of investigation:

First, the characteristics of events which have most potency for disorder have been specified so that the focus of investigation can be narrowed to those with the highest subsequent rates of ill health. Specific types of events that relate to particular illnesses have been identified ('loss' to depression and 'danger' to anxiety). In addition, the match between negative aspects of events and characteristics of the individual experiencing them has sought to predict the likely impact. For example, a severe life event in a domain of prior high commitment (such as losing a job in the context of marked work commitment) or in a domain of role conflict (child failing at school in the context of a mother's parenthood/employment role conflict) all carry increased risk for affective disorders such as depression. Thus, what appears to be a similar event can be experienced differently by different individuals, depending on their context. This can even be true for those living together; married couples have been shown to experience severe events differently with events involving children more often leading to disorder in mothers than fathers. This has been identified as a consequence of mothers' higher commitment to parenting and felt responsible for the event (Nazroo et al., 1997).

Second, those individuals with greater susceptibility to life events have been identified. The initial focus on life events has therefore led to an investigation of personal vulnerability characteristics, both ongoing and in early life, which render an individual more susceptible. The relationship of vulnerability and life events to disorder has been the focus of much investigation. Early identification of vulnerability factors (such as lack of close confidant, presence of three or more children, loss of mother in childhood and lack of employment) were argued to relate to loss of self-esteem. This was hypothesized as generalizing into hopelessness in the face of a severe life event and thus into depressive illness (Brown and Harris, 1978). Further prospective investigation showed attributes of such roles to be critical. Thus, negative relationships (including conflict with partner or child, or lack of close confidant) are associated with low self-esteem and together interact with a severe life event in causing depression.

Third, an individual's response to the event in terms of appraisal and coping has also proved critical in determining whether disorder ensues (Lazarus and Folkman, 1984). Problem solving and positive appraisal of coping options in relation to a life event relate to better health outcomes. Worse outcomes are related to coping behaviours such as self-blame, pessimism and denial. Vulnerable individuals exhibit poorer coping behaviours in response to severe life events, but characteristics of events themselves can influence response.

Certain methodological issues have dogged the study of life events in relation to disorder and required the development of sophisticated measurement, and prospective study design to avoid bias. These include issues of reporting bias, uncertainty of the timing of events in relation to onset of disorder, and the lack of clarity about the meaning of life events for different individuals. Measurement issues have thus proved critical. Early check list approaches examining total 'degree of change' score were based on the sum of self-report estimates of the number of event descriptions endorsed. These approaches, while showing a basic association of event score with illness, were unable to address any of the methodological issues which arose. Semi-structured interviews were thus developed which encouraged narrative accounts of events which, together with extensive probing questions, were able to elicit the full social context

47

of life events and their timing and sequence in relation to disorder (Life Events and Difficulties Schedule, Brown and Harris, 1978). Characteristics of these events were then assessed by the investigators, aided by manuals of precedent examples and consensus agreement to ensure reliability. Those events found to provoke depressive disorder were those objectively assessed as involving high threat or unpleasantness in the longer term, to be focused on the individual and independent from the illness itself. The latter is important in avoiding circularity in terms of illness related events being seen to bring about the disorder.

Although life events are defined by their discrete/acute occurrence, they are frequently related to longer-term stressful circumstances. Measures are needed to identify the longer-term stressors, or difficulties, which might have preceded, or followed from, life events. There is evidence that events arising from chronic difficulties have greater association with onset of depressive illness and create greater propensity to chronicity of disorder.

Life events can be more or less independent of the actions of the individual who becomes ill. This aspect can be critical in gauging the causal potency of the event in provoking disorder. If events are merely a product of vulnerability or the gradual onset of the disorder, then they have a lesser role in the aetiological process. The independence of events ranges from those non-independent (generated solely by the individual, such as voluntary change of job), those possibly independent (equally generated by the individual and others around him/her such as conflict or separation from a close relationship) and those fully independent (those not arising from any volitional act or past behaviour of the individual, such as redundancy following the closing down of a local factory or eviction due to demolition of a housing estate).

Debate has centred around the origin of life events. Life events are not evenly distributed, whether by individual, by gender, by family, by age, by socio-economic group or by location. Much can be attributed to social deprivation, resulting in increased numbers of stressors and lower resources to reduce their impact. However, explanations have also been sought in terms of individuals creating their own high-risk environments by generating events increasingly over the life course. The association of life events and difficulties to psychiatric disorder has been shown to hold throughout the life course. Lifetime studies of recurrent stressors and recurrent disorders show a longer-term trajectory of influence, with childhood adversity relating to greatly increased rates of lifetime events, difficulties and depression (Bifulco et al., 2000).

Investigators examining the role of individuals in creating high-risk environments have become interested in genetic influences. In particular, behavioural genetic approaches to the study of mental and physical disorders hypothesize that both the propensity to experience life events, and susceptibility to their effects, have significant inherited and genetic components. Studies of event similarity in adult twins demonstrate contributions from genetic and common environmental sources in addition to personal environmental influences (Kendler et al., 1993). However, twin studies, partly because of their scale, have failed to utilize the measurement sophistication common to sociological investigation of events. By reverting to check list approaches, attention to the context of events, their severity and independence are generally omitted, with all information based on self-report. The necessarily highly selected twin samples tend to be biased towards more affluent and better functioning families, thus failing to tap the events found in socially deprived groups. Thus, the well-documented greater preponderance of severe life events in low social class positions, in poor neighbourhoods, among socially excluded groups and in urban locations have failed to be integrated into such genetically-geared explanations.

The importance of studying life events in illness is not purely to understand social causation but also to influence intervention. Life events can be both positive and negative. Positive events have been shown to aid recovery from disorder. For example, in depression, hope-enhancing events (fresh start) and in anxiety, security-enhancing events (anchoring) have been associated with recovery. Help-seeking is also an important part of coping, with support from close others at time of life event crisis showing protective effects on onset and chronicity of disorders. Befriending interventions which provide support in dealing with events and ongoing difficulties have been shown to have a significant effect on recovery from disorder (Harris et al., 1999). Thus life events continue to be important components in both the disease and recovery process.

See also: *social support* and *psycho-social factors.*

REFERENCES

Bifulco, A., Bernazzani, O., Ball, C. and Moran, P. (2000) 'Lifetime stressors and recurrent depression: preliminary findings of the Adult Life Phase Interview (ALPHI)', *Social Psychiatry and Psychiatric Epidemiology*, 35: 264–75.

Brown, G.W. and Harris, T. (1978) *Social Origins of Depression*. London: Tavistock.

Brown, G.W. and Harris, T. (1989) *Life Events and Illness*. New York: Guilford Press.

Harris, T., Brown, G.W. and Robinson, R. (1999) 'Befriending as an intervention for chronic depression among women in an inner-city. 2: Role of fresh-start experiences and baseline psycho-social factors in remission from depression', *British Journal of Psychiatry*, 174: 225–232.

49

Kendler, K., Neale, M., Kessler, R., Heath, A. and Eaves, L. (1993) 'A twin study of recent life events and difficulties', *Archives of General Psychiatry*, 50: 789–96.

Lazarus, R.S. and Folkman, S. (1984) *Stress, Appraisal and Coping*. New York: Springer.

Nazroo, J., Edwards, A.C. and Brown, G.W. (1997) 'Gender differences in onset of depression following a shared life event: a study of couples', *Psychological Medicine*, 27: 9–19.

TB

lifecourse

> **Definition: In the context of health and illness, the lifecourse refers to the varying exposure to health risks experienced by individuals and groups either before or during birth, in childhood, or at various stages in adult life.**

In recent years approaches to health and illness using a lifecourse perspective have grown in popularity, especially among those working in the field of health inequalities. Instead of looking at data covering one point in time (for example, mortality data for 2001–2) and then correlating these with social factors (for example, occupational social class in the 2001 census), a lifecourse approach would seek, on a more continuous basis, to document early influences on outcomes in adulthood or in later life. Different kinds of data could be used to achieve this, but the perspective would likely to be a longitudinal one, mapping changes over time. Data collected regularly from birth cohorts (groups of people born at a particular time) are especially suited to lifecourse analysis.

The idea of the lifecourse differs from notions such as the life span, which denotes the maximum number of years a person may or does live, or life cycle, where fixed stages of birth, growth, adulthood, old age and finally death are marked by anatomical, physiological or cognitive changes. A lifecourse perspective makes less assumptions about fixed 'stages', though it may be concerned with some markers of transitions in people's lives, whether biological or social. Discontinuities in people's biographies and protective factors in long-term health outcomes can also be studied in a lifecourse perspective.

Much of the most recent debate about the lifecourse and health has stemmed from the so-called 'Barker hypothesis', following the work of the epidemiologist David Barker on the foetal origins of disease (1994, 1995). Barker's work was originally concerned with heart disease in men born in Lancashire and in Hertfordshire, England. By examining the health records of men born in the years before 1939, which provided details of birth weight and early growth, he showed that death from heart disease in later life was commoner in those who were smaller at birth and at one year. This work led to the idea that health and illness in adult life were 'biologically programmed' at birth. Studies of heart disease from other countries have shown similar patterns (e.g. Leon et al., 1998).

As Wadsworth (1996) has shown, this biological programming approach to health and the lifecourse includes developmental factors that act 'downstream' as the individual becomes exposed to (or protected from) behavioural and societal risk factors. The combination of poor foetal origins with later life factors such as obesity and smoking (both now strongly related to social class, being greater among poorer groups) significantly increases the risk for diseases such as diabetes and respiratory illness, as well as heart disease. However, the original Barker hypothesis placed special emphasis on events prior to and around the time of birth. Barker states that 'undernutrition and other adverse influences arising in fetal life or immediately after birth have a permanent effect on the body's structure, physiology and metabolism' (cited by Wadsworth, 1996: 153).

The idea that adult health and disease are already programmed at birth has become enormously influential in medicine, where Barker's ideas have been widely circulated. Barker's early papers on the subject were quickly collected and published in book form by the British Medical Journal (Barker, 1994). Part of the attraction of a biological programming hypothesis lies in its ability to redirect debates about health patterning and inequalities away from overtly controversial social and political issues, of the sort encountered by the Black Report and the Health Divide (Townsend et al., 1990) when they were published, and re-establish the causal primacy of individual level biological markers. For those in public health these factors can then be linked with social conditions such as those governing maternal health and health-related behaviours. The emphasis on biology also allows epidemiologists and others to connect their work with that going on in genetics and evolutionary biology, both of which have undoubted intellectual and cultural currency (as well as considerable research funding) at the present time.

Despite, or perhaps because of its emphasis on individual biological factors, medical sociology has also been drawn to the Barker hypothesis and a lifecourse approach. Much of what is now being argued about the

51

lifecourse follows Barker's approach, and in part constitutes a critical debate with it. The relative impact of biological and social factors follows the contours of this professional terrain. The medical sociologists Vågerö and Illsley, for example, have argued for the adoption of a lifecourse perspective in which 'biological and social influences are not mutually exclusive' (1995: 232). The task then is to tease out the relative impact of different biological and social factors on health across time. Sociologists have also been interested in the lifecourse as it demonstrates links between early biological development and *social* outcomes in adult life, some of which, in turn, may be linked with health.

Two examples can illustrate this latter point. The first concerns birth weight. Data from the 1958 birth cohort study, in England, covering birth weight in males and subsequent social standing as measured by housing and financial difficulties (Blane, 1999: 67) show consistent patterns. Housing difficulties are here defined as overcrowding or having to share basic facilities such as toilets or hot water supply. Financial difficulties are measured by indicators such as social class V at birth, reported financial problems or the receipt of free school meals. The evidence shows that low birth weight disadvantages the individual through both biological and social pathways. In this approach poor physical development is seen to 'select out' individuals over time, for example, in the job market, in such a way that life chances are adversely affected on a number of fronts. It may also be the case that mediating pathways include difficulties in making or sustaining personal relationships. It has recently been shown, for example, that birth weight is associated with marital status, with the finding that men (this time in Helsinki) 'who were small at birth are less likely to marry', an observation in line with Barker's original research in Hertfordshire (Philips et al., 2001).

The second example concerns the impact of height, about which there is much discussion in sociological as well as medical circles. Again data from various studies show a strong correlation between height in the early years of life and social outcomes such as unemployment. Height, like birth weight, appears to correlate with many social factors, from unemployment to social class. Height in women appears to predict social mobility as measured by 'achieved social class' in comparison with 'class of origin' (Illsley, 1986). Both biological and social processes are held to be at work here. Height may be a measure of thriving and thus physical and psychological capacity, or may be indirectly related to health, again, through a 'selection' processes acting on work and marriage chances.

For medical sociologists, bringing together biological data on foetal origin and early development, with social as well as health outcomes, offers a way of maintaining an emphasis on health inequalities in adult or later life (focusing on unemployment or poverty) while recognizing the significance of arguments about early influences on the lifecourse put forward by Barker and others. Wadsworth, for example, argues that research working across these boundaries can argue for the importance of the interaction between social and biological capital across the lifecourse, with an emphasis on the social. He states:

> A poor start in terms of health or social beginnings is likely to be a long-term problem, because health capital seems increasingly likely to be fixed, and although social capital develops more gradually and over a longer period, it becomes in later life the key to maximizing the benefits of health capital. (1996: 164)

Social influences can also, of course have an impact on health from the earliest of years. Wadsworth gives particular emphasis to the importance of education as a moderating influence on a 'poor start'. Education may be particularly important not just in terms of its potential contribution to social mobility and earning capacity (Wadsworth, 1991: 150–1) but also in such areas as health promotion and the development of healthy lifestyles. However, the impact of peer pressure and cultural fashions surrounding health-related behaviours remains important. Wadsworth argues that this needs to be recognized in devising better health education among young people if it is to have a lasting influence on development and the lifecourse (1996: 165).

Most of the current interest in lifecourse influences on health and social status has focused on physical illness, albeit among older groups on chronic illness as well as on life-threatening conditions such as heart disease. However, the study of mental health is also open to a lifecourse approach. The recent work of Bifulco and Moran (1998) can help to illustrate this point.

In their book, *Wednesday's Child*, Bifulco and Moran summarize data from community-based studies of samples of individual women in London and of sisters who have been interviewed about their early life. As far as depression in adulthood is concerned, evidence for the lasting influence of psychological and social factors in its occurrence and course seems clear. In particular, neglect and abuse early in childhood, especially in combination, lead to a significantly increased risk of depression later in life. The role of neglect is especially prominent in this work, alongside the much more widely recognized role of physical or sexual abuse.

These studies also show a clear relationship between neglect and abuse and the presence of family poverty. However, while the inequalities

53

literature has emphasized the role of poverty as playing a major role in adult physical health, Bifulco and Moran argue that neglect and abuse in childhood play a more important part in mental health. Though such processes often unfolded in the context of material hardship, such hardship alone could not, in their studies, explain the onset of disorder (Bifulco and Moran, 1998: 128). The point here is that lifecourse influences on health are not likely to be simple or mechanistic effects of either biological or social determinants, but involve complex processes that either raise the risk of health problems in later life or protect against it.

These important studies on mental health reveal a more general difficultly with the lifecourse concept. While the lifecourse undoubtedly directs attention to pathways that may be important for health, these may be variously causal, selective or confounding in character. When biological, social *and* psychological processes are considered, a plausible narrative thread in the argument may sometimes be difficult to sustain. Indeed, the researcher may be presented with a host of correlations of the sort that lead to no specific or useful conclusions. This may be especially the case where social outcomes, such as marriage or its absence, are the focus of study. It is difficult to see how birth weight or height, for example, 'selects out' some individuals and not others in the complex processes of marital decisions and relationships, despite the correlations found in the data.

If the lifecourse approach is to be developed by medical sociologists, it needs to be grounded in the lived experience of individuals and collectivities. This means studying the biographical and contextual nature of unfolding experience in particular historical and cultural circumstances, rather than relying on statistical data that are too distant from the issues being examined. Some of the best work on birth cohorts has done and is currently trying to do just this – piecing together the various influences that have affected individuals and collectivities (together with their own actions and agency) over time.

But the study of the intersection of biography and history presents a final difficulty. The experience of cohorts born 40 or 50 years ago may have limited value for those born in the current period, where low birth weight, for example, is much reduced, and where adverse social circumstances means something quite different from the experiences of those brought up in the pre- or post-1945 period. A lifecourse approach to health needs to be able to relate to a contemporary context if it is to be more than of historical interest.

See also: *social class* and *material and cultural factors.*

REFERENCES

Barker, D. (1994) *Mothers, Babies and Disease in Later Life*. London: BMJ Publishing Group.

Barker, D. (1995) 'Fetal origins of coronary heart disease', *British Medical Journal*, 311, 171–4.

Bifulco, A. and Moran, P. (1998) *Wednesday's Child*. London: Routledge.

Blane, D. (1999) 'The life course, the social gradient and health', in M. Marmot and R.G. Wilkinson (eds), *Social Determinants of Health*. Oxford: Oxford University Press.

Illsley, R. (1986) 'Occupational class, selection and the production of inequalities in health', *Quarterly Journal of Social Affairs*, 2: 151–65.

Leon, D.A., Lithell, H.O., Vågerö, D., Koupilova, I., Mohsen, R., Berglund, L., Lithell, U. and McKeigue, P.M. (1998) 'Reduced fetal growth and increased risk of death from ischaemic heart disease: cohort study of 15000 Swedish men and women born 1915–29', *British Medical Journal*, 317: 241–5.

Philips, I.W., Handelsman, D.J., Eriksson, J.G., Forsen, T., Osmond, C. and Barker, D.J.P. (2001) 'Prenatal growth and subsequent marital status: longitudinal study', *British Medical Journal*, 322: 771.

Townsend, P., Davison, N. and Whitehead, M. (1990) *Inequalities in Health: The Health Divide*. Harmondsworth: Penguin Books.

Vågerö, D. and Illsley, R. (1995) 'Explaining health inequalities, beyond Black and Barker', *European Sociological Review* 11 (3): 219–41.

Wadsworth, M. (1991) The Imprint of Time: Childhood, History and Adult Life. Oxford: Oxford University Press.

Wadsworth, M. (1996) 'Family and education as determinants of health', in D. Blane, E. Brunner and R. Wilkinson (eds), *Health and Social Organisation: Towards a Health Policy for the 21st Century*. London: Routledge.

MB

medical sociology

55

PART 2

Experience of Illness

medicalization

> **Definition: Medicalization describes a process by which non-medical problems become defined and treated as medical problems, usually in terms of illnesses or disorders.**

Medicalization is now established as a key sociological concept yet it is difficult to be specific about when it entered the social scientific lexicon. It seems that the process was first referred to by critics of the growing influence of psychiatry in the 1960s (although these critics did not use the term explicitly), and grew in popularity in the 1970s when linked with the concept of social control. Since then, medicalization has been applied to a whole variety of problems that have come to be defined as medical, ranging from childbirth and the menopause through to alcoholism and homosexuality.

According to Conrad and Schneider (1980), medicalization can occur on three distinct levels: (1) conceptually when a medical vocabulary is used to define a problem; (2) institutionally, when organizations adopt a medical approach to treating a problem in which they specialize; and (3) at the level of doctor–patient interaction when a problem is defined as medical and medical treatment occurs. As these distinctions illustrate, the process often involves physicians and their treatments directly. However, this is not necessarily so, as in the case of alcoholism where the medical profession may be only marginally involved or not involved at all.

Medicalization is often associated with the control of deviance and the ways in which deviant behaviours that were once defined as immoral, sinful or criminal have been given medical meanings. The process of medicalizing deviant behaviour is not straightforward, however, and can be seen as involving a five-stage sequential process (Conrad and Schneider, 1992). The first stage involves a behaviour being defined as deviant, usually before the emergence of modern medical definitions. For example, chronic drunkenness was defined as highly undesirable before any medical writer defined it as such. The second stage occurs when the medical conception of a deviant behaviour is announced in a professional medical journal. Descriptions of a new diagnosis (for example, hyperactivity) or the proposal of a medical aetiology for a type of deviant

59

behaviour (for example, alcoholism) are used to promote a deviant behaviour as a medical problem. Next comes claims-making by medical and non-medical interest groups. This stage is crucial if a new deviance designation is to emerge. Medical claims-makers are not usually organized specifically to promote a new medical deviance category but involve a loose alliance of people with similar professional interests. The activities of non-medical claims-makers (for example, pharmaceutical companies or self-help groups) may be more overt and involve engaging in publicity campaigns or political lobbying. They often align themselves with medical claims-makers and use these medical champions to lend scientific credibility to their claims. The fourth stage in the process involves the legitimation of a claim. This occurs when claims-makers launch an instrumental, as opposed to merely a rhetorical challenge to the existing deviance designation. Finally, medicalization occurs when the medical deviance designation is institutionalized. This can be when a deviance designation is codified in a medical classification system or when a bureaucracy is created to provide institutionalized support for medicalization. The value of this theoretical model is that it suggests that attempts to conceptualize deviance as a medical problem are often hotly disputed with the outcome uncertain. Perhaps surprisingly, however, there has been little attempt to evaluate its usefulness or to try and develop it (but see Conrad and Jacobson, 2003).

The logic of this model suggests that the degree to which a condition is medicalized will vary. For some conditions medicalization may be total whereas, for others, competing definitions may exist and medicalization remains incomplete or even minimal. According to Conrad (1992), we do not yet have a good understanding of which factors affect the degree of medicalization. As he notes, the support of the medical profession, the availability of interventions or treatments, the existence of competing definitions and the actions of groups challenging medical definitions may all be important. Nor should it be assumed that medicalization is only a one-way process. It is also possible for de-medicalization to occur if a problem ceases to be defined in medical terms and medical treatments are no longer seen as an appropriate solution. The most frequently mentioned example is homosexuality in America which, until 1973, was defined by the American Psychiatric Association (APA) as an illness. After protests and picketing by the gay liberation movement and support from some sympathetic psychiatrists, the APA voted to declassify it as an illness, a decision that was later endorsed in the UK. As a result, homosexuality became more widely recognized as a lifestyle choice. With the onset of the AIDS epidemic in the 1980s, however, it became partially remedicalized, although in a different form. Overall, the evidence to date is that medicalization is far more common than de-medicalization but it remains important to see it as a two-way process.

While there is now some consensus about the nature of medicalization, there is no such agreement about its cause. Some have argued that the expansion of medical jurisdiction is primarily a consequence of the medical profession exercising its power to define and control what constitutes health and illness in order to extend its professional dominance. Others have considered medicalization to be the result of broader social processes to which doctors are simply responding. Thus, Illich (1976), for example, attributes medicalization to the increasing professionalization and bureaucratization of medical institutions associated with industrialization. For him, the expansion of modern medicine has created a dependence on doctors and taken away people's ability to engage in self-care. Zola (1972) too, has argued that medicalization is rooted in the development of an increasingly complex technological and bureaucratic system and a reliance on the expert.

As the above discussion suggests, many writers tend to conceive of medicalization in a negative way, focusing on how the phenomenon has resulted in a form of medical social control that serves particular interests in society. For Marxists such medicalization is best seen as serving the interests of the ruling capitalist class. From this standpoint, the creation and manipulation of consumer dependence on medicine are merely examples of a more general dependence upon consumer goods propagated by that class. For feminists the focus has tended to be on how a male-dominated medical profession has increasingly defined women's problems in medical terms and advocated medical interventions. Women's experience of childbirth has been a particular focus of attention. Here it has been suggested that doctors' use of obstetric techniques such as foetal monitoring machines, pain-killing drugs, induction and forceps without telling women patients why such techniques are necessary or what the risks are has resulted in their experiencing childbirth as alienating. Moreover, as it is usually male doctors who often control such technology, its coercive utilization is seen as reinforcing existing patriarchal social relations.

In contrast, others have pointed to the real clinical and symbolic benefits of medicalization. Redefining a condition as appropriate for medical attention opens up opportunities for the alleviation of symptoms or a cure and also legitimates it, reducing the stigma and censure that may be attached. In the case of chronic fatigue syndrome, for instance, it seems that patients may benefit from a diagnosis simply because it makes meaningful an incoherent and disruptive experience, and opens up possibilities for managing and living with the syndrome (Broom and Woodward, 1996). Similarly, those with a drinking problem have benefited from the label of alcoholism as a disease as it has helped them to counter-act attributions of blame and moral weakness. Medicalization has also meant that they are now less likely to be arrested for being drunk in a public place and more likely to be medically treated in a potentially more humane way than would otherwise be the case.

The medicalization thesis has much to recommend it, including the creation of new understandings of the social processes involved in the development and response to medical diagnosis and treatment and the development of a critical framework to analyse medicine, health and health care. However, a number of important criticisms have also been levelled against it, especially its more negative variant. In particular, it has been criticized for portraying the individual patient and the lay public more generally as essentially passive and uncritical in the face of modern medicine's expanding jurisdiction. For example, Kohler Riessman (1989) in her discussion of women's experience of different conditions, ranging from childbirth to premenstrual syndrome, has drawn attention to the way in which women have at times actively participated in the medicalization process to meet their own needs and have not simply been passive victims of medical ascendancy. Williams and Calnan (1996) have developed this critique further by drawing on arguments about modernity as a reflexive social order, 'risk society' and lay re-skilling. They suggest that in late modernity there is a far more critical relationship between medicine and the lay populace and that trust in medicine increasingly has to be won and maintained in the face of growing public awareness of the risks as well as the benefits of medicine and the limits of medical expertise. It is in this context that re-skilling or re-appropriation of knowledge takes place as lay people interpret the information produced by medical experts, both individually and collectively. In addition, Strong (1979) has claimed that the negative portrayals of medical expansion found in the medicalization thesis, while containing important insights, are nevertheless in certain respects exaggerated and self-serving. Medical sociologists' failure to be self-conscious about their vested interests has resulted in a tendency to exaggerate the degree of medical power and ignore constraints on medicalization, such as state control.

While these criticisms are well made, medicalization remains a useful concept for sociologists of health and illness. There is, however, a need to go beyond the accumulation of different cases of medicalization to try and develop a more integrated theory of the process of medicalization, its

62

causes and consequences and to relate these to recent changes in medical organization and knowledge and the growing challenge to medical authority.

See also: *consumerism, risk* and *decline of medical autonomy.*

REFERENCES

Broom, D.H. and Woodward, R. (1996) 'Medicalisation reconsidered: toward a collaborative approach to care', *Sociology of Health and Illness*, 18: 357–78.

Conrad, P. (1992) 'Medicalization and social control', *Annual Review of Sociology*, 18: 209–32.

Conrad, P. and Jacobson, H. (2003) 'Enhancing biology? Cosmetic surgery and breast augmentation', in S.J. Williams, G.A. Bendelow and L. Birke (eds), *Debating Biology: Sociological Reflections on Health, Medicine and Society*. London: Routledge.

Conrad, P. and Schneider, J.W. (1980) 'Looking at levels of medicalization: a comment on Strong's critique of the thesis of medical imperialism', *Social Science and Medicine*, 14A: 75–9.

Conrad, P. and Schneider, J.W. (1992) *Deviance and Medicalization: From Badness to Sickness*. 3rd edn. Philadelphia, PA: Temple University Press.

Illich, I. (1976) *Medical Nemesis*. London: Calder and Boyars.

Kohler Riessman, C. (1989) 'Women and medicalisation: a new perspective', in P. Brown (ed.), *Perspectives in Medical Sociology*. Belmont, CA: Wadsworth.

Strong, P. (1979) 'Sociological imperialism and the profession of medicine: a critical examination of the thesis of medical imperialism', *Social Science and Medicine*, 13A: 199–215.

Williams, S. and Calnan, M. (1996) 'The "limits" of medicalisation? Modern medicine and the lay populace', *Social Science and Medicine*, 42: 1609–20.

Zola, I. (1972) 'Medicine as an institution of social control', *Sociological Review*, 20: 487–54.

JGA

63

illness behaviour

> **Definition: Illness behaviour refers to the way in which people define and interpret their symptoms and the actions they take in seeking help.**

One of the first sociologists to discuss illness as a social behaviour was Talcott Parsons (1951). Parsons suggested that for illness not to disrupt society's ability to function efficiently and effectively, a specific 'sick role' was necessary. Within the sick role the patient has an obligation to seek and be receptive to medical advice and treatment and, in return, they will be identified as 'sick' and released from their usual duties within society. In turn, doctors are placed in a position of authority, with the expectation that they will provide appropriate health care. However, as Bloor and Horobin (1974) suggest, Parsons' model of the sick role is an 'ideal type', being characterized by abstract generalizability and exaggeration of empirical reality. Thus, they argue that sick people do not always become patients and not all patients are sick.

Moreover, although Parsons saw the relationship between the patient and the doctor as reciprocal and, therefore, unproblematic, Bloor and Horobin suggested that a major source of potential conflict evolves from doctors' ambivalent expectations of how patients ought to behave when they consult. On the one hand, doctors expect patients to have the expertise to judge when their symptoms warrant medical help, and should therefore avoid bringing 'trivia' to the doctor. On the other hand, however, when patients arrive at the medical encounter, they are expected to surrender their medical knowledge and be guided by the medical 'experts'. This, Bloor and Horobin suggest, places patients in a 'double-bind'.

Although doctors often complain that patients come to see them with 'trivia', a recent study of community health care utilization (Rogers et al., 1999) revealed that the most common response to illness was to self-medicate with products purchased over the counter. Thus, it has been suggested that a 'symptom iceberg' exists, where around one-third of people experiencing symptoms do nothing, one-third self-medicate or seek alternative therapies and one-third consult the doctor. Further investigation into this mismatch between need and demand for health care has shown that a greater proportion of patients with significant symptoms do not consult the doctor than there are patients consulting with minor symptoms. Thus, patients who seek medical help are often not the sickest. Although Parsons (1951) believed that his model of the sick role was necessary to maintain social order, research shows that illness behaviour is much more complex, with many factors influencing decisions to seek medical help.

Indeed, noting the complexity surrounding decisions to seek medical help, Mechanic and Volkart were the first to describe the concept of illness behaviour. They used the term 'illness behaviour' to refer to 'the ways in which given symptoms may be differentially perceived, evaluated, and acted (or not acted) upon by different kinds of persons' (1960: 87).

Recognizing that people responded to illness in different ways, Mechanic and Volkart suggested that social factors such as education, religion and social class played an important role in shaping illness behaviour.

More recent work has also revealed the importance of social factors on the decision to consult the doctor. In particular, social class has been found to relate to illness behaviour, with people from a higher social class being more likely to view themselves as being ill and to seek treatment than their working-class counterparts. As Blaxter and Paterson (1982) found in their study of working-class mothers, illness was seen as a normal part of daily life. As long as their children could walk and play, the mothers in Blaxter and Paterson's study often did not define them as ill, even in the presence of symptoms. Other studies show social class differences in the reported experience of tiredness and backache. These symptoms are generally found to be key features of illness among middle-class respondents, whereas there is a tendency in working-class communities for people to accept these symptoms as a part of normal life. It has been suggested that this functional definition of health and illness among people from poorer backgrounds is based on an economic need to keep working, as well as/or as the result of low expectations of medical care.

Illness behaviour has also been found to be culturally patterned. Following field studies with patients in New York, Zola (1973) found that there were differences among the ways in which Irish and Italian respondents viewed illness. Irish patients in this study tended to perceive their illness in terms of a specific dysfunction and described their symptoms as interfering with physical functioning. In contrast, Italian patients perceived their illness in a more diffuse way and described their symptoms as causing disruption to their general mode of living. Other studies have shown similar findings, with Irish respondents being more stoical about pain and responding by withdrawing from social interaction and Italian respondents being more vocal about their pain and requiring social support from others.

In addition to the impact of social variables on illness behaviour, Mechanic and Volkart (1960) identified four dimensions of the illness itself that influenced the decision to seek medical help: (1) the frequency with which the illness occurs in a given population (its commonality); (2) the familiarity of the symptoms; (3) the predictability of the outcome of the illness; and (4) the amount of threat and loss that is likely to result from the illness.

In later studies, Mechanic (1978) identified a number of other factors relating to the type of illness that influenced help-seeking behaviour. These included the visibility or salience of the symptoms, the perceived

65

present and future seriousness of the symptoms, the extent to which symptoms disrupt social activities, the frequency of symptoms and interpretations of the cause of symptoms and availability of treatment. In addition, Mechanic recognized that the impact that illness had on those caring for the patient was an important determinant of illness behaviour. He suggested that when illness becomes so disruptive to everyday life that the carer is unable to cope any longer, medical help will usually be sought.

Like Zola and Mechanic, Herzlich (1973) also found that illness behaviour depended upon the extent to which symptoms interfered with a person's life. Following a study in Paris and rural France, Herzlich found that the effect that symptoms had on a person's normal activity influenced their perceptions of illness and, in turn, their decisions to seek medical help. Herzlich described three ways in which people viewed their illness: (1) illness as destructive; (2) illness as a liberator; and (3) illness as an occupation. Where illness was perceived as destructive, it was seen as a barrier to maintaining normal roles within society, which eventually resulted in exclusion from social groups. People perceiving illness in this way often used denial as a means of restricting social isolation and they therefore tended not to consult the doctor. Those who considered illness as a liberator viewed it as a positive experience where they were freed from their social obligations. Medical advice was generally sought as it provided legitimate entrance to the sick role. Where illness was seen as an occupation, it was considered as something that had to be worked at in much the same way as was required of paid employment or domestic work. The maximum medical advice was therefore sought in order to fight the illness.

Zola (1973) also saw the ability to cope with symptoms as an important determinant of illness behaviour. He suggested that rather than consulting when they are most sick, people often consult when their ability to accommodate symptoms breaks down. Zola identified five factors, or 'triggers', which initiate a person into consulting the doctor. First there is the occurrence of an interpersonal crisis, such as the death of relative. Although the patient may experience symptoms for some time, it often takes a crisis to occur before they seek medical help. Second is perceived interference with social or personal relations, where symptoms start to have an impact on a person's social life or their relationships with others. The third trigger is sanctioning, where family members or friends suggest that they seek medical help and thereby agree that there is a need to go to the doctor. Fourth is perceived interference with vocational or physical activity, where symptoms prevent the patient from carrying out their daily activities. Finally, there is the temporalizing of symptoms, where a time limit is placed on the illness. People will often say that they will consult the doctor if the symptom has not gone within a given time frame.

Although the decision to consult the doctor is shaped by the type of illness and a person's individual and social circumstances, it is unusual for a person to seek medical help without first discussing their symptoms with at least one other person. A number of studies have shown that most people talk with many different friends and family members before going to see a doctor. This line of communication about illness has been termed 'the lay referral system' and has been shown to influence illness behaviour. The size and type of social network have been found to have an impact on medical consultation rates. Large friendship networks tend to increase the medical consultation rate, whereas large family networks tend to support self-reliance. Close-knit networks, however, have been shown to work both in delaying and hastening the decision to seek medical help. Where a person receives adequate support from friends and family members, they are less likely to feel the need for support from health care professionals. Yet, repeated discussions about symptoms may also increase a person's anxiety level and therefore prompt them to seek reassurance from the doctor. It has been suggested that social networks have a changing relationship with health care utilization and family proximity may not be as important in the decision to consult as it has been in the past (Rogers et al., 1999).

The experience of illness involves more than the biophysical effect of symptoms. The interpretation of symptoms and action taken in response to illness are not only shaped by social and cultural factors but are also context-dependent, being influenced by specific aspects of the illness such as type, duration and visibility. In addition, social networks are frequently utilized in decision-making about seeking medical help. Thus, although Parsons saw access to the sick role as a necessary response to illness, patients have their own interpretations about their symptoms and what action, if any, should be taken.

See also: *lay knowledge* and *sick role.*

REFERENCES

Blaxter, M. and Paterson, L. (1982) *Mothers and Daughters: A Three Generation Study of Health Attitudes and Behaviour.* London: Heinemann Educational Books.
Bloor, M. and Horobin, G. (1974) 'Conflict and conflict resolution in doctor-patient relationships', in C. Cox and A. Mead (eds), *A Sociology of Medical Practice.* London: Collier Macmillan.

67

Herzlich, C. (1973) *Health and Illness*. London: Academic Press.

Mechanic, D. (1978) *Medical Sociology*. 2nd edn. New York: Free Press.

Mechanic, D. and Volkart, E.H. (1960) 'Illness behaviour and medical diagnosis', *Journal of Health and Human Behaviour*, 1: 86–94.

Parsons, T. (1951) *The Social System*. New York: Free Press.

Rogers, A., Hassell, K. and Nicolaas, G. (1999) *Demanding Patients? Analysing the Use of Primary Care*. Buckingham: Open University Press.

Zola, K. (1973) 'Pathways to the doctor: from person to patient', *Social Science and Medicine*, 7: 677–89.

KB

stigma

> **Definition: Stigma refers to a negatively defined condition, attribute, trait or behaviour conferring 'deviant' status, which is socially, culturally and historically variable.**

The term stigma has a long lineage, predating the advent of the social sciences as we know them today. The Greeks, in fact, originated the term to refer to bodily signs, cut or burnt into the body, which were designed to expose the bearer as a slave, a criminal or a social outcast; someone 'ritually polluted' who was to be avoided, especially in public places. Today, however, the term is applied more widely to any condition, attribute, trait or behaviour that symbolically marks the bearer off as 'culturally unacceptable' or 'inferior' and has, as its subjective referent, the notion of shame or disgrace.

Perhaps the key point of reference, for present purposes, is Goffman's pioneering study of 1963, tellingly entitled *Stigma: Notes on the Management of Spoiled Identity*. Part and parcel of his own inimitable dramaturgical perspective on the vicissitudes of self-presentation in everyday life, Goffman's concern in this book is with the maintenance and integrity of the self, or perhaps more correctly in this case, the presentation of a discredited or discreditable self. Taking such a stance, in other words, provides a 'special application of the art of impression management', revealing through its potential disruption, much about the taken-for-granted or tacit ways in which people organize their lives and the everyday encounters through which they unfold.

A full account of Goffman's study is beyond the scope of this brief chapter (see, for example, Williams, 1987). Suffice it to say that three distinct types of stigma are identified by Goffman: (1) namely stigmas of the body (such as blemishes or deformities); (2) stigmas of character (the mentally ill or the criminal, for example); and (3) stigmas associated with social collectivities ('racial' or tribal), all of which he stresses are socially, culturally and historically variable. Perhaps most importantly for this discussion, Goffman's social definition of stigma turns on the distinction he draws between 'virtual social identity' – normative expectations, that is to say, of what the person *ought* to be – and 'actual social identity'; the category or attributes the individual *actually* possesses. The stigmatized, from this perspective, are those who possess a deeply discrediting *discrepancy* between virtual and actual social identity *vis-à-vis* those 'normals' for whom no such discrepancy occurs. A stigma, then, 'is really a special kind of relationship between attribute and stereotype' (Goffman, 1963: 14); a meaning imposed on an attribute via negative images, stereotypes and attitudes that potentially discredits a member of a particular social category. This, in turn, maps on to another distinction which Goffman draws between the *discredited*, whose stigma is evident or 'known about', and the *discreditable* whose situation is the precise opposite. In the former case, the prime dramaturgical task is one of 'managing tension', in the latter case it is one of 'managing information': to tell or not to tell, to reveal or conceal, that is the question! (Goffman, 1963).

Goffman's treatment of these issues echoes labelling theory, which eclipsed Parsonian perspectives on illness as social deviance in the 1960s, stressing how stigma springs from the definitional workings of society, rather than the inherent qualities of the attribute or behaviour itself. The basic idea here, building on the work of Lemert and espoused by writers such as Becker, Erikson and Kitsuse, is one of 'primary deviance' (the original infraction), societal reaction (public/professional 'crisis'), and 'secondary deviance' (the person's response to the negative societal reaction), leading to a 'master-status' (which floods out all other roles and sources of identity) that is extremely difficult to disavow or shake off. In short, stigma as a societal reaction 'spoils identity', a phenomenon generated in social situations and the contingencies they entail by virtue of unrealized norms, which impinge on the encounter in more or less pressing and predictable ways.

Goffman, however, in typical iconoclastic fashion, adds a further twist. His penchant for mentioning troubling truths about individuals is clearly evident when he notes that the blind, the deaf, the ex-mental patient, the prostitute, the ex-convict, and many others discussed in the pages of his book, are not the only ones who experience stigmatization. Norms of identity, Goffman comments, breed deviations along with conformity. Stigma management is a general phenomenon, a process that occurs wherever there are identity norms. Few people are totally without discrediting attributes. The reader is led, therefore, to realize that 'stigma involves not so much a set of concrete individuals who can be separated into two piles, the stigmatized and the normal, as a pervasive two-role social process in which every individual participates in both roles . . . the normal and stigmatized are not persons but rather perspectives' (ibid.: 163–4). This provides Goffman with the rationale for claiming that if people are to refer to the stigmatized individual as 'deviant' they might more profitably regard them as a 'normal deviant'.

These ideas and arguments have translated more or less readily into sociological studies of the meaning and experience of illness, both mental and physical, over the years. The sociology of chronic illness, for example, has proved particularly fertile terrain upon which to explore these insights, developing and refining them along the way. A particularly notable study, for example, is Scambler's (1989) research on epilepsy in Britain. Once diagnosed as suffering from epilepsy – thereby officially making them, according to Scambler's respondents, into an 'epileptic' – individuals typically found themselves confronted with problems of information control. Scambler makes a useful distinction here between 'felt' and 'enacted' stigma. The former pertains to the fear of being discriminated against due to cultural 'unacceptability' or 'inferiority'. The latter, in contrast, refers to actual cases or enactments of discrimination. For Scambler's respondents it was fear of stigmatization, which was most disruptive of their lives, rather than actual cases of enacted stigma.

Faced with these dilemmas, various forms of adaptation emerge. Schneider and Conrad (1981), for example, in their American study, refer to 'adjusted' and 'unadjusted' responses to epilepsy, the former including the following sub-types: *pragmatic* attempts to minimize the impact of epilepsy (while concealing it); the concealment of one's epileptic status (the *secret* sub-type); and the '*quasi-liberated*' attempt to positively avow rather than disavow what others see as a discreditable attribute, thereby challenging others' conceptions and freeing an individual from the need for concealment or secrecy due to 'felt' stigma. For those displaying 'unadjusted' responses, in contrast, the defining feature was a sense of being 'overwhelmed' or 'overcome' by the condition, which included the 'debilitated' sub-type (Schneider and Conrad, 1981: 215–17).

Another more recent treatment of these issues, for comparative purposes, concerns a study by Navon (1996) of leprosy destigmatization campaigns in Thailand. Interestingly, the study found that educating the public about leprosy only increased the risks of stigmatization. An explicit message not to be afraid of the disease, for example, suggests an implicit message that most people are still afraid of it (1996: 271). The stigma itself, however, Navon argues, bears the potential for destigmatization; a paradox explained by the fact that the worse the image of the disease, coupled with policies of secrecy or concealment by sufferers, the less likely its identification with people diagnosed today, thereby avoiding actual negative reactions. The discrepancy, in other words, between leprosy's image and the reality of the patients' lives today (given advances in medical treatment) is 'already so great that even when an actual case leprosy is diagnosed, society's reaction tends to be one of scepticism' (ibid.: 271). This implies that an analysis of destigmatization processes that considers the difference between 'images and actual reactions, as well as changes in the stigmatized phenomenon itself, may completely undermine the view of all stigmatization as harmful and all destigmatization as helpful' (ibid.: 273). Constructionist perspectives that take a pessimistic view of the possibility of destigmatizing illness, are therefore criticized by Navon, despite the difficulties of destigmatization campaigns. Pessimism, it is argued, is 'not the inevitable conclusion' of the destigmatization process, be it leprosy or some other less stigmatized condition (ibid.: 273).

Enough has been said to indicate the abiding importance of stigma as a social scientific concept, in medical sociology as elsewhere, and its importance to those within medical, health and other welfare settings. A few critical points are nonetheless worth making. First, the interactionist paradigm, within which much of this work on stigma is located, has itself been criticized for its predominantly micro-oriented concerns and a-structural biases. Early work on these issues, moreover, grew out of what Gerhardt (1989) terms the 'crisis' model of illness – illness as a public crisis in which (professional) labelling soon follows – which in contrast to latter-day 'negotiation' models – the negotiation of illness within and beyond the medical encounter – tended to paint a largely passive picture of the person, overwhelmed by the stigmatizing consequences and effects of their newfound 'master status'. These criticisms perhaps are somewhat uncharitable in Goffman's case, particularly in view of his other landmark book *Asylums* (1961), itself part and parcel of the anti-psychiatry movement, in which the power of (total) institutions and the variable, sometimes ingenious, responses of inmates to these 'mortifications' of self

71

is very much to the fore. A final point of criticism concerns a questioning of the notion of illness as deviance, be it the Parsonian or interactionist formulation, given the prevalence of illness within the community, much of which never reaches the doctor's surgery (illness as the norm?); the possibility of conformity to the sick role when ill (Pflanz and Rhode, 1970); and the need to focus not simply on the negative (stigmatizing) consequences of illness, but also on other more positive responses, meanings and styles of adjustment. A balanced, multi-dimensional and multi-layered approach, in short, is clearly required in order to capture the meaning and experience of illness in its manifold guises, stigmatizing or otherwise, and the settings and contexts in which it occurs and unfolds. The potential, in the era of genetic testing and predictive medicine, for new forms of discrimination and stigmatization, alerts us nonetheless, to the abiding importance of this concept across the lay/professional divide.

See also: *chronic illness and disability, illness behaviour* and *social constructionism.*

REFERENCES

Gerhardt, U. (1989) *Ideas About Illness: An Intellectual and Political History of Medical Sociology.* London: Macmillan.

Goffman, E. (1961) *Asylums: Essays on the Social Situation of Mental Patients and Other Inmates.* New York: Doubleday Anchor.

Goffman, E. (1963) *Stigma: Notes on the Management of Spoiled Identity.* New York: Doubleday Anchor.

Navon, L. (1996) 'Beyond constructionism and pessimism: theoretical implications of leprosy destigmatisation campaigns in Thailand', *Sociology of Health and Illness,* 18 (2): 258–76.

Pflanz, M. and Rhode, J.J. (1970) 'Illness: deviant behaviour or conformity?', *Social Science and Medicine,* 4: 645–53.

Scambler, G. (1989) *Epilepsy.* London: Routledge.

Schneider, J. and Conrad, P. (1981) 'In close with illness: epilepsy, stigma potential and information control', *Social Problems,* 28: 32–44.

Williams, S.J. (1987) 'Goffman, interactionism and the management of stigma in everyday life', in G. Scambler (ed.), *Sociological Theory and Medical Sociology.* London: Tavistock, pp. 134–64.

SW

embodiment

> **Definition:** *Embodiment refers to the lived body, our body being-in-the-world, as the site of meaning, experience and expression.*

The philosophical roots of a concern with embodiment, as a challenge to Western dualism, can be traced to the rise of phenomenology in the twentieth century, particularly the work of Merleau-Ponty (1962/1945) in which the mind/body duality is effectively overcome. Embodiment, in this respect, concerns the lived experience of our bodies in the world, including our emotional relations with other similarly embodied beings or agents.

The importance of embodiment has taken some considerable time to filter through to sociology, itself a peculiarly disembodied enterprise until quite recently. This past corporeal neglect, however, has now given way to a burgeoning (some may say excessive) field of sociological work on the body and society, thereby helping put minds back into bodies, bodies back into society and society back into the body. Frank (1991), for example, has been a key exponent of this viewpoint, contrasting his own embodied approach to social action (which may be seen as a 'bottom-up' approach) with Turner's (1984) earlier pioneering sociological formulation of the body as a 'problem' for society (a 'top-down' approach, that is to say) – one focused on the (internal) *restraint* and (external) *representation* of bodies and the *reproduction* and *regulation* of populations in time and space respectively. Turner's (1992) own subsequent work, in fact, has moved more fully to this embodied viewpoint, in keeping with many other writers in this newly emerging field of inquiry. It is not, as these debates suggest, solely or simply a question of the body as a product of society or society as a product of the body, but of bodies both as *shapers of* and *shaped by* the society and social relations of which they are a part. Embodiment, then, provides a crucial missing link between structure and agency, the macro and the micro.

Nowhere are these embodied matters more clearly demonstrated than in relation to health and illness. The sociological conceptualization of chronic illness, for example, as Kelly and Field state, requires a conceptualization of the body, which acknowledges biological and social

73

facts. Biological and physical facts, in this respect, are sociologically significant because they impinge directly on self; provide signals for identity construction; and act as limiting factors on social action for the sufferer (1996: 251). This, in turn, brings to the fore the experiential and expressive dimensions of embodiment.

Pain, for instance, calls into question our normal taken-for-granted relationship to the world and the embodied basis upon which this rests: 'problematizing' our bodies in various ways. The existentially charged and emotionally laden nature of such events – itself inflected through factors such as class and gender, age and ethnicity – is all too apparent here, underlining the importance of biography, self and identity (Williams and Bendelow, 1998). Attempts to reintegrate body, self and society, in this respect, include the search for meaning through narratives – themselves embodied stories and stories of embodiment – together with various strategies and styles of adjustment. While biographical themes of disruption and negative meanings of pain as displeasure abound in such contexts, other more positive renderings of pain are nonetheless possible, responses which may be more or less likely depending on the meaning and context, nature and severity, of the condition in question. Here again we glimpse the material and intentional, physical and emotional dimensions of mindful embodiment and their inextricable intertwining across culture, time and place. We also come to appreciate how the biological body is not so much lost sight of, but placed within a broader embodied, non-reductionist perspective grounded in our being-in-the world: one which a medicine of the lived body, *vis-à-vis* a reductionist biomedicine, must actively take up and dwell within.

Lawton's (2000) recent study of the dying body in the hospice sheds further corporeal light on these issues, drawing attention, *inter alia*, to the inescapably material dimensions of our embodiment, the literal loss of bodily boundaries which the ravages of (malignant) disease may bring and the centrality of bodily integrity to Western notions of selfhood. The modern Western self, as Lawton's case studies on 'unbounded' bodies and 'dirty' dying so clearly reveal, cannot be understood apart from the irreducible fact of embodiment, a body not simply concerned with the superficial arts of impression management or 'display', but one which can 'act' and be 'self-contained'. The deterioration of the body in palliative care – one which may quite literally rot away through malignancy – and the dissolution of the social web are often inseparable here, leading to the 'non-negotiable' or 'inexorable disintegration of self' (Lawton, 2000: 184–5). This moreover, as Lawton emphasizes, involves the sequestration

74

of bodies, both materially and symbolically, within the confines of the modern hospice, thereby enabling certain cherished ideas about living, personhood and the hygienic, sanitized body to be symbolically reaffirmed within society at large (ibid.: 144).

A focus on embodiment in the context of health and illness, also helps bridge the structure–agency, micro–macro divide, opening up many black boxes in doing so. Freund (1998), for instance, in his work on the 'expressive' body, draws attention to the manner in which differing modes of emotional being are, in effect, differing embodied ways of feeling empowered or disempowered in contemporary Western society. The dramaturgical stresses and strains of role performance, he suggests – themselves an index of social hierarchies of power and status, domination and control – translate more or less readily into the health and illness of embodied agents, including neuro-physiological perturbations of many different sorts, whether consciously experienced or not. These processes, in turn, weigh most heavily on those in subordinate positions, via the invalidating definitions of others and the threats to selfhood and ontological insecurity these engender, thereby revealing yet another powerful pathway through which the negative effects of inequality take their toll. A 'geography' of emotions, in Freund's terms, emerges here, spanning both social–physical and psychosomatic space, linked through the vicissitudes of emotion work and the deleterious consequences of dramaturgical stress. In these and other ways, Freund suggests, the expressive body provides a 'common ground' for the sociology of emotions and the sociology of health and illness; an approach, we may add, which meshes well with current debates on inequalities in health.

Attention to fleshy matters of lived embodiment, as these brief illustrations suggest, provides a more promising way forward than (strong) constructionist approaches in which the body is seen, solely or simply, in discursive terms. Both approaches, of course, have their merits and attempts to reconcile them are now very much on the agenda. For some critics, nonetheless, the focus on embodied experience and expression draws attention away from other, more macro-oriented concerns and extra-corporeal sociological matters. This, however, as shown above, is not inevitable; some of the most promising work, indeed, is located precisely at this juncture. As both structured and structuring, the body is central to these debates and their attempted resolution. Other classic sociological themes, moreover, can themselves be re-read in this new more embodied light, augmenting (rather than replacing) former concerns and insights along the way.

One particularly important issue to confront, within and beyond the sociology of health and illness, concerns whether or not we wish to advocate a sociology *of* the body, a sociology *of* embodiment or an *embodied* sociology. A sociology of the body, for example, may reflect on the body as an object of sociological analysis. A sociology of embodiment, in contrast, would take the lived meanings and experiences of bodies seriously, in health as elsewhere. An embodied sociology, however, very much in keeping with the general thrust of this entry, would go one step further, taking the embodiment of its practitioners, as well as those we seek to study, seriously (Williams and Bendelow, 1998). This, in turn, opens up related questions concerning the relationship between reason and emotion, the role of emotions in social life and the emotional underpinnings of sociology itself as a supposedly 'rational' or 'dispassionate' enterprise.

Whatever one's view of these embodied matters, the implications are clear. Sociology's own somewhat disembodied past is now being critically redressed, breathing new corporeal life into its classically rationalist bones.

See also: *chronic illness and disability, illness narratives* and *social constructionism.*

REFERENCES

Frank, A.W. (1991) 'For a sociology of the body: an analytical review', in M. Featherstone, M. Hepworth and B.S. Turner (eds), *The Body: Social Process, Cultural Theory*. London: Sage.

Freund, P.E.S. (1998) 'Social performances and their discontents: the biopsycho-social aspects of dramaturgical stress', in G. Bendelow and S.J. Williams (eds), *Emotions in Social Life: Critical Themes and Contemporary Issues*. London: Routledge.

Kelly, M. and Field, D. (1996) 'Medical sociology, chronic illness and the body', *Sociology of Health and Illness*, 18 (2): 241–57.

Lawton, J. (2000) *The Dying Process: Patients' Experiences of Palliative Care*. London: Routledge.

Merleau-Ponty, M. (1962) *The Phenomenology of Perception*. London: Routledge.

Turner, B.S. (1984) *The Body and Society*. Oxford: Blackwell.

Turner, B.S. (1992) *Regulating Bodies: Essays in Medical Sociology*. London: Routledge.

Williams, S.J. and Bendelow, G. (1998) *The Lived Body: Sociological Themes, Embodied Issues*. London: Routledge.

SW

chronic illness and disability

> **Definition:** **Chronic illness refers to those forms of long-term health disorders that interfere with social interaction and role performance. Disability is a more controversial concept, defined as physical functioning by some, and as social discrimination by others.**

Medical sociology has long had an interest in the study of illness experience and especially of chronic illness. The public health and demographic reasons for this are not hard to find. In the last 40 to 50 years most developed countries (and now many 'developing' nations) have undergone a 'demographic transition'. A decline in mortality at all ages, but especially in infancy and early adulthood, has led to an increase in average life expectancy from birth and (in the presence of low fertility rates) an ageing population. Today the majority of men and women can expect to live into old age. As deaths from infections have declined and as a greater proportion of the population comprises the elderly, those disorders associated with adult and later life have grown in prominence. Many of these are chronic disorders, such as arthritis, stroke, dementia, Parkinson's disease and some forms of heart disease and cancer.

Sociological interest in chronic illness has, in part stemmed from the limitations of medical treatment for chronic disorders. While some forms of treatment are very effective, for example, hip replacement and cataract surgery, many disorders can only be treated palliatively, to relieve pain and to help physical functioning. The long-term implications of chronic illness inevitably bring social and psychological factors to the fore and many physicians have looked to wider forms of collaboration in order to understand the issues more clearly.

Sociological interest has stemmed from key work carried out in the 1960s and 1970s, especially in the USA. Initially, research focused on the social patterning of chronic illness and whether this differed from life-threatening conditions that produced high mortality. Conover (1973) reviewed and re-analysed data that had been the subject of a debate between two sociologists, Kadushin and Mechanic, and concluded that the occurrence of chronic illness was, indeed, related to social class and poverty.

However, most sociological work has been on the consequences of chronic illness, and the steps taken to mitigate its effects. Perhaps the most significant publication in the 1970s, in this regard, was Strauss and Glaser's book, *Chronic Illness and the Quality of Life* (1975). Although Strauss and Glaser begin by noting the health care implications of chronic illness, especially the need for professionals to widen their horizons from their preoccupation with acute conditions, the main thrust of the chapters in the book is strongly interactionist in tone. From this viewpoint, chronic illness is not just a given biological entity, patterned by social conditions, but is itself a 'negotiated reality'. Chronic illness and its outcomes are shaped by the decisions, tactics and organization of 'work' carried out by patients and others, over the 'trajectory' of the illness. The contingent nature of this process is part of a general view of society, which is seen to be the product of interaction and negotiation.

In Britain, Bury (1982) developed this position to argue that chronic illness might be conceptualized as a form of 'biographical disruption'. The impact of serious and persisting symptoms on everyday life was seen to threaten a sense of the taken-for-granted world. Modern medical categories, the medical understanding of disease and the treatment it could offer might be appropriated by patients, and employed in legitimating and explaining their altered condition to family and fiends. At the same time, the diagnosis and its implications for the future might confirm the fact that the individual is suffering from a progressively disabling condition from which there is no escape. In the absence of a medical cure, the individual must negotiate and manage their altered state with what support they can muster.

In a later paper, Bury (1991) went on to distinguish between three dimensions of this process. First, he argued that 'coping' refers to the cognitive processes employed by the chronically ill to sustain a sense of self-worth and to come to terms with an altered situation and an altered body. Second, the term 'strategy' refers to the actions and processes involved in the management of the condition and its impact on interaction and life chances. The strategic management of the disorder and its effects requires decisions about how to mobilize resources and how to balance demands on others and remaining independent. Third, chronic illness involves the adoption of a particular 'style' of living, or different 'styles of adjustment'. Lifestyle for the chronically ill often means deciding how much should be disclosed or disguised about the condition, how far

78

the person should 'come out' and in what way, in interacting with others. For some groups, withdrawal from all but essential interaction has been observed. For others 'normalization' has meant integrating the disorder into an altered and public identity. Biographical disruption may not, therefore, be the only outcome. Depending on outlook and circumstance, biographical reinforcement may also be possible.

Though it is clear from available evidence that most chronic disorders are disabling in their effects, the relationship between chronic illness and disability is a complex and sometimes vexed question. The term 'disability', here, refers to activity restrictions or functional limitations, in movement and dexterity for example. In most official schemas used for assessment and epidemiological purposes, distinctions are usually made between 'impairment' involving changes to the body through illness or trauma, 'disability' in terms of functional and activity limitations, and 'handicap' referring to social disadvantage consequent on impairment and/or disability. Not surprisingly, many national surveys of disability reveal the importance of age, with significant increases in disablement over the age of 75.

In recent years, however, disability movements in a number of countries have sought to challenge such concepts. In many of these alternative arguments, an attempt is made to break the link between chronic illness and disability. Whatever the realities of illness, it is held, 'disability' is essentially a question of social oppression and discrimination (Oliver, 1996). Impairments caused by illness or traumas are accepted as physical realities, but the inability to participate in social or economic activities is strongly argued to be a function of physical and social barriers. From this viewpoint, disability is seen to be the product of a capitalist society that distinguishes between the 'able-bodied' and the 'disabled', with the medicalization of disability adding to the negative responses of the dominant society.

At the far end of this argument, chronic illness and bodily states are completely separated from 'disabling structures' and 'disabling societies'. Oliver argues that disablement has 'nothing to do with the body. It is a consequence of social oppression' (1996: 35). The tendency to treat disability as a characteristic of the individual, it is further argued, reinforces an ideology of individualism and thus a failure to locate the source of disability squarely in society.

However, it is important to note that not all disability activists share these views in total. French (1993), for example, has argued that the specific experiences of groups of disabled people need to be taken into account in any rounded approach to the subject. While it seems clear, she argues, that 'social solutions' are needed to tackle the problems disabled people face, this is not always a straightforward matter. As an individual with a particular form of visual impairment, French recognizes that changes to the environment that might help her might 'disable' someone else. How should the need for brightly light public places by some, for example, be reconciled with the needs of others to have dimmed lights? French states: 'perhaps I am simply lacking in imagination but I have yet to find even a specialized setting for visually impaired people where issues such as this have been resolved' (1993: 21).

Views such as this act a corrective to an 'oversocialized' view of disability, in which social structures and disability rights squeeze out all other considerations. Though dialogue between those documenting the experience of particular groups of people, and those emphasizing the political dimensions of discrimination and oppressive practices has been difficult to pursue, some have sought to re-examine the relationship between chronic illness and disability. Barnes et al., for example, have recently made the point that as work in disability studies progresses, 'the complexities in the relationship between environment/society and impairment/disability will have to be confronted' (1999: 66). The growing diversity within each tradition (medical sociology and disability studies) suggests that a more fruitful exchange may occur in the future.

As far as medical sociology is concerned, one final point should, perhaps, be noted. That is, there is likely to be a continuing tension between a 'problems' perspective, in which the difficulties people face are documented and brought into view, and one in which chronic illness and disability can be approached in a positive, if not always an overtly political, light.

If medical sociology has been largely 'reformist' in tone and disability activists more 'radical', a recent emphasis on a postmodern culture of illness and disability moves beyond these positions. Charmaz (2000), for example, suggests that sociology needs to go further than document the 'patient's perspective' and the normalization processes that 'contain' the effects of illness and disability on everyday life, important though these are. Significantly, she goes on to say that 'chronic illness can mean embarking on an odyssey . . . to integrate the self on a different level . . . facing such losses moves them [the chronically ill] towards transcending loss' (Charmaz, 2000: 287).

As with other sociological writers, especially in North America, the dividing lines between chronic illness, disability and health appear to become blurred in such arguments. Here a form of 'biographical reinvention' may be seen, whether among disability activists, patients' groups or others, in what Frank calls the 'remission society'; a society where large numbers of people may be experiencing or recovering from a variety of bodily ills. What in the earlier literature was seen to be a process of stabilization and normalization by the chronically ill now becomes a ceaseless and nomadic journey with no clear end point. The links between body, self and society, in this viewpoint, are not simply the outcome of interactional difficulties or 'social oppression', but constitute a shifting terrain, on which individuals and groups attempt to construct new identities and new realities.

There is a need for medical sociology to examine empirically the salience of this postmodern approach, as well as the more political stance of some disability researchers, by conducting studies among representative samples of the chronically ill and disabled. Without this, both medical sociology and disability studies may be caught up in forms of rhetoric that are difficult to evaluate. The testing of many of the ideas that have grown in recent years would seem to be the most urgent task facing medical sociology in relation to chronic illness and disability.

See also: *medicalization* and *social movements and health.*

REFERENCES

Barnes, C., Mercer, G. and Shakespeare, T. (1999) *Exploring Disability: A Sociological Introduction.* Cambridge: Polity Press.

Bury, M. (1982) 'Chronic illness as biographical disruption', *Sociology of Health and Illness,* 4 (2): 167–82.

Bury, M. (1991) 'The sociology of chronic illness: a review of research and prospects', *Sociology of Health and Illness,* 13 (4): 451–68.

Charmaz, K. (2000) 'Experiencing chronic illness', in G.L. Albrecht, R. Fitzpatrick and S.C. Scrimshaw (eds), *The Handbook of Social Studies in Health and Medicine.* London: Sage.

Conover, P. (1973) 'Social class and chronic illness', *International Journal of Health Services,* 3 (3): 357–68.

French, S. (1993) 'Disability, impairment or something in between', in J. Swain, V. Finkelstein, S. French and M. Oliver (eds), *Disabling Barriers – Enabling Environments.* London: Sage.

Oliver, M. (1996) *Understanding Disability: From Theory to Practice.* London: Macmillan.

Strauss, A. and Glaser, B. (1975) *Chronic Illness and the Quality of Life.* St Louis, MO: Mosby.

MB

illness narratives

> **Definition: Illness narratives refer to the story-telling and accounting practices that occur in the face of illness. Narrative analysis seeks to understand the 'plot' of the account given and its social and motivational dimensions.**

It is a common observation that human cultures are rooted in myths and narratives, that is, in the construction and telling of stories. Narratives provide the opportunity for using metaphors and other linguistic devices to convey and produce meaning, especially in difficult or threatening circumstances. Anthropologists and sociologists have themselves frequently produced long accounts of the stories other people tell. Lévi-Strauss (1963), for example, has provided a detailed account of a myth held by the Cuna people of Southern America. In his account, this myth is shown to be not only meaningful but also useful. A shaman is described invoking the myth in front of a woman going through a difficult childbirth. The incantation and singing of the myth help the woman produce her baby, without the shaman touching her. Lévi-Strauss drew parallels between this process and psychoanalytic practice in the Western world, demonstrating, he believed, the presence of 'deep structures' underlying all human cultures.

Whether this structural approach is adopted or not, those interested in illness narratives are concerned to make intelligible the meanings produced in one cultural setting for an audience in another. Recently, for example, the idea that patients' narratives could be useful in clinical practice has gathered ground in the USA, the UK and other countries. At a time when 'evidence-based' practice has become the watchword in many medical systems, analysts have argued that the 'patient's view' is likely to be downplayed in favour of scientifically based and statistically oriented 'evidence'. Greenhalgh and Hurvitz (1999), for example, have advocated attending to illness narratives especially in general practice, where close contact with the patient's everyday life and the meanings attached to symptoms may be just as important as evidence-based guidelines.

However, sociologists and anthropologists interested in illness narratives have adopted a somewhat wider perspective, to include the multi-layered character of illness narratives, as well as their possible practical usage. Perhaps the best-known advocate of this approach is Kleinman (1988). Dealing with clinical practice first, Kleinman argues that illness narratives are important for two reasons. Despite the scepticism which Kleinman believes many practitioners hold concerning illness narratives, patients with chronic disorders need to have a 'witness to suffering' and to their existential fears. Attention to illness narratives is also important in assisting in the practical management of such disorders. It is for these reasons that patients will turn to doctors, even when they know that medical treatment may be limited.

But Kleinman goes on to show that illness narratives have many other functions, outside of the clinical situation. Most importantly, illness narratives help to deal with the altered situation and sometimes fundamental disruption which illness can create. In essence, illness narratives can help to address and fashion responses to the questions: Why me? Why now? and 'What can be done? – the question of order and control' (Kleinman, 1988: 29). These are questions which the medical model often finds difficult to answer, especially, again, in chronic illness where many disorders have unknown aetiologies and are difficult to treat.

Illness narratives thus construct meaning at a number of levels. Through an example of an elderly businessman with chronic heart disease Kleinman outlines a type of palimpsest, where each layer of meaning is written over another (1988: 32). So, what begins with the 'internal' reality of the illness soon connects with other areas of the man's life, including serious alcohol problems, and the long-standing effects of having had a brutal father. On top of this, the man indicates, through his narrative, the need to work out both his own experience of loss and his relationship with his children, who openly wish him to go into a nursing home. In such accounts, Kleinman suggests, it is possible to see that narratives are more than a 'reporting' of illness (whether to practitioners or others), but are efforts to integrate or reintegrate individuals into their social worlds. There is in many such cases a 'narrative reconstruction' occurring, in which disturbance and suffering are brought under some form of meaningful control.

Illness narratives inevitably take particular forms as well as having specific contents. Each narrative will be fashioned by individuals in unique ways and to some extent in unique circumstances. Yet the sociological study of illness, especially chronic illness, has shown that narratives may involve one of a limited number of formal properties. These forms, may, so to speak, exist prior to the construction or the telling of the story. They

83

are 'accessed' through membership of a culture, where common understandings allow, indeed, constrain meanings to be fashioned in specific ways. The forms that illness narratives take will also be shaped by underlying psychological needs and motivations concerning the presentation of self to others in particular contexts (for example, in an interview setting).

In a recent paper, Bury (2001) has outlined three forms of illness narratives that subsume some aspects of schemes developed by other authors. The first of these is what Bury calls 'contingent narratives'. These narratives are descriptions of the events surrounding the onset and early course of a disorder. They may deal with 'life events' such as bereavement or loss (particularly of a younger member of a family), or the 'external' circumstances of difficult or stressful work situations. They may also deal with the assimilation of medical explanations for the disorder and how these seem to tie in with the life experience of the individuals concerned. Contingent narratives deal with proximate causes and proximate effects. They often outline the steps taken to deal with the illness and the strategies being employed to manage its effects. Such narratives tend to be practical and descriptive in nature, dealing with events as they unfold and the immediate impact these have on the relationship between self and others.

In dealing with 'biographical reconstruction' individuals will often feel the need (not always consciously) to present themselves as culturally competent. In doing so they may employ 'moral narratives', the second form discussed by Bury. This moves the account a person may give from the descriptive to the evaluative. Narratives, in this sense, not only help to order experience but also help to express the 'dynamic relations' between self and others. Moral narratives may include social apologia in which the person tries to close the gap between their previous self-image and what they perceive or experience as failures in self-presentation or role performance, resulting from the effects of the illness. Moral narratives may also be a means to portray the self as active and socially engaged. Bury points out, however, that narratives may often be ambiguous; some may be ways of presenting the self as virtuous in comparison with others, sufferers or not. By praising oneself, one criticizes others. How the listener meets such claims to virtue is, of course, a different matter.

This brings us to Bury's third narrative form, what he calls 'core narratives'. These include 'genres of expression' through which the narrator 'emplots' themselves in a more or less dramatic fashion. Such narratives may be epic or heroic, tragic, comic or didactic (Bury, 2001: 278). Research on chronic illness has, again, furnished many examples of

84

these illness narratives. Bury quotes Kelly and Dickinson's (1997) study of colitis where, even in the face of radical surgery, or perhaps because of it, some respondents present themselves as quietly heroic and sometimes with a dark humour. These authors note that the trope of courageously 'fighting' the illness has become frequently invoked in public as well as private accounts.

Core narratives may also convey the underlying trajectory of the illness and the feelings associated with it. In this case, Robinson's (1990) study of multiple sclerosis illustrates how illness narratives may convey stable, progressive or regressive qualities. Robinson summarizes his analysis by saying that: 'a progressive narrative moves towards the personally valued goals, a regressive narrative away from such goals, and a stable narrative evaluatively sustains . . . the valued goals' (1990: 1176). Progressive narratives, in particular, convey a positive and more engaging response by the individual. Such narratives also chime in with a postmodern culture surrounding illness, one where 'restitution' and the search for a more positive identity through suffering may be found (Frank, 1995).

The analysis of illness narratives may be seen as part of the broadly interpretative wing of sociology. Clearly, eliciting and recording of patients' narratives require the employment of qualitative methods, especially extended interviews and life histories. Narrative analysis differs from other qualitative methods, however, in its stress on the need to examine long sequences of text and whole accounts, rather than breaking the text up, as in thematic analysis. Whole narratives across a sample of respondents can then be compared for their similarities and differences. Though such narratives may take on the properties of one of the forms discussed here, it is likely, of course, that they will combine more than one element in constructing an account.

The concept of illness narratives has been important in eliciting key dimensions of the experience of illness and its various meanings. In particular, it has suggested that the form of talk may constrain as well as facilitate expression in important ways, revealing key elements in a given culture. The study of illness narratives has also shown important variations in responses to illness and helped to understand the reasons why this should be the case. In particular, illness narratives have shown how the presentation of self in the face of illness frequently involves claims to moral as well as social competence.

However, as writers such as Riessman (1993: 2) have pointed out, the employment of interpretive methods in analysing illness narratives involves tackling 'the inevitable gap between the experience . . . and any communication about it'. This cautions against recent sociological approaches to illness narratives, which regard them as a move in reclaiming illness from a dominant medical model and from a 'colonial' medical practice. For example, illness narratives are, according to Frank, 'stories that are their own truth'. Frameworks of analysis are, from this viewpoint, merely devices to 'heighten attention' to these truths (Frank, 1995: 24). While, in one sense, it must be the case that individuals have a unique insight into their own experience, Riessman's methodological considerations suggest the need to proceed with care.

If illness narratives are treated as a 'revealed truth', then all claims take on equal weight. Yet the gap between experience and communication discussed by Riessman leads the researcher to ask the question 'why was the story told that way?' (1993: 2). This question may reveal, in the analysis, contradictions and ambiguities in expression and in the relationship between the accounting procedures and the motivations for presenting matters in one way and not another. Motivational elements suggest that in sociology, and in clinical practice, illness narratives need to be interpreted and not taken as given. The ethic of the sociologist must be governed by the recognition that the teller 'has the first word on which the interpretation depends' (Riessman, 1993: 52) but, at the same time, that illness narratives are 'always edited versions of reality, not impartial or objective descriptions of it' (Riessman, 1990: 1197).

See also: *chronic illness and disability* and *medical model.*

REFERENCES

Bury, M. (2001) 'Illness narratives, fact or fiction?', *Sociology of Health and Illness,* 23 (1): 263–85.

Frank, A. (1995) *The Wounded Storyteller: Body, Illness, and Ethics.* Chicago: University of Chicago Press.

Greenhalgh, T. and Hurwitz, B. (1999) 'Why study narrative?', *British Medical Journal,* 318: 48–50.

Kelly, M. and Dickinson, H. (1997) 'The narrative self in autobiographical accounts of illness', *The Sociological Review,* 45 (2): 254–78.

Kleinman, A. (1988) *The Illness Narratives: Suffering, Healing and the Human Condition.* New York: Basic Books.

Lévi-Strauss, C. (1963) *Structural Anthropology.* New York: Basic Books.

Riessman, C.K. (1990) 'Strategic use of narratives in the presentation of self and illness: a research note', *Social Science and Medicine,* 30 (11): 1195–2000.

Riessman, C.K. (1993) *Narrative Analysis.* Newbury Park, CA: Sage.

Robinson, I. (1990) 'Personal narratives, social careers and medical course: analyzing life trajectories in autobiographies of people with multiple sclerosis', *Social Science and Medicine,* 30 (11): 1173–86

MB

> *Definition: Risk involves exposure to a given danger or hazard.*

The language of risk is now frequently used in both popular and expert discourse especially when it comes to discussing health issues. This has not always been so, however. In pre-Renaissance times the dominant popular discourse was that of 'fate' – in which personal misfortune and disaster were explained in terms of chance, personal destiny and the will of the Gods. In this period, dangers such as floods and epidemics were perceived as natural events and the idea of human fault or responsibility was not considered. With the emergence of modernity in the seventeenth century a new materialistic and deterministic discourse was established, premised on the belief that the social and natural world followed causal laws. From this standpoint, risks were the products of such determinism and the vagaries of nature. Subsequently, risk was scientized as a result of the growing influence of mathematical explanations relating to probability. In the nineteenth century it became possible to measure the risk of an event by calculating its statistical probability, thereby taming chance. Risk also came to be located in human beings as well as in nature and unintended outcomes were acknowledged as being a possible consequence of human action. According to Lupton (1999), modernist notions of risk also recognized that risk could be either 'good' or 'bad', involving gain or loss, and could thus been seen in neutral terms. Since the nineteenth century, however, the meaning of risk has been transformed and has now come to be seen as involving only negative outcomes. Risk now means danger, and the greater the risk, the greater the danger.

Traditionally, research on risk has been the preserve of the risk industry, drawing primarily on disciplines such as engineering, toxicology, biostatistics and actuarial science. Assessing public health risks has also become a major issue for epidemiologists who aim to calculate the 'relative risk' or numerical odds of a population developing an illness when exposed to a risk factor, compared with a similar population that has not suffered such exposure. It is on the basis of these risk assessments that governments have conducted health education campaigns, for example, about AIDS, to warn the public about the dangers of 'risky

87

behaviour'. It is expected that the provision of information about such risky behaviours will lead to their reduction.

It is only recently that more attention has been given to developing social analyses of risk. In what follows, a variety of such analyses will be discussed starting with the cultural approach, inspired by the anthropologist Mary Douglas. Douglas was one of the first to draw attention to the need for an analysis that challenged the status of risk as an objective measure, as argued by members of the risk industry. Instead, she took a weak constructionist view, like many others after her, and considered that objective hazards were inevitably mediated by cultural processes and could only be known in relation to these processes. She was interested in why some dangers were selected as risks while others were not and how risk acts as a symbolic boundary between groups. For her, what was of significance was that groups of people identify different risk attributes and even types of risk as a result of their particular form of social organization and interaction in the wider culture. In her view, the way in which such collectivities respond to risk is functional for the maintenance of their form of social organization. The argument was formalized in an analytic scheme that has come to be known as grid/group analysis. For Douglas the degree of collectivism found in groups and the degree of internal difference within groups impact on perceptions of risk. Collectivism, whether strong or weak, is defined in terms of 'group', while the degree of difference is defined in terms of 'grid'. By linking grid and group, Douglas, along with her colleague Wildavsky (1982), identified four distinct world-views which justified different ways of behaving towards a hazard. These were called hierarchist (high grid/high group), egalitarian (low grid/high group), fatalist (high grid, low group) and individualist (low grid, low group). Hierarchists, for example, are considered to be well integrated (group axis), and to accept externally imposed risk assessment by experts (grid axis), while egalitarians, although being well integrated too, tend to challenge the experts' assessments on the grounds that these experts' calculations threaten their group's way of life (grid axis). Douglas also believed that when people feel they are at risk, they tend to blame outsiders rather than focus on dangers from within their own community. In the health field grid/group analysis has been applied to studying differences in response to hazards in contexts ranging from hospitals to transport. While the approach has been criticized for being too static and for failing to explain how organizations and individuals can change their perception of risk over time, it nonetheless offers a way of exploring how conflicts over risk can be understood in terms of plural constructions of meaning that are culturally framed.

Other more sociological work on risk perception has adopted an interpretivist approach and generally concentrated on two broad areas: perceptions of risk and risk behaviour and the relationship between lay and expert knowledge of risk The first of these has emphasized the role of contextual factors in risk perception. For example, Hallowell (1999) examined the risk perceptions and behaviour of women attending a genetic counselling clinic for hereditary breast and ovarian cancer. She found that while the women perceived themselves as at risk of cancer, these perceptions were not the only influence on their behaviour. They were also profoundly influenced by their sense of family obligation to other family members (dead, alive or unborn) and were therefore prepared to compromise their own needs of 'not knowing' for the sake of others. Others have focused on the relationship between lay and expert perceptions of risk. For instance, Davison et al. (1991) explored the extent to which lay beliefs about the risk of coronary heart disease both mirror and diverge from expert views. While lay people agreed with health promotion experts that they should accept some responsibility for their health to minimize the risks of heart disease, they differed by referring to the social circumstances surrounding this disease and to more fatalistic ideas when either personalistic or social types of explanation seemed inadequate.

In addition to this interpretivist work on group risk perceptions and behaviour, there have also been more macro-level studies about the role of social institutions and structures in the framing of risk. One key institution involved in shaping risk perception is the mass media. As Nelkin (1991) has shown with regard to AIDS in the USA, the media serve as filters through which both lay people and experts receive news and interpret events. She goes on to argue that media messages about AIDS have made the disease visible to lay people and turned it into a public issue requiring a regulatory response. To construct these media messages journalists rely on external sources of information, including those from social movements. These campaigning groups make claims about the risk status of what they perceive to be environmental, technological or medical developments, and in the process help construct such dangers as social problems worthy of public attention. In the health field one example is the work of Brown (1995) who shows how campaigning groups in the USA have used popular epidemiology – the process of lay people marshalling the knowledge and resources of experts to understand the epidemiology of disease, its treatment and prevention – in order to detect environmental health hazards and seek solutions to them.

The relationship between lay and expert knowledge has also been explored more broadly by social theorists in the context of declining trust in expert authority in late modern society. Giddens (1990), for example, has suggested that the judgements of experts are now under increasing scrutiny and are either accepted or rejected by lay people who are making pragmatic calculations about the risks involved. In these circumstances the most cherished beliefs underpinning expert systems are open to revision and alteration, thereby challenging a dominant source of authoritative interpretation. The degree to which people feel alienated from or at least ambivalent towards experts also relates to the German sociologist Beck's (1992) argument that we now live in a 'risk society': that is one that is increasingly vulnerable to major socio-technical disruption and growing global interdependency. Social and economic developments have created global hazards, ranging from nuclear accidents to ecological disasters, for which there is no adequate aftercare. These structural features highlight the need for trust in expert authority at a time when greater reflexivity and awareness of the indeterminate status of knowledge about risk combine to undermine it. One of the main criticisms of this 'reflexive modernization' thesis is that it is based on broad generalizations of structural and organizational processes that lack grounding in actual processes and experiences of institutional and everyday life. Nonetheless, this approach has been enormously influential and has provided valuable insights into the structural and political aspects of risk.

While the risk society, like the other approaches outlined above, has adopted a weak constructionist position about risk, accepting that risk is an objective hazard that is mediated through social and cultural processes, there is one approach that takes a strong constructionist position – that concerned with risk and governmentality. From this standpoint there is no such thing as an objective risk; rather, risks are solely a product of discourses, strategies, practices and institutions around phenomena that turn them into risks (Lupton, 1999). This Foucauldian-inspired perspective is particularly interested in the way in which risk operates in relation to the political ethos of advanced liberalism. The latter conceptualizes individuals as rational agents who should take responsibility to protect themselves from risks rather than rely on the state to protect them. Health promotion, or what Petersen (1997) calls the 'new public health', is seen as a case in point. This health risk discourse is said to focus on internalizing risk in the consciousness of individuals, encouraging them to be active in maintaining their bodies and their health. Making the right choice is central to constructing the self as 'normal' and distinguishing the self from risky others. If individuals take risks or manage them poorly, then the blame lies with them as individuals. While this approach has the merit of relating risk to a current political ethos, it can be criticized for paying too much attention to discourse and strategies and not enough to how people actually respond to risk in their everyday lives.

In sum, the social analysis of risk now incorporates a variety of approaches ranging from Douglas' grid/group analysis through interpretivist and structural approaches to Foucauldian analyses of risk and governmentality. Each has something to offer in helping us make sense of the meaning and nature of risk as a dominant feature of late modern society.

See also: *lay knowledge, social movements and health* and *surveillance and health promotion.*

REFERENCES

Beck, U. (1992) *Risk Society*. London: Sage.

Brown, P. (1995) 'Popular epidemiology, toxic waste and social movements', in J. Gabe (ed.), *Medicine, Health and Risk*. Oxford: Basil Blackwell.

Davison, C., Davey Smith, G. and Frankel. S. (1991) 'Lay epidemiology and the prevention paradox', *Sociology of Health and Illness*, 13: 1–19.

Douglas, M. and Wildavsky, A. (1982) *Risk and Culture: An Essay on the Selection of Technological and Environmental Dangers*. Berkeley, CA: University of California Press.

Giddens, A. (1990) *The Consequences of Modernity*. Cambridge: Polity Press.

Hallowell, N. (1999) 'Doing the right thing: genetic risk and responsibility', *Sociology of Health and Illness*, 21: 597–621.

Lupton, D. (1999) *Risk*. London: Routledge.

Nelkin, D. (1991) 'AIDS and the news media', *The Milbank Quarterly*, 69: 293–307.

Petersen, A. (1997) 'Risk, governance and the new public health', in A. Peteresen and R. Bunton (eds), *Foucault, Health and Medicine*. London: Routledge.

JGA

the sick role

Definition: *The sick role refers to the set of rights and obligations that surround illness and shape the behaviour of doctors and patients.*

The origins of the concept of the sick role are to be found in Talcott Parsons' description of 'The case of modern medical practice' in *The Social System*, published in 1951. In that work Parsons outlines what he takes to be the functional character of modern medical practice. This approach regards the role of medical care as meeting certain 'prerequisites' which are deemed to be necessary for the functioning of all social systems, especially modern ones. 'Health' is included in the functional needs of the individual members of the society so that from the point of view of the functioning of the social system, too low a general level of health, too high an incidence of illness, is dysfunctional' (Parsons, 1951: 430). The function of medical practice, therefore, is to help maintain an optimal level of health in society.

While Parsons recognized that health and illness have a basis in biology, his contribution to the development of medical sociology was to provide a thorough-going account of the sociological implications of health. For Parsons, the sick role occupied a pivotal place in this account, encapsulating those forms of behaviour surrounding illness, when normal role obligations are relinquished or suspended.

As Gerhardt has shown, it is possible to identify two models of illness in Parsons' work. Both are important to an understanding of the sick role. The first model is what she terms the 'capacity model' (1989: 16) in which there is a 'failure to keep well'. Occupying the sick role under these circumstances, is 'negatively achieved' through incapacity to perform roles. In this model, illness is a 'natural phenomenon', like the weather, and not the result of human motivation (Parsons, 1951: 430). Gerhardt (1989: 16) points out that occupying the sick role can operate as a 'niche' in which the incapacitated person is able to recover without 'enforced normalization with punitive overtones'.

The second is in many respects a more complex and interesting model. This treats illness as deviance, and the sick role as a mechanism of social control. The issue of deviance arises for Parsons because, while some forms of illness may not involve psychological elements, most do. As far as the causes of illness are concerned, Parsons mentions, for example, 'differential exposure' to infections or injury (1951: 430). People may more or less consciously expose themselves to health risks, such as continuing to smoke, even in the face of known harm.

For Parsons, part of the psychological element in illness stems from responses to 'social pressures'. In so far as modern systems create considerable strain for individuals, illness may be one result. The sick role allows the individual temporary exemption from role obligations, and provides the mechanism for returning to health and therefore to normal role performance. But in providing such exemption, the sick role may become an attractive alternative to everyday pressures, providing a way of 'evading social responsibilities' (ibid.: 431) and offering 'secondary gain'. It is for this reason that the sick role is a 'contingent' one so that malingering, or motivated avoidance of role responsibilities, does not become too easy or 'dysfunctional' from a system viewpoint. It should be noted in this context that in all modern societies absence from work due to ill health is heavily regulated, often requiring medical certification.

In this second, deviancy or motivated model of illness, psychological and social processes are also at the heart of medical practice. As Gerhardt (1989: 35–6) notes, this emphasis in Parsons' formulation may have stemmed from his interest and training in psychoanalysis. In *The Social System*, Parsons (1951: 431) predicted that, as the twentieth century progressed, the dominance of a biological model of illness would give way to a 'psychosomatic' model, dealing with a wide range of 'social actions' involved in illness states. Nevertheless, medical practice helps to regulate illness and is thus part of society's social control apparatus.

What, then, are the social actions and psychological processes which go to make up the sick role in modern societies? Parsons identifies two sets of four, mutually reinforcing, dimensions to the sick role; four for the performance of the doctor's role and four for the patient's role. Together they constitute the necessary elements for a functional 'sick role'.

Doctors, like patients have obligations and rights. First, Parsons argues that doctors have the obligation to be technically competent and meet 'selection criteria' separate from other elements of the persons's social status (ibid.: 434). In other words, the appointment of doctors and their practice should be based on technical expertise not on personal or social background. Second, the practitioner should be 'affectively neutral', tackling the medical problem in an 'objective way'. The doctor should thus have the welfare of the patient at heart and not personal or commercial considerations – 'the "profit motive" is supposed to be drastically excluded from the medical world' (ibid.: 435). Parsons was keen, in this respect, to contrast medicine in the USA with the world of business (Bury, 1997: 84). Doctors should be 'collectivity oriented' and serve the community.

In return for meeting these obligations, two rights flow. The first is that doctors are treated by society as professional practitioners, with a degree of independence and self-regulation. This flows from the exercise of 'functional specificity' and 'universalism' in that doctors are expected to be expert in specific areas and to relate to a body of knowledge which has universal application. The exercise of these skills allows doctors to claim a degree of freedom from the organizational and commercial constraints in which they work. Second, doctors are allowed access to tabooed areas such as the sick person's body. This access may involve physical examination or, more dramatically, surgery (Parsons, 1951: 451–2).

The exercise of this set of obligations and rights on the part of the doctor provides the basis for the patient entering the sick role. If the patient felt, for example, that the doctor was technically incompetent, was acting because of personal feelings, or crossing boundaries in tabooed areas such as access to the body, then the sick role would be likely to break down immediately. Indeed, many recent high profile controversies in countries such as the UK have involved just such elements.

In the presence of effective and safe medical practice, however, the patient can enter the sick role with some degree of confidence. Here, for patients, Parsons identifies four dimensions of the sick role: two obligations and two rights. Let us deal with the rights first.

According to Parsons, the sick role provides, as has already been noted, exemption from normal role responsibilities. This right has to be legitimated, often by a doctor in the last analysis, protecting the patient against the charge of 'malingering' (Parsons, 1951: 437). Second, the individual has the right not to be expected to get well by an act of will, 'pulling himself (*sic*) together'. Rather, his 'condition must be changed and not just his attitude'. Such a view helps individuals seek or accept help, even when there might be a motivation towards not doing so.

As far as obligations are concerned, the patient must want to get well. Although illness is usually thought to be an undesirable state, this is not always clear-cut. The rights of the sick role are conditional on demonstrating a motivation to get well. Second, the individual has the obligation to seek technically competent help, if the sick role is to be securely legitimated. Not only that but the person must cooperate with the doctor, producing a 'complementary role structure'. In this way the 'secondary gain' of the sick role is limited, and the return to health maintained as a primary goal.

It has been the fate of the sick role concept to be criticized as often as it has been explicated. The concept clearly raises many questions, especially concerning its relevance to the wide range of illness states and forms of medical practice that exist in modern societies. Gallagher (1976) has provided a useful summary of some of the most problematic areas. These can be summarized in three main ways.

The first involves the place of chronic illness in Parsons' scheme. It is clear from what has already been said that the sick role is essentially a temporary one. Whether one employs the incapacity or the deviancy

94

model, both assume that the sick role will be occupied for a period leading to recovery and the resumption of normal roles. In chronic illness, Gallagher argues, this is often not the case, as here the possibility of a return to health is reduced. Second, as Bloor and Horobin (1975) have also argued, not all forms of illness lead to the adoption of the sick role. In many cases being 'legitimately ill' does not need the sanctioning of a doctor, and much self-treatment and self-help are employed in dealing with illness. Gallagher (1976: 210) makes the point that in adapting to chronic illness patients are not just 'compliant' but active in dealing with their problems, most notably in the context of 'family and lay social support'.

Third, Gallagher makes several points concerning what he takes to be an overly 'medico-centric' view of illness, the sick role and medical practice in Parsons' approach. In particular, Gallagher notes that while Parsons sets out a clear case for the centrality of doctors (especially hospital doctors) in health care organizations, other health care workers (including family practitioners) as well as lay support and family structures are equally important (ibid.: 213). Moreover, claims about the need for an optimal level of health in the social system are contradicted by the low priority given by the medical profession to prevention, where 'training and orientation are attuned to illness rather than toward the maintenance of health' (ibid.: 215). The growth of primary care and health promotion perhaps marks some change in emphasis today.

While Gallagher's critique points up some of the weaknesses of Parsons' position, it is arguable that the sick role still retains some strengths for medical sociology. For example, despite Gallagher's telling points about the sick role's *temporary* character, the situation is often more complex than he allows. In a defence of his argument, Parsons (1978: 28) pointed out that even in the case of chronic disorders, such as diabetes, the physician has an obligation 'to reinforce the patient's motivation to minimize the curtailment of his capacities' and he recognized that a 'full-time' occupancy of the sick role does not apply to all forms of illness, especially chronic illness.

And while Parsons may be too prone to present the sick role as a means of providing an asymmetrical but complementary role structure (playing down its potential for conflict), when it is placed in his full discussion of health and medicine, it does address issues of abiding concern. As Gerhardt (1979) has pointed out, these range from the psychodynamic aspects of illness and treatment, to the structural issues of illness and incapacity, and thus to issues of social control and power inherent in the sick role. For Gerhardt, the sick role is part of a 'structural'

95

view of illness, locating individual needs in the wider society. Recently, Shilling (2002) has revisited Parsons and explored his relevance for the sociology of the body and health. It is for these reasons, perhaps, that the sick role remains an important concept in medical sociology.

See also: *illness behaviour, medical model* and *practitioner–client relationships.*

REFERENCES

Bloor, M. and Horobin, G. (1975) 'Conflict and conflict resolution in doctor-patient relationships', in C. Cox and A. Mead (eds), *A Sociology of Medical Practice*. London: Collier-Macmillan.

Bury, M. (1997) *Health and Illness in a Changing Society*. London: Routledge.

Gallagher, E. (1976) 'Lines of reconstruction and extension in the Parsonian sociology of illness', *Social Science and Medicine*, 10: 207–18.

Gerhardt, U. (1979) 'The Parsonian paradigm and the identity of medical sociology', *The Sociological Review*, 27 (2): 229–51.

Gerhardt, U. (1989) *Ideas About Illness: An Intellectual and Political History of Medical Sociology*. Basingstoke: Macmillan.

Parsons, T. (1951) *The Social System*. London: Routledge and Kegan Paul.

Parsons, T. (1978) *Action Theory and the Human Condition*. New York: Free Press.

Shilling, C. (2002) 'Culture, the sick role and the consumption of health', *British Journal of Sociology*, 53 (4): 621–38.

MB

practitioner–client relationships

96

> *Definition: Practitioner–client relationships refer to the ways in which health workers and lay people interact during a medical consultation. Many factors such as the context of the consultation and communication styles influence the type of relationship.*

In 1956, Szasz and Hollender argued that doctors had traditionally been concerned with bodily structures or functions and that the concept of the 'relationship' was novel in medicine. They proposed that *types* of doctor–patient relationship took on distinctive forms, each being influenced by technical procedures, the nature of the intervention and the social setting in which it occurred. In the first type, characterized by *activity–passivity*, the doctor was seen as a 'parent' treating an 'infant', for example in a situation where the patient was in a coma. In the second, *guidance–co-operation* was more in evidence, for example, during a period of acute infection where the doctor treated the patient in a parent–adolescent relationship. In the third type, *mutual participation* was seen in an 'adult–adult' interaction, for example, in the context of managing chronic illness. Two main properties of the doctor–patient relationship were observed in these different types. First, that it is a *process*, the relationship changing with symptoms and the way the patient wishes to relate to the doctor; and, second, that it is *fluid* in that a patient in a coma may see the same doctor when he/she has recovered.

Sociological studies from the 1950s to the 1980s have tended to work within the broad framework outlined by Szasz and Hollender, though Freidson argued that the activity–passivity relationship could, theoretically, be reversed, where the patient could be active and the doctor passive (Freidson, 1970: 317). As will be discussed below, recent changes in the organization and availability of health care bring the idea of practitioner–client relationships to the fore, and are associated with the emergence of new types of relationship, where the patient (or client) is more active. First, however, following the discussion provided by Bury (1997) and developing the approach of Szasz and Hollender and Freidson, three models of the doctor–patient relationship are outlined.

The first model is the consensus model of practitioner–client relationships. Bury defines this as 'the ability of the system to fashion values and roles which could provide the necessary basis for a shared "consultation" on what [is] proper conduct and what the goals of the action [are]' (1997: 83–4). The work of Talcott Parsons (1951) is most closely associated with this model, where general social expectations and obligations are brought into the medical encounter. Here doctors have legitimate authority, commanding and receiving respect from patients and, in return, acting in the best interests of the patient. Doctors possess knowledge that is scientific and uncontested; 'The patient has a need for technical services because he [*sic*] doesn't – nor do his lay associates, family members etc. – "know" what the matter is or what to do about it' (ibid.: 439).

Second, there is the conflict model, in which differences are inherent in the relationship. Bury uses Freidson's work (1970) to argue that patients and doctors live in different social worlds. Patients have personal

97

and social agendas, being concerned with the effects of illness on daily activities and relationships. In contrast, doctors operate with a biomedical agenda, narrowly focusing on treating the disease. Following Freidson (1970), it is possible to identify the main points of conflict as involving the following: doctors and patients coming from two different worlds that are always in conflict, if only 'latently'; patients wanting more information than the doctor is willing to give; doctors handling cases conventionally, whereas the patient may doubt that their case is typical; and, finally, patients struggling to gain a mode of individual care, irrespective of demands of the system as a whole.

Another source of potential conflict is that doctors may complain, paradoxically, that patients consult them inappropriately with trivial complaints, but also that they delay in seeking early help for medical problems (Bury, 1997). Indeed, campaigns continue to this day try to 'educate' the lay person in appropriate referrals.

Third, the negotiation model of doctor–patient relationships emphasizes both patient and doctor as active and the consultation as shared. As Bury argues, 'Negotiation implies both the presence of conflict and the willingness to work towards an agreement, if not in establishing a consensus' (1997: 92). Studies such as that by Stimson and Webb (1975) showed that patients may exert 'countervailing power' outside, if not inside the consultation, but other studies have shown that a negotiated relationship is difficult to achieve. Tuckett et al.'s (1985) study of 108 GP surgery sessions found that although doctors usually shared some of their reasons for thinking as they did, it was discovered that: doctors and patients rarely talked to each other about the consequences of the patient's illness; doctors did little to encourage patients to present their views; and, finally, doctors did not tailor their advice to what they already knew about the patient's life.

In summing up their research, Tuckett et al. suggested, 'Patients are not treated as competent "experts" in their own health care, at least to nearly the degree that might be possible. Their ideas, explanations and opinions are not sought in any systematic or thorough way and tend to be devalued as not useful or relevant' (1985: 211).

In addition to these three models of the doctor–patient relationship, a fourth, contractual model needs to be added, taking into account changes in population and healthcare since the 1980s. Bury contends 'Such a model is emerging from the long-term trend in the reduction of the power of professionals, related to the erosion of hierarchical relationships in late modern cultures more generally' (1997: 101). In this model, the patient and doctor may be more open to each other's perceptions and to

98

each other's role in managing ill health, especially chronic disorders. However, some of the dynamics driving such a change come from factors other than the desire for reform. Doctors, mindful of litigation and clinical governance, are increasingly practising 'defensive medicine' where, for example, many tests may be ordered to ensure that every option is covered. Patients, in turn, may be more active in deciding what treatment to have by weighing the risks and benefits. They may refer to hospital league tables in deciding where to be treated. Consumerist, managerial and government-driven issues are clearly relevant to this model. However, many of the challenges to doctors' dominant position come from demographic changes and changes in health service organization; these are now briefly outlined.

By 2016 it is expected that the number of people in the UK aged 65 or over will exceed those aged under 16; a trend that will be mirrored across Europe and in other parts of the world. An increase in the prevalence of chronic illness, fuelled in part by improvement in mortality rates, will ensure that many people will have multiple consultations about a particular health problem. Studies such as Tuckett et al.'s (1985) will therefore need to be planned longitudinally to measure changes in relationships over time, as both age and course of disease influence the nature of the relationship between practitioners and their clients.

The rise of chronic illness and patient-led self-help groups, together with multiple sources of medical information, has led to an increase in awareness and self-care. Patients are becoming 'experts' in their diseases and more confident during the consultation, such that what they need from the practitioner at each visit may change. The nature of compliance has also changed focus, from patients abiding by 'doctors orders' (Parsons, 1951: 464) to managing treatment regimes to fit in with their personal life. In this continuity of care, practitioners and clients may know each other over a long period, such that consultations will draw on prior knowledge as the relationship between individuals develops further.

The *context* of the meeting is an important factor in the doctor–patient relationship, for example, the place of the meeting and the number of meetings with the same (or other) professional prior to the interaction. In hospital settings the relationship between practitioner and client has been affected in many ways, for example, reduced total bed numbers with a reduced length of stay coupled with changes in medical knowledge and advice, and the rise of new technologies. 'Hospital at home' programmes, whereby care is given in the patient's home for conditions traditionally treated in hospital, shifts the boundary of care and will almost certainly affect interaction with heath professionals as they are 'invited' into the patient's home. Through these programmes, many carers have taken over roles traditionally belonging to health professionals, such that a 'service-recipient' relationship exists, whereby many practitioners, both lay and professional, give care and more than one individual is affected by that care.

The introduction of health centres and specialized clinics in the UK has meant, too, that professionals other than doctors will be interacting with patients in these settings. Many nurses in Britain now prescribe a range of drugs and nurse consultants are responsible for running their own outpatients clinics and discharging patients from hospital care. A multidisciplinary approach means that patients may see a team of professionals during one visit to the hospital, or primary care clinic, making the doctor–patient relationship just one aspect of patients' interaction with professionals in these settings.

Part of the UK government's NHS Plan 2000 was to have modern information technology (IT) systems in every clinical setting; trials of remote foetal screening whereby the doctor and patient are not even in the same county during the consultation have been carried out. Here a practitioner transmits foetal ultrasound images in real time over the telephone to the consultant, presenting a wholly new context in which the practitioner–client relationship can be explored. Through IT advances, sections of the lay public are increasingly demanding convenience. NHS Direct, a 24-hour, nurse-led telephone helpline covering England and Wales was launched in 1998, providing advice on a number of health conditions and on the availability of self-help groups. Appropriate courses of action may be given according to local computer-assisted guidelines. NHS Direct may herald a shift in traditional British health care where more care can be delivered without face-to-face contact and with no continuity of care. Indeed, Heath Maintenance Organizations in the USA have also used the telephone service as a convenient and cost-effective part of primary care.

The GP's ability to prescribe certain expensive medicines for patients living in some areas of the UK has been referred to in the media as a 'postcode lottery'. The newly formed National Institute of Clinical Evidence (NICE) now issues guidelines to clinicians about which treatments are most effective; this may further restrict doctor's clinical freedom. Furthermore, evidence-based medicine – amalgamating an individual doctor's expertise with the 'best available' clinical evidence – together with 'clinical governance', a framework through which the NHS is now accountable for improving service quality and maintaining high standards, will also affect how lay people and health professionals interact.

Despite these managerial and governmental controls, cases of medical

100

error are now regularly reported in the media, affecting the trust that was once assumed to exist in practitioner–client relationships (Parsons, 1951). In Britain, for example, recent concern regarding 'avoidable deaths' of babies following cardiac surgery at Bristol Royal Infirmary in the early 1990s highlighted failures among senior staff to take action. Events such as these may also push forward changes in practitioner–client relationships. Whether this will be in the direction of 'partnership' or a 'shared' relationship (Charles et al., 1999) or to a more legalistic 'contractual' model, outlined above, will be a matter of continuing debate.

See also: *consumerism, managerialism* and *malpractice.*

REFERENCES

Bury, M. (1997) *Health and Illness in a Changing Society*. London: Routledge.
Charles, C., Gafni, A. and Whelan, T. (1999) 'Decision-making in the physician-patient encounter: revisiting the shared treatment decision-making model', *Social Science and Medicine*, 49: 651–61.
Freidson E. (1970) *Profession of Medicine: A Study of the Sociology of Applied Knowledge*. Chicago: University of Chicago Press.
Parsons, T. (1951) *The Social System*. New York: Free Press.
Stimson, G. and Webb, B. (1975) *Going to See the Doctor: The Consultation Process in General Practice*. London: Routledge and Kegan Paul.
Szasz, T.S. and Hollender, M.H. (1956) 'A contribution to the philosophy of medicine: the basic models of the doctor–patient relationship', *Archives of Internal Medicine*, 97: 589–92.
Tuckett, D., Boulton, M., Olson, C. and Williams, A. (1985) *Meetings Between Experts*. London: Tavistock.

KL

uncertainty

Definition: **Uncertainty refers to an element of medical training and practice that mediates the management, delivery and reception of medical knowledge in clinical situations.**

Uncertainty is, and always has been, a feature of everyday life. It is the gap between knowing and not knowing which, when related to the sociology of health and illness, has implications for the way medical professionals and patients communicate with each other. Comprising both doubt and anxiety, uncertainty has been identified as a pervasive element of medical education, the clinical consultation and the experience of illness. By distinguishing three forms of uncertainty – clinical, functional and existential – it becomes possible to explore how doctors and patients attempt to control uncertainty in medical situations.

Talcott Parsons (1951) is often cited as introducing the concept of medical uncertainty to a sociological audience through his analysis of doctors' management of medical knowledge. Parsons argued that the uncertainty that doctors experience when practising medicine is an inevitable consequence of the rapid and continued progress of science and medicine. The doctor is faced with managing clinical uncertainty while also responding to his or her own and the patients' emotional needs. For Parsons, the combination of uncertainty and the personal and interpersonal demands of the medical consultation results in 'not merely institutionalization of the roles [of doctors and patients], but special mechanisms of social control' (1951: 450).

Renee Fox (1999) extended Parsons' work concerning clinical uncertainty in a recent review of studies into how medical students were 'trained for uncertainty'. She found that students were subject to three types of uncertainty that had implications for future practice. Fox distinguished these types as emanating from the inadequacy of medical knowledge, the difficulties in acquiring a command of current and continually changing skills and knowledge and, finally, from not knowing whether uncertainty was due to limitations of current medical knowledge or the limitations of the student's capabilities. Overall, she claimed that clinical uncertainty is a key aspect of both medical knowledge and culture.

Through her observations of medical students, Fox identified ways that doctors attempt to handle uncertainty in practice. In order to master as much knowledge as possible, they may reduce medical problems to probability-based, scientifically defined issues, disregarding the affective, personal nature of the patient and the consultation. At the same time, doctors learn to ignore the existence of uncertainty altogether, an approach that Fox argued is implicitly sanctioned by the medical educational system that oversees their 'socialization' into the profession. Conversely, the stress of dealing with clinical uncertainty is sometimes dispelled, or at least hidden, through the use of dark humour to avoid the difficulties that doctors may have when talking seriously of their fears about uncertainty.

Atkinson (1984) disputed Fox's claim that medical students are trained for uncertainty, arguing that the culture of medical education serves instead to insulate trainees and doctors from issues of uncertainty through the process of professional socialization. Medical knowledge, for Atkinson, far from being presented and accepted as problematic in terms of scope and complexity, instead is assimilated by medical students as established facts to be memorized and mastered. Moreover, even in clinical situations, dependence on the personal experience of doctors serves to minimize any uncertainty he or she might feel, and in effect 'guarantee[s] knowledge which the student and practitioner can rely on' (Atkinson, 1984: 953). Thus, as an outcome of what Atkinson termed 'training for certainty', doctors become less likely to acknowledge uncertainty in the clinical situation, either as it affects them or their patients.

Empirical studies of doctors' practice in the consulting room have highlighted that issues about uncertainty are not confined to educational settings and dilemmas, but may be used by the doctor for functional ends. Doctors, therefore, may actively manage uncertainty in the professional–lay encounter, often as an avoidance tactic, raising issues of power and control in the clinical setting. A classic work in this area of functional uncertainty in everyday clinical contexts has been written by Fred Davis (1960). In the 1950s he examined patterns of communication between doctors and the parents of children with poliomyelitis. He was particularly interested in how the prognosis, or probable outcome, of the illness was conveyed to the parents of the ill child.

Davis devised a model for understanding interaction between doctors and patients in clinical settings, which suggested that, when the prognosis is not clinically certain or substantiated, two scenarios can be expected. The doctor will either share his or her uncertainty with the patient (*admission of uncertainty*), or withhold it (*dissimulation*), adopting instead delaying tactics or providing treatment in spite of uncertainty. Dissimulation was particularly notable when doctors felt that their own reputation and clinical ability might be damaged if they appeared uncertain because, as Davis noted, indecision is not widely tolerated in our society, particularly in the area of medicine.

Conversely, doctors may maintain the pretence of uncertainty despite being sure of the medical facts and probable outcome. Davis proposed two main reasons that might lie behind the doctors' decision to withhold a certain prognosis and thereby maintain uncertainty in the consultation. First, doctors simply do not want to give bad news, preferring to allow the parents to believe their children might recover at some point in the future. In essence, uncertainty was viewed as a

103

means of maintaining hope. Second, to tell parents that their child might be disabled for life creates an emotional situation with which the doctor might not want to deal. Davis described this as an attempt to 'avoid scenes with [parents] and having to explain to and comfort them, tasks . . . often viewed as onerous and time-consuming' (1960: 44–5). Thus, Davis found that doctors used scientific and medical uncertainty to manage the interaction and communication with their patients and the patients' families.

Davis concluded by noting that previous approaches to uncertainty proposed by medical sociologists, such as that by Fox, predominantly attribute problems of communication between doctor and patient to the current state of scientific and clinical knowledge. Alternatively, Davis' study demonstrated that 'other values and interests also influence the doctor–patient transaction' (ibid.: 47), and therefore place the relationship and the way it is managed firmly in the social sphere.

Another application of the concept of functional uncertainty in medical work was that of Glaser and Strauss (1965), who looked at *awareness contexts* of terminally ill patients and their carers during the period when death was imminent. Glaser and Strauss defined awareness contexts as 'what each interacting person knows of the patient's defined status, along with his [*sic*] recognition of others' awareness of his own definition' (1965: 10). Deployment of functional uncertainty in the care of the dying is best illustrated by the case of *closed awareness*. In this case it is the patient who is kept unaware about the probability and timing of their own imminent death, even though the doctor, and possibly the patient's family, is fully knowledgeable about what will happen and when. Like Davis (1960), Glaser and Strauss found that doctors used uncertainty to maintain a distance from patients' experiences of illness and death.

By the 1980s there was little evidence to suggest that doctors' use of functional uncertainty was threatening their power and authority in the medical consultation, or that clinical uncertainty had reduced either doctors' control of the agenda in clinical situations or patients' acceptance of the legitimacy of modern medicine. However, where the patient was chronically ill and particularly well informed, or was in regular contact with the general practitioner, uncertainty did appear to become more difficult for doctors to manage. In these circumstances, negotiation rather than professional domination was instrumental in shaping the clinical agenda (Calnan, 1984).

Other findings suggest that clinical uncertainty can increase lay ambivalence about the value of biomedical science, particularly when doctors are unable, 'on the basis of available knowledge, to provide clear bio-medical guidelines about how to face the uncharted course of ... illness' (Comaroff and Maguire, 1981: 118). Focusing on the families of children with leukaemia, Comaroff and Maguire found that the availability of new forms of treatment served to increase parents' sense of uncertainty about the prognosis of the disease, and also highlighted the failure of medical knowledge to keep pace with technical developments. Consequently, the ambiguities inherent in both the clinical and personal knowledge of this chronic and life-threatening illness resulted in 'oscillations in perception and mood from unreflective hope to fear and depression' (ibid.: 121).

A more recent but related account of the interaction between clinical and lay uncertainty comes from Adamson, who separated the concept of uncertainty into two identifiable types, in this case, clinical and existential. Adamson defined clinical uncertainty as 'the socially organised realisation by a member of the medical community that the knowledge needed to diagnose a disease and predict an outcome is missing' (1997: 135). Many of the issues already discussed, such as those in Fox's and Davis' work, illustrate this concept both in terms of the extent of medical knowledge and one's personal mastery of it.

Conversely, existential uncertainty is that which patients experience when the cause of their illness is unknown, for example, with inflammatory bowel disease (which Adamson had), multiple sclerosis and osteoarthritis. Adamson recognized that existential uncertainty and clinical uncertainty naturally co-exist, but argued that the patient's experience of doubt, worry and anxiety differs significantly from the experience of the doctor (1997: 154).

By separating clinical from existential uncertainty, Adamson was able to highlight the interactive nature of the lay–professional relationship. Like Davis, he argued that, for the patient, uncertainty can bring hope and opportunity as well as despair and confusion, although misdiagnosis and incorrect treatments may lead to unfulfilled expectations of being cured (Adamson, 1997: 152; Davis, 1960: 44). Adamson's work, like that of Comaroff and Maguire (1981), has also brought to the fore patients' perceptions of the problems that arose through the limitations of scientific and medical knowledge, issues which have often been overlooked in other sociological analyses of uncertainty.

Adamson's work, as well that by Fox, Davis and others, raises some points to consider for the future study of medical uncertainty. With the onset of genetic testing for inherited diseases, public health issues such as BSE and illnesses like chronic fatigue syndrome and post-traumatic stress disorder, it is likely that clinical, functional and existential uncertainty will escalate rather than abate. Fox (1999) notes that the scope for clinical uncertainty has increased in the past 20 years, with genetics, the re-emergence of infectious diseases, the recognition of the iatrogenic effects of treatments and the advent of evidence-based medicine all contributing to the problems that doctors face in the practice of medicine. Furthermore, with the increased use of the language of risk in medical and health care discourses, the concept of uncertainty moves outside of the consulting room and becomes incorporated into the larger community of scientific and medical experts, and in lay experience and knowledge. All these issues raise questions over whether uncertainty is now an expected, but still difficult, part of thinking about how new techniques, illnesses and sources of information will be managed in the future.

See also: *medical autonomy and medical dominance, practitioner–client relationships* and *professional socialization.*

REFERENCES

Adamson, C. (1997) 'Existential and clinical uncertainty in the medical encounter: an idiographic account of an illness trajectory defined by Inflammatory Bowel Disease and Avascular Necrosis', *Sociology of Health and Illness*, 19 (2): 133–59.

Atkinson, P. (1984) 'Training for certainty', *Social Science and Medicine*, 19: 949–56.

Calnan, M. (1984) 'Clinical uncertainty: is it a problem in the doctor–patient relationship?', *Sociology of Health and Illness*, 6 (1): 74–85.

Comaroff, J. and Maguire, P. (1981) 'Ambiguity and the search for meaning: childhood leukaemia in the modern clinical context', *Social Science and Medicine*, 15B: 115–23.

Davis, F. (1960) 'Uncertainty in medical prognosis: clinical and functional', *American Journal of Sociology*, 66 (1): 41–7.

Fox, R. (1999) 'Medical uncertainty revisited', in G. Albrecht, R. Fitzpatrick and S. Scrimshaw (eds), *The Handbook of Social Studies in Health and Medicine*. London: Sage.

Glaser, B. and Strauss, A. (1965) *Awareness of Dying*. Chicago: Aldine.

Parsons, T. (1951) *The Social System*. London: Routledge and Kegan Paul.

SR

compliance and concordance

> *Definition: **Compliance refers to the extent to which a person's behaviour coincides with medical advice. Concordance refers to an agreement between the patient and the doctor about whether, how and when medical treatment will be used.***

The concept of compliance, or non-compliance, is not new. Even physicians in the ancient world, such as Hippocrates (*c.* 460–377 BC), recognized that patients did not always follow the treatment instructions that they were given by the doctor. Although compliance relates to the extent to which any medical advice is followed, the main focus of research has been on the use of medicines. A number of different types of non-compliance with medicines have been identified, including: receiving a prescription but not having it made up at the pharmacy; taking a dose different to that prescribed; taking drugs at different times to those recommended; forgetting one or more doses or increasing the frequency; and stopping the drugs too quickly.

Early research on compliance tended to concentrate on how many people are non-compliant with medicines and their characteristics. One way of measuring non-compliance is by calculating the difference between the number of prescriptions issued by the doctor and the number presented to the pharmacist. Where this approach has been used, a non-compliance rate of around 7 per cent has been found. Other measures such as pill counting and urine testing have shown that around a third to a half of patients do not take their medicines according to the terms of the prescription. However, rates of compliance vary depending on the type of drug being prescribed, the length of time that it is meant to be taken and the complexity of the drug regime. For example, around 30 per cent of patients have been found to be non-compliant with antibiotics, whereas up to 70 per cent of patients are not compliant with certain drugs for arthritis (Stimson, 1974).

Determining the characteristics of patients who are most likely to be

107

non-compliant has proved to be complex. Numerous studies that have aimed to examine the impact of social factors such as gender, age, marital status and social class on compliance, have failed to produce consistent results. While some authors identify people from a working-class background and young women as being less likely to comply, others fail to find a relationship between compliance and any socio-demographic factors.

Implicit in the early studies of compliance was the idea that the 'problem' of non-compliance is situated within the context of the doctor–patient relationship and that patients are passive recipients of health care. This corresponds with Parsons' (1951) vision of the need to maintain social order through the adoption of specific social roles. One of the pre-requisites of entering the 'sick role', according to Parsons, is that a person must follow the advice of the medical expert. Thus, patients who fail to comply with medical instructions were viewed as 'deviant' or 'defaulting'.

Following investigation of 19 studies published in the 1950s and 1960s, Stimson (1974) found that non-compliant patients were widely described as 'defaulters', 'disobedient', 'unco-operative' and as not 'obeying' instructions. Stimson, however, questioned the underlying assumption in these studies, that patients were passive recipients of medical instructions. Rather than accepting the notion that patients ought to receive instructions from the doctor and follow them unquestionably, Stimson believed that patients had their own ideas about illness and the use of medicines, which they brought to the medical encounter. Thus, he suggested that the focus of research should be on the social context in which illnesses are experienced and treatments used.

Having questioned the 'passive patient' approach to compliance, Stimson also carried out interviews with patients and found that their decisions about taking drugs were shaped by the experience of the medical encounter, discussions with lay social networks and previous experiences with other drugs. Moreover, rather than being one-off decisions, patients were shown to continue with their evaluation of the experience of illness and their use of prescribed drugs after they left the medical consultation. Stimson's respondents often described how, having consulted with the doctor, they then sought further information, speaking with friends and family members about their treatment. Rather than simply disobeying the doctor's instructions, therefore, patients were found to be using the information that they gathered over time to help inform decisions about their use of medicines.

Following Stimson's insightful study, research turned to investigating patients' beliefs about medicines and how these influenced their usage. Not only were patients found to hold their own beliefs about medicines, but also, these were shown to be quite different from the beliefs held by health care professionals. Moreover, a recent qualitative study, where patients and general practitioners were interviewed before and after the medical consultation, revealed that a number of misunderstandings exist between doctors and patients concerning the use of medicines (Britten et al., 2000). These misunderstandings were generally found to arise because of a lack of communication between the doctor and the patient, with both being reluctant to voice their personally held views about their preferences concerning medicines. Thus, based on what often turned out to be an inaccurate belief that a patient was expecting a prescription, doctors prescribed medicines that they did not regard as strictly necessary, or even particularly beneficial.

In a further interview-based study with patients referred to a rheumatology clinic, Donovan and Blake (1992) found that patients' beliefs about medicines and the personal and social circumstances within which they lived had an impact on the decisions they made about their treatment. Although almost half of the patients were not taking the drugs according to the terms of the prescription, they had made their decisions after weighing up the expected risk of taking the prescribed drugs against the perceived benefits of the treatment. Instead of arriving at the clinic to receive instructions from the doctor, Donovan and Blake found that patients had their own ideas about treatments, which were influenced by information from others such as family members and the media.

A number of other studies have shown that specific drug attributes shape a person's perceptions of the treatment. In particular, the colour of a drug, its name, shape and mode of delivery have all been found to be important in influencing the way in which drugs are seen and used. While tablets that are coloured red are generally viewed to be more powerful than those of other colours, green tablets have been shown to be most effective in the treatment of anxiety, and yellow tablets appear to be more suitable for treating depressive symptoms (Schapira et al., 1970). In addition, drugs that are administered in injection form are perceived to be stronger than those that are swallowed.

Studies have also looked at the wider social context in which medicines are taken. For example, Conrad (1985) found that patients with epilepsy self-regulated their medicines in order to ensure normality and to be able to live what they considered to be a normal life. Helman (1981) described how long-term users of psychotropic drugs could be classified according to their different perspectives, symbolic meanings and

109

modes of usage. Helman described three models of psychotropic drug use: 'food', 'fuel' and 'tonic'. Where patients were classified as using drugs as 'food', they saw them as necessary for daily living. They perceived themselves as having minimal control over the use of the drug and therefore took them as instructed by the doctor. Patients who perceived the psychotropic drugs as a 'fuel' saw them as a means of enhancing their relationships with others. They expressed some degree of control over their use and took them when they were thought to be necessary for maintaining the status quo. Where patients saw the drugs as a 'tonic', they perceived them as useful for their own benefit only. They had maximum control over their use and chose to take them only when they perceived them to be required. Helman states that the use of drugs in this flexible way, as a tonic, most closely represents what Stimson (1974) identified as the patient as a decision-making individual.

Having shown that patients hold their own beliefs about medicines and are therefore active in treatment decisions, the term 'compliance' becomes problematic. The concept of compliance is built on the idea that it is rational for patients to adhere to medical advice. Thus, the concept denies the legitimacy of behaviours that deviate from the doctor's instructions. It has therefore been suggested that in order to recognize the doctor–patient interaction involved in the use of prescribed medicines, the concept of 'concordance' needs to be developed. A report produced by the British Royal Pharmaceutical Society's working party on concordance describes the concept as an open negotiation and subsequent agreement between patients and doctors about the use of medicines (Royal Pharmaceutical Society, 1997). Acknowledging that both patients and doctors have equally cogent health beliefs, the working party suggested that concordance can best be achieved where patients are able to express their health beliefs to the doctor and doctors are able to convey their medically informed health beliefs to the patient. The working party defines concordance as:

> a new approach to the prescribing and taking of medicines. It is an agreement reached after negotiation between a patient and a health care professional that respects the beliefs and wishes of the patient in determining whether, when and how medicines are to be taken. Although reciprocal, this is an alliance in which the health care professionals recognize the primacy of the patient's decisions about taking the recommended medications. (www.concordance.org)

Concordance therefore suggests an open and informed discussion between the patient and the doctor about treatment options, which leads to an agreement about the way in which a condition will be treated. By recognizing that the patient is an active participant in decisions about health care, with guidance from the doctor, acceptable treatment options can be considered. Rather than 'disobeying' the doctor's orders, patients leave the consultation with an agreed decision about their treatment. As already mentioned, perceptions about treatments do not remain static and newly learnt information, often from discussions with friends and family members, leads to a re-evaluation of treatment decisions. In order that concordance can be achieved, therefore, the patient may need to return to the doctor for further discussion about treatment options.

Although the concept of concordance is relatively new, it is a reflection of a much wider debate among sociologists concerning a shift towards a more equal relationship between the doctor and the patient. In addition to beliefs about medicines, patients have been found to hold individual beliefs about health and illness, which shape their decisions about treatment. Thus, within this context, the concept of compliance, or non-compliance, where patients are viewed as passively following (or disobeying) medical instruction is problematic. The extent to which patients are equal partners within the doctor–patient relationship, however, needs further consideration. In particular, research needs to focus on determining whether patients wish to participate in negotiations about their medicines and, if so, whether doctors are prepared to relinquish some of their autonomy surrounding the prescribing of medicines. Unless both the doctor and the patient are able to move towards a more equal partnership, the concept of concordance will have little more value than being a 'politically correct' term for compliance.

See also: *practitioner–client relationships* and *the sick role.*

REFERENCES

Britten, N., Stevenson, F., Barry, C., Barber, N. and Bradley, P. (2000) 'Misunderstandings in prescribing decisions in general practice: qualitative study', *British Journal of Medicine*, 320: 484–8.

Conrad, P. (1985) 'The meaning of medications: another look at compliance', *Social Science and Medicine*, 20 (1): 29–37.

Donovan, J. and Blake, D. (1992) 'Patient non-compliance: deviance or reasoned decision-making?', *Social Science and Medicine*, 34 (5): 507–13.

Helman, C. (1981) '"Tonic", "fuel" and "food": social and symbolic aspects of the long-term use of psychotropic drugs', *Social Science and Medicine*, 15B: 521–33.

Parsons, T. (1951) *The Social System*. New York: Free Press.

Royal Pharmaceutical Society of Great Britain (1997) *From Compliance to Concordance: Towards Shared Goals in Medicine Taking*. London: RPS.

111

Schapira, K., McClelland, H.A., Griffiths, N.R. and Newell, D.J. (1970) 'Study on the effects of tablet colour in the treatment of anxiety states', *British Medical Journal*, 2: 446–9.

Stimson, G.V. (1974) 'Obeying the doctor's orders: a view from the other side', *Social Science and Medicine*, 8: 97–104.

KB

quality of life

> Definition: **Quality of life refers to an individual's sense of social, emotional and physical well-being which influences the extent to which she or he can achieve personal satisfaction with their life circumstances.**

The term 'quality of life' has been used in many contexts. It first came into common parlance in the USA at the end of the Second World War and referred to the possession of material goods, for example, a car, telephone, or washing machine, which made life 'better'. Following the social movements of the 1960s, material 'standard of living' was more clearly distinguished from the experience of personal freedom, autonomy and fulfilment, and quality of life eventually came to signify the experience of 'a good life' in contrast to mere material success. At the same time, concern that, despite increasing economic prosperity, groups in the population continued to experience poverty and limited opportunities led to the development of objective social indicators as alternatives to the traditional economic measures such as GNP per capita. Statistics on such matters as divorce, crime rates, housing standards, or environmental pollution were used as a form of social monitoring to show changes in quality of life at a societal level and to serve as a basis for policy interventions.

The increasing concern with quality of life in social research was soon matched by an interest in quality of life in a health context and, by the 1970s, measures of quality of life began to supplement traditional clinical measures in the evaluation of health care interventions, particularly in relation to cancer, psychiatry and rheumatology. In this context, concern for quality of life represented a broadening of the aims of health care from a traditional focus on survival and 'quantity of life' to include the impact of health problems on personal well-being and life satisfaction. As more people experienced the limitations imposed by chronic illness and disability, and as many pondered the benefits of technologies which prolonged life in a diminished condition and struggled with the escalating costs of health care, quality of life became an increasingly important measure of the outcomes of health care interventions.

Despite its widespread use, quality of life has remained a vague and abstract concept. It has been viewed as the extent to which basic human needs have been satisfied; as the degree of satisfaction or dissatisfaction felt with various aspects of life; and as the extent to which pleasure and satisfaction characterize human existence. From a phenomenological perspective, quality of life is seen as reflecting the gap between the hopes and expectations an individual holds and his or her present experience. Other definitions have variously emphasized the capacity of an individual to realize his or her life plans; the ability of an individual to manage life as he or she evaluates it; or the ability to lead a 'normal' life. A particularly influential definition within social gerontology identifies two objective conditions – general health and functional status, and socio-economic status – and two subjective evaluations – life satisfaction and self-esteem – as at the core of quality of life.

Within the health field, interest has focused on health-related quality of life (HRQL), a term which refers to a loosely related body of work on functional ability, health status and subjective well-being. The conceptual framework for this work derives largely from the WHO definition of health which points to the need to take physical, mental and social well-being into account in assessing the health of individuals and populations. The concept itself, however, is not well developed theoretically and debate continues over the specification of the domains which comprise HRQL. Patrick and Erickson (1993), for example, present it as characterized by resilience, health perception, physical function, symptoms and duration of life, while others employ related concepts such as health status, cognitive function, emotional state, social function, role performance and subjective well-being to define and assess HRQL.

Although HRQL has been investigated using qualitative methods, most effort in this field has focused on the development of quantitative measurement instruments (Bowling, 1997). While some early measures were designed to be used by clinicians to obtain 'objective' assessments of physical or mental functioning, more recent measures have been designed to obtain the patient's subjective assessments and to reflect lay perceptions of the impact of illness on their lives. Generic instruments – for example, the Sickness Impact Profile (SIP), the Nottingham Health Profile (NHP) and the Short-Form 36 (SF-36) – are designed for use with any population group and provide a broad-based assessment. Disease-specific instruments have also been developed to provide greater sensitivity in measuring aspects of symptoms and functioning relevant to particular conditions. A concern sometimes expressed about these instruments, which aim to obtain standard information from all patients, is that they impose on individuals an external value system, which may not reflect their own. In an attempt to address this, individualized measures have also been developed, which ask people to specify for themselves the domains of life that are most affected by their condition and the degree of disruption they experience. Such measures are more sensitive to differences between individuals or population groups with regard to the significance of illness and its effects on day-to-day life but are also more difficult to interpret and analyse.

Measures of HRQL have been used in a variety of ways, from screening for and monitoring psycho-social problems in individual patients to assessing perceived health problems in population surveys. They are most commonly used, however, in clinical trials and evaluation research where they provide subjective, patient-based assessments for evaluating the effects of health care interventions. In this context, they have been invaluable in drawing attention to outcomes which may be missed by more traditional clinical measures, in highlighting differences in assessments between patients and clinicians and in demonstrating the limitations and deleterious side-effects of medical interventions. For example, in an early influential study, Croog et al. (1986) carried out a randomized control trial on 625 men with moderate hypertension to determine the effects of three commonly used drugs which act in different ways to control blood pressure. After six months, patients in all three treatment groups had similar levels of blood pressure control. However, clear differences were found between the groups in a range of measures of quality of life, including general well-being, physical symptoms and sexual dysfunction, cognitive function, work performance and satisfaction with life. These findings demonstrated that anti-hypertensive drugs had an effect on wider aspects of patients' lives and that these effects could reliably be measured. The authors also suggested that, by giving due attention to quality of life measures in clinical practice, doctors could better address the needs and concerns of their patients.

More controversially, quality of life measures have been used by health economists to provide a single index of the benefits of medical interventions, the quality adjusted life year (QALY). QALYs are a measure of life extension gained by a specific medical treatment adjusted by a 'utility' weight, which reflects the relative value of the health status attained. For example, a year with side-effects of anti-hypertensive treatment has been judged to be equivalent to 0.98 of a year of full health. Calculations of costs per QALY gained can then be made for different health care interventions. Perhaps not surprisingly, there has been much scepticism about the meaningfulness of QALYs and much unease about using them in making complex choices in resource allocation (Carr-Hill, 1989).

In an effort to develop a theoretical foundation for HRQL research, Wilson and Cleary (1995) have outlined a model that attempts to link traditional clinical measures, measures of HRQL and measures of quality of life at a more global level. The model proposes causal linkages between five types of outcome of health care, which move from the cell to the individual to the interaction of the individual as a member of society. At each subsequent level, concepts are increasingly integrated and increasingly difficult to define and measure and the factors influencing them become increasingly complex and outside the control of the health care system.

According to Wilson and Cleary's model, 'biological and physiological measures' assess the function of cells and organs and are usually made by clinicians. 'Symptom reports' shift the focus to the individual and depend on subjective assessments. 'Measures of functional status' assess the ability of the individual to perform particular tasks and are influenced by symptom experience and other factors in the individual (for example, personality, motivation) and the social environment (for example, income, housing, social support). 'General health perceptions' are the global perceptions that individuals hold about their health and take account of the weights or values that they attach to different symptoms or functional impairments. Finally, 'overall quality of life' is a measure of life satisfaction that represents a synthesis of a wide range of experiences and feelings that people have, including health-related quality of life but also other salient life circumstances such as economic, political and spiritual factors.

This model highlights the complex factors which influence quality of life and which may at times produce what appear to be counter-intuitive or paradoxical assessments. For example, in a study of individuals with moderate to severe disabilities, Albrecht and Devlieger (1999) found that more than half reported a good to excellent quality of life despite experiencing severe difficulties performing daily tasks, being socially isolated and having limited incomes and benefits. Such findings point to

115

the way the range of social and psychological processes involved in accommodating to illness or disability can produce changes in the internal standards for appraising current health status, or a redefinition of notions of what constitutes a good quality of life, which may in turn influence perceptions of quality of life independent of 'objective' health status or functional ability. Albrecht and Devlieger describe this process in terms of a balance theory, where the experience of well-being and life satisfaction derives from the individuals' ability to reconstitute a balance between body, mind and spirit and to build a harmonious relationship with their social environment. In a critique of this work, Koch (2000) questions the assumption that underlies the perception of a disability paradox, that 'diminished physical (or mental) capacity' necessarily precludes a good quality of life. In reply, Albrecht and Devlieger (2000) point out that their respondents themselves identified a paradox and in doing so provided insights into the social and psychological processes that contribute to a good quality of life.

In summary, health-related quality of life represents an attempt to treat health as multi-dimensional, social and subjective in ways that sociologists have long advocated. Because much of its development has been in the context of applied policy considerations, theoretical and conceptual developments have been ignored. The emphasis has also been on quantitative assessment that misses out the rich descriptions of patients' experience provided by more qualitative approaches. Nevertheless, attention to quality of life in assessing the outcomes of medical care has served to draw attention to the broader impact of illness and health care on patients' daily lives and to provide a framework for incorporating a wider range of social and psychological factors in considerations of health and health care.

116

See also: *chronic illness and disability* and *evaluation.*

REFERENCES

Albrecht, G. and Devlieger, P. (1999) 'The disability paradox: high quality of life against all the odds', *Social Science and Medicine*, 48: 977–88.

Albrecht, G. and Devlieger, P. (2000) 'Disability assumptions, concepts and theory: reply to Tom Koch', *Social Science and Medicine*, 50: 761–2.

Bowling, A. (1997) *Measuring Health: A Review of Quality of Life Measurement Scales.* 2nd edn. Buckingham: Open University Press.

Carr-Hill, R. (1989) 'Assumptions of the QALY procedure', *Social Science and Medicine*, 29: 469–77.

Croog, S., Levine, S., Testa, M., Brown, B., Bulpitt, C., Jenkins, C., Lerman, G. and Williams, G. (1986) 'The effects of antihypertensive therapy on the quality of life', *The New England Journal of Medicine*, 314: 1657–64.

Koch, T. (2000) 'The illusion of paradox: commentary on Albrecht, G.L. and Devlieger, P.J. (1998). The disability paradox: high quality of life against all the odds, *Social Science and Medicine*, 48: 977–988', *Social Science and Medicine*, 50: 757–9.

Patrick, D., and Erickson, P. (1993) *Health Status and Health Policy: Quality of Life in Health Care Evaluation and Resource Allocation*. New York: Oxford University Press.

Wilson, I., and Cleary, P. (1995) 'Linking clinical variables with health-related quality of life: A conceptual model of patient outcomes', *Journal of the American Medical Association*, 273: 59–65.

MBO

dying trajectories

> **Definition:** *A dying trajectory refers to the temporal dimension of dying, which has the two properties of duration (how long it takes to die) and shape (a variable number of episodes of slow or fast decline).*

The idea that dying can be understood in terms of a trajectory is the particular contribution of Glaser and Strauss (1968), whose book *Time for Dying* was devoted to elaboration and illustration of the concept. This was one of several books that arose from experience of a research project undertaken in the early 1960s, employing the method of participant observation in hospital wards where different kinds of dying were going on, in which the ideas of grounded theory were used (Glaser and Strauss, 1967). The notion of a dying trajectory has in a general sense influenced subsequent analysis of illness experience, being one of a number of such concepts (for example, 'stage', 'career', 'status passage', 'scheduling') representing the idea that such experience can be broken down into parts that can then be opened up for inspection.

In retrospect, it is possible to see that this is a concept firmly rooted in interactionist sociology, being very close to the concept of 'career'. The claim of grounded theory to construct concepts inductively from inspection of data, suspending the researcher's analytic preconceptions, is thus exposed as somewhat unrealistic, although this in no way diminishes the value of the concept of trajectory. In its focus on the consequences for interaction of variable dying trajectories, the concept is distinctively sociological when compared with the equivalent psychological concept of

117

'stages' of dying (Kubler-Ross, 1969). This latter concept, though, has had more influence on health care professionals, perhaps because it requires less reflection on the motives of health care staff, firmly locating any 'problems' within the patient.

Glaser and Strauss began from the observation that care of dying people involves a considerable amount of planning and emotional adjustment, on the part of staff as well as relatives, and that temporal predictions figure large in this. Staff come to recognize familiar trajectories in which, typically, there are critical junctures. These can involve an initial definition of a patient as 'dying', enabling preparation for the death by those who know (the issue of whether such knowledge was desirable for patients being a major issue at the time of the original study). Typically, a juncture at which it is considered that there is 'nothing more to do' might then be reached, followed by a final descent of variable duration and speed, the 'last hours', the 'death watch' and finally death itself. At any point, however, trajectories can be disrupted, with consequences for the organization and sentimental order of both formal health care work and the 'work' of relatives in planning visits and adjusting emotional states.

The prediction of dying trajectories is therefore a preoccupation for both staff and relatives and much depends on getting this right, with periodic adjustments to predictions often being necessary, although the communication of these to all involved is not always guaranteed. A case where a dying patient killed herself unexpectedly while in hospital is used to demonstrate the severe disruption of trajectory expectations, occasioning much retrospective work to construct a satisfactory account of the event that absolved staff from responsibility. Three main trajectories are delineated by Glaser and Strauss: the 'lingering', the 'expected quick death' and the 'unexpected quick death'. Each will be considered in turn.

Lingering trajectories have been the subject of much subsequent sociological work that investigates 'dying', being typically associated with cancer, where researchers (like others who attend dying people) have time to plan and carry out their work of interviewing and observation. Such trajectories may occupy different sites – home, hospital, hospice, nursing home – and be an opportunity for much helpful preparation for death by all concerned in terms of anticipatory grief. Facing death and planning for it are feasible under these circumstances and are an opportunity for a typically modern form of self-identity to be expressed. This is one that makes the self into a reflexively formed project, as described by Giddens (1991) and elaborated in relation to dying by Seale (1998) who points out that such trajectories have an heroic quality, representing admirable qualities of self-direction, courage and awareness for onlookers, who incorporate these qualities in their own re-telling of the death.

Yet Glaser and Strauss record that there are also disadvantages to lingering trajectories. Here we begin to see in the work their hallmark qualities of great sociological investigations: the capacity to balance detachment and involvement in the analysis of matters of sentiment and morality. Indeed, it is this that distinguishes Glaser and Strauss from the sentimentally immersed Kubler-Ross. Glaser and Strauss point out that the conjuncture of 'social' with 'biological' death may be an issue if trajectories are 'too long' and carers become weary of their tasks. Patients can then die socially before they expire biologically, involving abandonment by staff or relatives. Sudnow (1967) famously explored this issue at around the same time as Glaser and Strauss and the relevance of his analysis for today has been established by Timmermans (1998) who observed negative consequences for poorer patients in hospital care. Additionally, lingering trajectories can involve emotional identification by staff with their patients, particularly where younger patients are involved, where the 'social loss' is experienced as greater and therefore more distressing.

When lingering trajectories take a downturn, making increased demands on family resources, considerable anxiety over the suitability of placement in an institution can be generated. Concern about the humanity of institutional care associated with badly managed dying trajectories inspired the hospice movement, and in Chapter 4 of *Time for Dying*, Glaser and Strauss record a fruitful visit to observe the work of Cicely Saunders shortly before St Christopher's hospice was founded in South London. An aim of hospice-style terminal care is summarized by them as being the joint management by patient, staff and relatives of a lingering dying trajectory, premised on an open awareness context. Here, the authors (unusually) show their colours in a personal endorsement of the desirability of such care.

The 'expected quick' trajectory gives less time for anticipatory mourning, so may be experienced as particularly disruptive by relatives, but is a relatively routine event in hospitals so presents few problems of management for staff. The chief potential issue is that of prolonging life by artificial means. Here (as in trajectories that are judged 'too lingering') issues of euthanasia may arise. Chambliss (1996), in a more recent observational study of dying in hospitals, found that this not only occasions complex negotiations with families, but can also promote divisions between staff, with nurses generally being more likely to advocate 'pulling the plug' in order to reduce suffering, in the knowledge that it is not they who must do this.

The 'unexpected quick' trajectory is perhaps the most difficult for all concerned to manage, particularly if it occurs in an institutional setting devoted to the construction of dying as an orderly passage. Everyone is less prepared for such events, and Glaser and Strauss record some quite elaborate stage management activity by staff to place these events in order retrospectively. The death of a woman in childbirth, the unexpected heart arrest, the unexpected death of a person on the operating table: these all occasion a degree of alarm and may threaten staff with accusations of negligence or incompetence. Much of the work done by staff in these circumstances involves turning a 'crisis' into a routine 'emergency' situation of the sort we are all familiar with through contemporary television dramas. Thus *ER* has contributed to the perception that there are 'standard' responses that routinize a crisis (for example, the arrival, actions and equipment of the resuscitation team).

One elaborate subterfuge to manage relatives' emotional responses, observed by Glaser and Strauss in the case of unexpected deaths in the operating theatre, involved telling relatives that the operation had been extended due to dangerous 'complications'. After a suitable period of waiting with the body behind closed doors, while the relatives took in the implications of this, a doctor would emerge to break the bad news. Additionally, autopsies are conducted, both of the physical and psychological sort, in which staff involved in quick, unexpected dying trajectories seek to achieve what Glaser and Strauss call 'a solid feeling about what is happening' (1968: 121). The observation that these events caused such subsequent narrative reconstruction influenced Seale (1998), who reports a study of the stories of relatives and friends of those who died alone, in which the moral reputation of speakers is continually at stake in constructing satisfactory explanatory tales.

The concept of the dying trajectory has not entered the general sociological literature as successfully as the concept of 'awareness contexts' (Glaser and Strauss, 1965) or come anywhere near the phenomenal success of the 'grounded theory' approach to research, perhaps because the interactionist notion of 'career' is adequate for most similar purposes. In a search through sociological dictionaries and introductory textbooks and key recent works on the sociology of dying, there are few references to the concept (that of 'awareness contexts' appears more frequently). But the kind of thinking that the notion of a 'dying trajectory' involves has been influential, because it represents a moment when the experience of dying (and caring for dying people) could for the first time be considered as a process deserving systematic sociological analysis. As has also been noted above, the concept does not stand alone, being part of a web of ideas in the original work (awareness contexts, social death, sentimental order, social loss, grounded theory), many of which have influenced subsequent work, or been subject to further elaboration.

See also: *illness narratives* and *emotional labour.*

REFERENCES

Chambliss, D.F. (1996) *Beyond Caring: Hospitals, Nurses and the Social Organization of Ethics*. Chicago: University of Chicago Press.

Giddens, A. (1991) *Modernity and Self-identity: Self and Society in the Late Modern Age*. Cambridge: Polity Press.

Glaser, B.G. and Strauss, A.L. (1965) *Awareness of Dying*. Chicago: Aldine.

Glaser, B.G. and Strauss, A.L. (1967) *The Discovery of Grounded Theory: Strategies for Qualitative Research*. Chicago: Aldine.

Glaser, B.G. and Strauss, A.L. (1968) *Time for Dying*. Chicago: Aldine.

Kubler-Ross, E. (1969) *On Death and Dying.* New York: Macmillan.

Seale, C.F. (1998) *Constructing Death: The Sociology of Dying and Bereavement*. Cambridge: Cambridge University Press.

Sudnow, D. (1967) *Passing On: The Social Organization of Dying*. Englewood Cliffs, NJ: Prentice-Hall.

Timmermans, S. (1998) 'Social death as self-fulfilling prophecy: David Sudnow's "Passing On" revisited', *Sociological Quarterly*, 39 (3): 453–72.

CS

121

PART 3

Health, Knowledge and Practice

medical model

> **Definition:** *The medical model refers to the conception of disease established in the late nineteenth and early twentieth centuries, based on an anatomo-pathological view of the individual body.*

The concept of the medical model is frequently used by sociologists and others as a shorthand way of describing the dominant approach to disease in Western medicine. This approach, based on a pathological anatomy of the body, broke away in the nineteenth century from earlier conceptions to establish the idea of specific diseases with specific causes. Before then, disease in Western societies had been largely based on humoral theories and on exhaustive descriptions of symptoms. Thomas Sydenham, the seventeenth-century English physician, for example, would have no truck with dissection and the emerging field of anatomy. He declared, 'and as for anatomy, my butcher can dissect a joint full and well; now young man, all that is stuff; you must go to the bedside, it is there alone you can learn disease' (cited by Porter, 1997: 229). Such scepticism about a scientific and laboratory-based medicine was common in the early modern period and in some forms persists to this day.

However, by the mid-nineteenth century various alternative models of disease, including those based on observation and 'bedside medicine' (Jewson, 1976) were made to give way to a view that located disease in specific organs. Indeed, in 1800, Bichat had argued that pathological processes giving rise to disease might not even be located in an organ, but in a specific tissue. By the 1880s bacteriology had begun to show that specific micro-organisms were responsible for specific diseases, for example, the tubercle bacillus for tuberculosis and the vibrio cholera for cholera. Predictably perhaps, these findings were resisted by many physicians who were wedded to the idea that such disease clearly involved the whole person and therefore must be systemic in origin and character.

The new model of disease contained three dimensions: (1) that a specific aetiology could be found underlying specific diseases; (2) that diseases caused lesions in the body which altered its anatomy and physiology; and (3) that these two processes, in turn, gave rise to

125

symptoms. Though successes in applying this new approach were not immediate, by the end of the nineteenth century antitoxin for diphtheria, for example, was showing dramatic results and the adoption of antisepsis was beginning to make hospital care and especially surgery safer. The development of antibiotics, especially following the identification by Fleming of penicillin in 1928, and its final introduction in 1941 (Porter, 1997: 457) showed that the medical model of disease could produce lasting and beneficial results.

The impact of the medical model on the doctor–patient relationship was equally profound. As the conception of disease focused on processes inside the body, the task of the doctor was to elicit information about the signs and symptoms of the disease and then locate these in the new nosology. Thus, the ability to diagnose became highly prized and was based on test results and judgements about deviations from 'the normal', rather than on observations of departures from the patient's 'natural state' (Lawrence, 1994: 45). From the patient's viewpoint, the task now was to recognize signs and symptoms of disease and present them to the doctor at the appropriate time. As disease was seen to reside in the individual body, it could best be diagnosed and treated in a one-to-one situation by the clinician. Doctors were increasingly oriented towards individual 'presentation', rather than tackling the complexities and heterogeneity of the patient's familial, social or moral worlds. The medical model can be seen, therefore, as reinforcing individualism as a dimension of modern experience.

The growing allegiance of doctors to the medical model in the late nineteenth and especially early twentieth centuries is also partly explained by the association of the new approach to disease with social and sometimes political reform. Even in the early nineteenth century, as novels such as George Eliot's *Middlemarch* made clear, the reforming medical man, increasingly under the influence of the medical model, was part of the changing fabric of (in this case) English society. Hence, as with the growth of individualism, the medical model did not simply develop in a social context: it was an important constitutive part of society's changing character. Progress in medicine was but one of a range of practices linked to changing cultural and social structures.

Lawrence (1994) argues that, by 1920, the idea of disease as individual pathology had become almost entirely dominant, pushing other theories and approaches aside. This underpinned and legitimated the development of a 'bounded' medical profession which increasingly exercized jurisdiction over medical matters (Lawrence, 1994: 77). State regulation of medicine and a ceding of quasi-judicial powers to the profession, for example, its ability to register or de-register ('strike off') practitioners, gave it enormous powers of autonomy and control. Senior hospital doctors, in particular, and those organized in the various Royal Colleges had, and arguably still have, particular access to these levers of power.

Not surprisingly, therefore, the development of the medical model has not always been met with unqualified acceptance, even by those doctors sympathetic to a scientific medicine. There are some within the profession, especially those in specialties such as public health and psychiatry, and in general practice, who have argued against the complete subsuming of medical practice under the medical model.

The 1960s and 1970s saw a number of critiques emerge from within medicine. Thomas Szasz, a medically trained psychoanalyst and R.D Laing, an ex-army psychiatrist, among many others, issued broad critiques of the application of the medical model to mental illness. In addition, the 1970s saw strong reactions by leading epidemiologists in public health to what they perceived as the over-reliance on (unevaluated) curative medicine by the public, and too great an influence on the part of the medical establishment. McKeown (1976), for example, examined the historical role of medicine and showed that for many if not all infections, mortality had fallen substantially before the medical model had uncovered their causes or, indeed, fashioned any preventative or curative responses. McKeown demonstrated that public health measures and better living standards were responsible for improvements in health in the nineteenth and twentieth centuries. Part of the problem of the 'mechanistic' medical model's focusing on the individual, McKeown argued, was that broader determinants of health were overlooked.

In medical sociology, early theorizing about health and medicine, especially that by Parsons, regarded medicine as largely functional in social terms. Parsons (1951) regarded medicine and the medical model of disease to be rational, counteracting the 'needs dispositions' of the ill. By addressing the individual's problems in medical terms, the tendency towards deviance, represented by illness states, could be safely channelled, pending the return of the individual to their former roles.

However, by the 1970s, medical sociologists were also becoming highly critical of the medical model and its application by the medical profession. Freidson (1970), in particular, set out a full-blown critique of the profession and, quite unlike Parsons, sought to challenge the apparent objectivity of the medical model. The belief in illness as an objective entity, Freidson argued, stemmed from the perception of 'viruses and molecules . . . [as a] physical reality independent of time, space and changing moral evaluation' (1970: 208). But, Freidson insisted, 'biological deviance or disease is defined socially and is surrounded by social acts that condition it' (ibid.: 209). The failure of the medical profession to recognize this situation meant that far from acting as a socially functional institution, it left the patient in a passive position, where lay constructions were given little or no credence. The 'clash of perspectives' between the patient's world and that of the doctor led to an underlying conflict: 'Given the viewpoints of the two worlds, lay and professional, in interaction, they can never be wholly synonymous' (ibid.: 321).

As can be seen from the above, Freidson's argument rested on a distinction between illness (the experience of the patient) and disease (the conception of the doctor). While the application of the medical model of biological disease could vary depending on the cultural context, Freidson was more concerned to contrast the different perspectives of patients and doctors than follow through a detailed critique of the 'social construction' of disease.

It has perhaps been Foucault's critique of the medical model that has taken this question much further. In a number of writings on 'bio-power' Foucault set out what he took to be the social significance of the pathological anatomy view of disease. In his book, *The Birth of the Clinic*, Foucault (1976) centres his argument on Bichat and his dictum 'open up a few corpses'. The significance of this move was, as noted earlier, to locate disease in what Foucault terms the 'volumes and spaces' of the body. This individuating and the internalizing of disease, for Foucault, were the hallmarks of the 'new' medical model. The growing dominance of this model, together with the associated growth in power and influence of the medical profession, demonstrated for Foucault the intimate relationship between knowledge and power.

Like Freidson, medicine's monopoly over disease and illness for Foucault stemmed from the power to name and locate disease in the individual. Bringing the individual under 'the gaze' of medical perception was part of a growing tendency of modernity to rely on the 'discursive practices' of experts in achieving social control. These practices divided populations according to their 'disciplinary' codes. In fact, in Foucault's work the term 'discipline' had a double meaning. The 'discipline' of medicine at one and the same time located the individual in a scientific schema, and, on the other, added to the tendency to create 'docile bodies' by regulating them in specific ways. The growth of medicine, psychology and the human sciences in general, no less than the growth of the clinic and hospital (like the school and the prison) were the institutional expression of 'disciplinary power' shaping and reshaping modern life.

The point of Foucault's critique is that the enormous growth in the power of medicine and the medical conception of disease was neither inevitable or irreversible. He states: 'this order of the solid, visible body is only one way – in all likelihood neither the first, not the most fundamental – in which one spacialises disease' (Foucault, 1976: 3). The message is clear: things could have been otherwise, and therefore can be otherwise in the future. The apparent objectivity of the body and the permanence of the medical model are open to question and change.

These critical views of the medical model have done much to challenge the power of the medical profession and to fuel some of the challenges to 'medical dominance' now found in public as well as academic circles. However, despite the persuasiveness of these critiques, there are limitations which suggest that the medical model is more complex than envisaged. Two must suffice here.

First, the idea that the medical model is neither the first nor likely the last way of conceptualizing disease may be superficially true, but paradoxically it understates the transformations that the medical model and other features of modernity have created. While alternative ways of conceptualizing disease and illness may emerge (health promotion, public health and the myriad of 'alternative practices' have all grown in recent years), the medical model shows little sign of disappearing. Developments in pharmacology, immunology and especially genetics suggest that the power of medical knowledge and of the profession show little sign of significant erosion, at least in the scientific realm, however problematic it sometimes appears.

Second, the changing pattern of disease in Western countries, and especially the decline in infections, have meant that many areas of medical practice have moved away from a complete reliance on a narrow, 'mechanistic' view of the body or of illness, if they ever accepted it fully. Many of those working with the chronically ill, for example, are as concerned with physical, social and psychological functioning of the individual and with the pattern of informal care, as they are with diagnostic or medical treatments. The medical model may never have been so fundamental to the everyday practice of medicine as Foucault and others believed.

Such caveats concerning the medical model suggest that its role is at one and the same time more powerful and more limited than critics have recognized. These complexities need to be addressed in future work on the medical model.

See also: *practitioner–client relationships, professions and professionalization* and *social constructionism.*

REFERENCES

Foucault, M. (1976) *The Birth of the Clinic*. London: Tavistock.

Freidson, E. (1970) *Profession of Medicine: A Study of the Sociology of Applied Knowledge*. Chicago: University of Chicago Press.

Jewson, N. (1976) 'The disappearance of the sick man from medical cosmology 1770–1870', *Sociology*, 10: 225–44.

Lawrence, C. (1994) *Medicine in the Making of Modern Britain 1700–1920*. London: Routledge.

McKeown, T. (1976) *The Role of Medicine: Dream, Mirage or Nemesis?* Oxford: Blackwell.

Parsons, T. (1951) *The Social System*. New York: Free Press.

Porter, R. (1997) *The Greatest Benefit to Mankind: A Medical History of Humanity from Antiquity to the Present*. London: HarperCollins.

MB

—social constructionism—

> *Definition:* **Social constructionism refers to the view that scientific knowledge and biological discourses about the body, health and illness are produced through subjective, historically determined human interests, and are subject to change and reinterpretation.**

Social constructionism is a forceful and sometimes contentious approach, which regards all knowledge as created through human interaction and interpretation. Social constructionists maintain that knowledge is neither universal, fixed nor neutral, but is always changing in response to social relations. In relation to medicine, this thesis argues that medical knowledge about the body and its pathology, such as physical disease entities or mental illness, cannot be understood as standing apart from material society, as objective and detached scientific knowledge.

An important precursor of social constructionist thought in medical sociology was the commentaries in the 1960s on the role of the psychiatric profession in the diagnosis and treatment of those labelled mentally ill. A decade later, Freidson's (1988) analysis of the power and authority of the medical profession suggested that the way medicine was practised served to promote and maintain the social and political interests of doctors. The dominant status of the doctor allowed him 'extraordinary autonomy in controlling ... the definition of the problems he [*sic*] works on' (ibid.: 337). Illness therefore becomes a social state, constructed through the power of doctors to create labels and meanings for lay experiences.

However, Freidson held back from suggesting that bio-scientific knowledge itself was socially constructed; rather, it was its utilization that was subject to human interpretation. He contrasted 'neutral scientific concepts like that of "virus" or "molecule"' with the 'inherently evaluational concept of medicine' (ibid.: 208). Essentially, he argued that disease categories reflect objective diagnoses, while illness is a subjective state capable of manipulation by doctors who had the power to define illness and therefore determine what counts as being sick (ibid.: 206). While Freidson put medical practice under the sociological microscope, social constructionists went on to maintain that medical knowledge itself must be critically scrutinized as well.

The origin of a distinctive and self-defined social constructionist perspective in medical sociology lay in interpretations of the work of Foucault, particularly *The Birth of the Clinic* (1973). Based on an appraisal of practices in hospitals in nineteenth-century France, Foucault critically examined the relationships between scientific knowledge, medical training and clinical practice, focusing his analysis on the way medical discourses have developed and altered over time. Within this analysis, Foucault noted that, prior to this era, the body was not always a given certainty. He argued that it was 'created' by the biomedicine process of objectification, effected through a new form of surveillance that Foucault termed the 'clinical gaze'. Therefore, following Foucault, illness and the body cannot be reduced to a physical reality, but must be viewed as a consequence of the clinical gaze adopted by physicians to make the body and its mechanisms available and subject to medical scrutiny.

In his interpretation of the work of Foucault, David Armstrong took an explicitly social constructionist approach and explored the construction of discourses about public health measures, the body and professional–lay interaction. For example, in Armstrong's (1983) analysis of the sanitary movement of the mid-nineteenth century, he asserted that it should not be seen as the scientific victory of man over nature, or of the scientific understanding of contagion and infection. Rather, it was representative of the changes in political and social discourses in which the human body became open to increased surveillance by those with political and medical power. The physical body, by becoming an object to be bounded and quarantined, represented 'a psycho-social space ... determined by the contemporary new sciences of psychology and sociology' (Armstrong, 1983: 407).

Foucault also inspired work by Arney and Bergen (1983). For them, as for Foucault, it was not enough to define power as being held by one or more groups or individuals. They argued that sociologists need to look at the nature of power, the rules that govern it and how those rules are applied to shape the surveillance techniques used in medical discourses. Arney and Bergen examined the creation of the patient as person and considered the ways in which alcoholism, pain, chronic illness and handicap were conceived of and treated from the 1950s onwards. They also charted the changes in the focus of medical practice over the past two centuries, from the treatment of the body as a physical object to the incorporation of social and psychological aspects into the clinical gaze. In doing so, Arney and Bergen demonstrated that mid-nineteenth-century medical thought heralded the 'reformulation of medical work and medical power' which in turn 'invented the patient who was also a person' and, consequently, an expansion in the domain of the doctor (1983: 11–12).

Not all medical sociologists who take a social constructionist approach necessarily adhere vigorously to the Foucauldian view that questions the underlying reality of biological understandings of the body and the experience of disease. To be sure, there remains a tension between Foucauldian social constructionism and other approaches that attract or adopt the social constructionist label. Those who follow Foucault are not directly concerned with the professional–lay power struggle, or with the privileging of social and experiential knowledge over its scientific counterpart, but instead seek to deconstruct accepted histories and discourses about medical knowledge, practice and power. Alternatively, those not directly drawing on Foucault focus on questioning the development of scientific and medical knowledge and interpretations of disease. They take a more direct look at how traditional sociological areas of enquiry, such as power relations and political and economic considerations, can be applied to understanding the basis of medical knowledge and the role of medical practitioners.

These accounts are more explicitly related to how the interests of particular groups can influence the production and application of scientific and medical knowledge. In general, proponents of this approach argue that disease categories are the result of social, political and professional debates and power struggles and are not simply the result of medical and scientific investigation.

For example, Arksey (1998) examined how competing versions of medical knowledge about repetitive strain injury (RSI) have been constructed by various professional and lay interest groups. She argued that, rather than being objective, neutral and value-free, medical knowledge about RSI is the product of 'occupational turf wars' between specialists vying for 'autonomy, status and resources' (Arksey, 1998: 9). Drawing on Fleck's model of the process by which a disease entity becomes recognized as a medical fact, Arksey found that the construction of medical knowledge is not always consensual, but is subject to controversy about cause, treatment and the very legitimacy of certain conditions. Thus, medical 'facts' are not necessarily based on irrefutable biological evidence, but are instead the outcome of collective interaction within a group. Such an analysis is particularly timely with the advent of other contentious illnesses such as chronic fatigue syndrome (CFS), Gulf War syndrome and attention-deficit hyperactivity disorder (ADHD).

Although social constructionist perspectives have become a significant strand in the sociology of health and illness, they have nevertheless engendered an ongoing debate among sociologists, principally among those who question the validity and relevance of Foucault's arguments. One of the most comprehensive criticisms of the use of social constructionism to explain the development and uses of medicine came from Bury (1986). Bury made a series of points about the limitations of social constructionism, some of which were disputed by Nicolson and McLaughlin (1987). Of Bury's many points, three will be discussed here, along with Nicolson and McLaughlin's responses.

First, Bury contended that social constructionism does not fully acknowledge the real impact and experience of illness. No matter how knowledge of the diseased body is developed and implemented by medical professionals, sickness, pain and disability remain a reality for those who suffer them. Nicolson and McLaughlin (1987) countered that a social constructionist approach does not deny that people have bodies, but that the body can only be understood through the discourses that surround it. According to Nicolson and McLaughlin (ibid.: 111), perceptions of the human body cannot be standardized and homogeneous, despite the efforts of modern science to 'produce consensual agreement about physical reality'. Instead, they drew on the neo-Kantian tradition that proposed that human knowledge is not based on rational observation of the data of the world, but rather is mediated by 'a priori' beliefs held by individuals. Thus, Nicolson and McLaughlin argued that perspectives on physical phenomena must be recognized as shaped by the cultural, social and personal knowledge of the actors involved.

Second, Bury alleged that social constructionism, by denying the

133

element of discovery, negates past medical progress and denies the prospect of future progress. He claimed that the constructionist view sidesteps recognition of medical advances, most notably the eradication of many fatal infectious diseases such as smallpox and the suppression of others like polio (1986: 145). Although Bury acknowledged that Western medicine and science have brought threat as well as progress, he insisted that the modern quality of life has been transformed for the better through medical work. Nicolson and McLaughlin also argued that progress is not always necessarily wholly positive, but maintained that it is imperative that sociological investigation examines the context in which progress is claimed, as well as its underlying and consequent meanings.

Finally, Bury took issue with the relativist standpoint of social constructionism. Relativism holds that there is no one truth, and knowledge is only capable of being assessed against criteria set in specific cultures, eras and social conditions. Of course, this presents a significant dilemma: if no one form of knowledge is more valid than any other, then the social constructionist analysis of the development of medicine cannot be accepted as more accurate than any other viewpoint.

Nicolson and McLaughlin responded to this by claiming that it is an aim of sociological enquiry to explore and question the cultural and contextual biases in the creation of knowledge (1987: 117–18). Although social constructionism maintains that knowledge may be the product of human, professional and political interests, it does not deny people the right to judge knowledge as true or false. However, it also does not accept that individuals or groups are entitled to privilege their own beliefs in determining the value of others' viewpoints.

In conclusion, social constructionism has contributed to a change in the way medical sociologists look at the development and application of medical knowledge. It provides tools with which subsequent analysis can examine the assumptions that underlie the acceptance or rejection of medical history and discourse. Through a social constructionist lens, a different framework from that proposed by the medical establishment can be used to assess the role of scientific knowledge, medicine and medical professionals, as well as to understand the experience of health and illness.

See also: *medical autonomy and medical dominance, medical model* and *the new public health.*

Arksey, H. (1998) *RSI and the Experts: The Construction of Medical Knowledge*. London: UCL Press.

Armstrong, D. (1983) 'Public health spaces and the fabrication of identity', *Sociology*, 27 (3): 393–410.

Arney, W. and Bergen, B. (1983) 'The anomaly, the chronic patient and the play of medical power', *Sociology of Health and Illness*, 5 (1): 1–24.

Bury, M. (1986) 'Social constructionism and the development of medical sociology', *Sociology of Health and Illness*, 8 (2): 137–69.

Foucault, M. (1973) *The Birth of the Clinic*. London: Tavistock.

Freidson, E. (1988) *Profession of Medicine*, 2nd edn. London: University of Chicago Press.

Nicolson, M. and McLaughlin, C. (1987) 'Social constructionism and medical sociology: a reply to M.R. Bury', *Sociology of Health and Illness*, 9 (2): 107–26.

SR

lay knowledge

> **Definition: Lay knowledge refers to the ideas and perspectives employed by social actors to interpret their experiences of health and illness in everyday life.**

The concept of lay knowledge within medical sociology is a recent development of the idea of lay beliefs. The study of people's beliefs about illness, health and medical care initially provided a way of understanding different forms of 'illness behaviour' and 'lay referral', particularly where 'non-compliant' behaviour suggested differences between the patient's perspectives and those of his or her physician. Research on these themes provided an empirical foundation for the argument that a patient's behaviour was influenced by his or her beliefs, and that these beliefs were a reasoned attempt to deal with the sometimes intensely contradictory demands of illness and its treatment in everyday life (Robinson, 1973). However, beliefs are more than antecedents to individual behaviour, and a second line of thought was beginning to conceptualize lay beliefs about health and illness as social representations. Drawing on the Durkheimian tradition of sociological theorizing about the *conscience collective*, Herzlich's (1973) 'socio-

135

psychological approach' provided an important bridge between the interesting but highly focused empirical studies of individual patients within medical sociology, and the panorama of social theorizing about the relationships between self and society.

With a respectful but sociologically critical eye on her respondents' accounts, Herzlich was able to move away from the methodological individualism characteristic of much work on lay beliefs at the time. She argued that individual beliefs about health and illness are representations of the culture and society in which people live. While these representations may include medical ideas about pathology and aetiology, lay perspectives express a certain cultural autonomy and embody a wider theorization of health and illness in relation to society. In analysing her material in this way Herzlich marked out a set of themes that would remind future social scientists that lay beliefs represented far too fecund a field to be left to the withering attention of health services researchers or government civil servants.

The work of Herzlich provided the intellectual foundation for two key arguments about lay beliefs. First, that lay ideas are not 'primitive' residuals stuck in the otherwise smoothly functioning bowels of modern 'scientific' societies, but complex bodies of knowledge or contextualized rationality that are central to our understanding of culture and society (Good, 1994). Second, 'lay knowledge' has two key dimensions. On the one hand, it contains a robust empirical approach to the contingencies of everyday life required by people trying to make sense of health and illness in themselves, their families and the wider communities in which they live. On the other, it displays a search for meaning that goes beyond the straightforwardly empirical, situating personal experiences of health crisis in relation to broader frameworks of morality, politics and cosmology. It represents, in Max Weber's terms, understanding in terms of both cause and meaning.

An illustration of the complexity of this can be found in Comaroff and Maguire's (1981) insightful study of 'the search for meaning' in childhood leukaemia. Modern medicine, they argue, supplies an empirical basis for explaining to parents what is happening to their children, but it provides no overarching framework through which parents can 'make sense' of what is happening. The parents in their study were asking not only what causes childhood leukaemia, but why has my child developed this disease, and why now? Perhaps it is not the business of good doctoring to answer these questions, but it does point to the tension between 'evidence-based' and 'narrative-based' approaches to health knowledge. Lay people need the evidence, but the evidence itself will not be enough to support the wider framework of interpretation needed to make sense of their child's illness.

With the increasing emphasis during the 1990s on public health and health promotion there has been a growing interest in how lay knowledge relates to ideas about health risks. For Herzlich's middle-class Parisians the 'way of life' in modern societies produces ill health, with way of life being defined more in terms of social and environmental circumstances than individual behaviour. Later work on this theme showed a tendency for personal responsibility explanations for ill health to be prevalent in both 'rich' and 'poor' populations, possibly reflecting the enduring values of Protestant non-conformity in some of the communities studied, and the effects of the ideology of 'possessive individualism' that were ripping through western societies at the time.

However, the key characteristic of lay knowledge is that it is integrative and holistic: drawing on multiple factors in a syncretic but not indiscriminate fashion; bringing together 'scientific' or other professional sources of knowledge and reflecting the ideological climate of the times, but also providing an incisive moral and political critique of them. A good example of this is to be found in Davison et al.'s (1991) study, based on the collection of extensive interview and observational data from naturalistic settings, examining the relationships between lay perspectives on coronary heart disease and the orthodox doctrine being promulgated in a nationwide health promotion campaign – Heartbeat Wales.

Davison et al. uncovered a strong strand of lay thinking that emphasized personal responsibility for health. They also identified a close correspondence between lay views and the simple, linear causal models of health educators, highlighting the links between diet, exercise, blood pressure, serum cholesterol and heart disease. There was no clear-cut clash of perspectives between lay people and professionals. However, Davison and his colleagues also argued that in situations in which a person becomes ill or a relative dies, when explanation is needed, these lay views become more complex. They coined the term 'lay epidemiology' to describe the way in which people may use a combination of personal, familial and social sources of knowledge, alongside professionally delivered information, to try and make sense of an event or problem. People develop a notion of who is a 'candidate' for a coronary that corresponds quite closely with risk factor epidemiology. However, the reality of lay experience is that people know many individuals who smoke, eat fatty foods, drink too much alcohol, have a stressful life, take no exercise, and live to a ripe old age (the 'Uncle

Norman' character); and, conversely, there are those who live an Aristotelian 'good life' of balance, frugality, virtue and restraint but collapse and die in their forties. Like Comaroff and Maguire's parents faced with their child's leukaemia, abstract descriptions of 'risk factors' are not enough to explain why a much-loved mother or brother has died so young.

Much risk factor epidemiology also assumes a freedom to make healthy choices that is out of line with what many lay people experience as real possibilities in their everyday lives. For example, in a study of a deprived inner-city area in the north-west of England (Williams et al., 1995), it was shown that lay people are only too well aware of the 'political' context of explanations for ill health in the community. In this instance, and in stark contrast with much risk factor epidemiology, the lay accounts reported illustrate the need to contextualize risks – smoking, diet, alcohol, lack of exercise – by reference to the wider material and environmental conditions in which the risks are embedded. The respondents understood the behavioural risk factors that made ill health more likely and for which they were, in a limited sense, responsible, but they were also aware that the risks they faced were part of social conditions that they could do little to change. For these working-class Salfordians, as for Herzlich's middle-class Parisians, the 'way of life' – in this case unemployment, poor housing, low income, stressful and sometimes violent lives – provided a context for 'making sense' of smoking, drinking and drug-taking and all the other 'behaviours' that risk factor epidemiologists calculate and correlate.

This more political expression of lay knowledge finds its most challenging form in the 'popular epidemiology' examined by Phil Brown (1995) and others. Studies of popular epidemiology take situations in which members of local communities have become concerned about a public health problem in their locality – the numbers of children with cancer, the high prevalence of asthma, or an increase in road traffic accidents – and seek some explanation for it. In these circumstances popular epidemiology begins with lay people linking the observed increase in the health problem to some kind of social or environmental hazard – road safety, factory emissions, toxic waste, nuclear power, and so on. Having made the connection, the community then tries to take action to do something about it and finds itself in conflict with local politicians, business corporations or professional experts who disagree, for one reason or another, with the view being expressed by the community. In these situations, local people are forced to move beyond the statement of a point of view to a process in which a social movement develops, evidence is systematically collected and analysed and scientific arguments are developed and sometimes tested in the courts. In popular epidemiology the boundaries are blurred between 'lay people' and 'experts' and the nature of the complex relationships between scientific rationality, personal beliefs and political interests.

The exploration of lay knowledge throws into sharp relief some of our major social concerns – the relationship between authority and expertise, the problem of meaning in a secular society, the incommensurability of different frameworks of interpretation and the difficulties involved in developing a society that is both democratic and knowledge-based. It is impossible to study lay beliefs as forms of knowledge without first acknowledging, as did the late Roy Porter, that universities and laboratories are not the only places in which evidence is debated and knowledge generated. Knowledge is found in the home, the street, the pub and the workplace, often revealing itself only at times of personal or community crisis when the taken-for-grantedness of everyday life is disturbed.

See also: *illness behaviour, the new public health* and *surveillance and health promotion.*

REFERENCES

Brown, P. (1995) 'Popular epidemiology, toxic waste, and social movements', in J. Gabe (ed.), *Medicine, Risk and Health*. Oxford: Blackwell.

Comaroff, J. and Maguire, P. (1981) 'Ambiguity and the search for meaning: childhood leukaemia in the modern clinical context', *Social Science and Medicine*, 15B: 115–23.

Davison, C., Davey Smith, G. and Frankel, S. (1991) 'Lay epidemiology and the prevention paradox: the implications of coronary candidacy for health promotion', *Sociology of Health and Illness*, 13: 1–19.

Good, B.J. (1994) *Medicine, Rationality and Experience: An Anthropological Perspective*. Cambridge: Cambridge University Press.

Herzlich, C. (1973) *Health and Illness: A Socio-Psychological Approach*. London: Academic Press.

Robinson, D. (1973) *Patients, Practitioners and Medical Care*. London: Heinemann.

Williams, G., Popay, J. and Bissell, P. (1995) 'Public health risks in the material world: barriers to social movements in health', in J. Gabe (ed.), *Medicine, Health and Risk*. Oxford: Blackwell.

GW

reproduction

> **Definition:** *Within sociological theory and research, reproduction, referring to pregnancy, birth and the use of reproductive technologies, is regarded as a social and cultural process as well as a biological process.*

The ways a society copes with the major events of birth, illness and death are central to the beliefs and practices of that society and reproduction is an area that reveals the relations between health care and dominant social values. There is considerable cultural variation in the way in which pregnancy and childbearing are defined and managed in everyday life. In some societies, pregnancy is a normal life event, a status passage, in others, it is regarded as an illness.

It is crucial to the sociological view of reproduction that it happens to, and within, society, as well as to an individual, who may, or may not be the subject of medical control. Thus, the way reproduction is 'managed' has important implications for society as a whole; for its view of reproduction, for the position of women, for family relationships. Furthermore, from the point of view of the individual woman, her career as a pregnant woman is not isolated from her other social roles.

An examination of work in this field shows that an early narrow definition of the sociology of human reproduction relating to conception, pregnancy, birth and motherhood has been broadened to encompass the study of sexuality, reproductive technologies and the social relations involved. This has resulted in work examining the sexual politics of reproduction and the construction of medical knowledge. Such work has aimed to get away from definitions of reproductive processes as biological events, isolated from social reality. At the same time, writers stressing social aspects have been cautious not to mask the effect biology has on women's lives.

Macintyre's (1977) early review identifies four types of sociological approach to the management of childbirth and sets out a sociological research agenda. These are: (1) historical, drawing on the sociology of professions and science perspectives; (2) anthropological, focusing on the management of birth in different cultures; (3) patient-oriented, focusing on user views and experiences; and (4) patient–services interaction. Her review highlights two key themes directly related to areas of debate within the sociology of reproduction. The first has been the concept of medicalization, and the second has been a dualistic notion of competing ideologies of reproduction (with the caveat that the theme of medicalization versus normalization does not turn into ideological mudslinging between 'forward with technology' and 'back to nature' lobbies).

The term 'medicalization' refers to a key concept in the field of sociology of health and illness and draws attention to medicine as a powerful instrument of social control. For example, Zola (1972: 487) notes that, historically 'medicine is becoming a major institution of social control, nudging aside, if not incorporating, the more traditional institutions of religion and the law'. The term has generally been used in a negative way to depict increasing medical control over everyday life and the construction or re-definition of aspects of everyday life as medical problems. It can occur on several levels, through language, institutionally or in the professional–patient relationship. It is a critical concept because it emphasizes that medicine is a social as well as a scientific exercise, which can have mixed effects. People may be treated with greater humanity when medical definitions replace criminal ones, but deviance is implicit in medical definitions, which make it more likely that medical treatments will be applied.

Women have been seen as particularly vulnerable to medicalization, and it is in relation to childbirth that the concept has been most fully developed. Sociologists have drawn attention to the medicalization of various aspects of the reproductive process. For example, an entire issue of the *International Journal of Health Services* (1975, 52) was devoted to a critique of medical imperialism and the medicalization of reproduction.

An early development of the medicalization concept has been the work of feminists who identified patriarchal society and its extension – patriarchal medicine – as a key force behind the medicalization of women's health issues. These scholars analysed how previous religious justifications for patriarchy were transformed into scientific ones, and described how women's traditional skills for managing birth were expropriated by medical experts at the end of the nineteenth century. Such work examined the way services are organized, reproductive technologies controlled, and sexuality constrained as particular manifestations of patriarchal control that shaped women's reproductive experiences. This early feminist literature identified the sexual politics of women's health and provided a theoretical basis for reclaiming knowledge

141

about, and control over women's bodies. It was polemical, intentionally political and was critical of the medical model imposed on pregnancy and birth.

Ann Oakley's (1980) studies of pregnancy and childbirth in Britain have, unusually for sociological texts, provoked wider public and professional debate. She demonstrated the ways in which the discourse of the medical world differs from the everyday language of women and their relatives, and how different understandings are associated with unequal authority and power. She theorized a dualistic notion of competing ideologies of reproduction, where women see pregnancy as a social process over which they should exert active control, and medicine as a potentially pathological event to be controlled and managed. This perspective assumed that women of all classes and ethnicities share the same view and was later challenged. Subsequent work has shown that such discourses cannot be reduced to dichotomies but are multiple and complex.

In 1983, Riessman pointed out in a review of women and medicalization that this literature has highlighted the negative consequences of modern birth technologies, and had a tendency to romanticize the midwife and pre-technological childbirth. She grounded her thesis by examining childbirth and reproduction, premenstrual syndrome and mental health. Importantly, she noted that what has not been documented is what women have gained and lost with the medicalization of life problems. Nor has it been noted how women have actively participated in the construction of new medical definitions, or the reasons that led to such participation. She argued that both physicians and women have contributed to the redefining of women's experiences into medical categories. Furthermore, physicians have sought to medicalize experience because of beliefs and economic interests, depending on specific professional developments and market conditions. Women, in turn, have collaborated in the medicalization process because of their own needs, which grow out of the class-specific nature of their subordination.

This investigation of the management of labour and childbirth in the 1970s and the 1980s has provided the background for more recent work on New Reproductive Technologies (NRTs). By the mid-1980s the focus was moving away from the experiences of the majority of women during pregnancy and birth to a fiercer critique of NRTs, spurred on by the birth of Louise Brown, the first test tube baby, in 1978.

It is important to define what technology is. According to the US Office of Technology Assessment, medical technology is the set of technologies and drugs used in health care, including those used in reproduction. Thus, the social relations of reproductive technology are key. NRTs include surrogacy, assisted fertility techniques, prenatal screening and diagnosis, cloning, and are derived from a scientific approach to reproduction, from which older technologies such as contraception have been derived, to 'manage' pregnancy and childbirth. Questions asked about NRTs have been on two levels. The first is the micro-level that describes their nature and function; the second is the macro level and the triad of women, gender and science.

Drawing on feminist criticisms of scientific knowledge and the medicalization of women's lives, studies of reproduction have highlighted the power relations such practices mediate. Criticisms are that women are used as experimental material; women's bodies are commodified and an oppositional status of women and foetuses constructed. Such writings have critiqued state control over access to services, and have asked in whose interests technological developments such as prenatal screening and testing, and infertility treatments, test tube babies, foetal imaging, surrogacy, and infertility treatment have been developed. The debate has focused on the extent to which these new technologies have been beneficial or a form of oppression to women setting up a binary divide of 'salvation or damnation'.

In the United States, Barbara Katz Rothman (1986) reported that prenatal testing changed the way people thought about childbirth and parenthood. An open mind about pregnancy outcome has been replaced with a new norm of 'tentative' pregnancy, even though perfection could not be offered. She concluded that prenatal testing has increased women's choices, but placed women in a position as genetic gatekeepers, which has consequences for the acceptance of all sorts of variations which children present.

In the 1990s there was a growing concern to examine boundaries between bodies and society, how bio-medicine is concerned with constructing the procreative body and the role of associated regulatory practices, and how technology allows medical professionals greater jurisdiction over larger areas of reproduction. Stacey (1992) has argued that the new reproductive technologies, such as IVF and GIFT and the 'new genetics' that are based on the discovery of DNA, have opened up new possibilities and created a 'scientific revolution in human reproduction', i.e., the teaming of real science with obstetrics, with implications for the way such technologies are managed and controlled.

There has been a concern that women are not just seen as passive recipients of reproductive technology, and that efforts should be made to explore how women contest and contribute to the construction of new

143

medical definitions and the use of NRTs. Such work has disavowed technological determinism and pushed towards the identification of agency. This has involved the delineation of the role of experts and the identification of female resistance. The work of Margaret Lock (Lock and Kaufert, 1998) has pointed out how women make pragmatic use of reproductive technologies and has challenged the representation of women as passive victims of surveillance. Further work is needed on the different strategies that women use in a proactive way to empower themselves/or not, and their relationship with the complex notion of 'control'.

A more recent debate has raised questions about the underlying perspectives of writers in the field of the sociology of reproduction, 'oppositioning' writers who expect the outcomes of their work to contribute and develop sociological theory, and writers with an explicit aim that their work will improve the experiences of women. Annandale and Clark (1996) have critically reviewed many of the underlying assumptions of writings in the domain of the sociology of childbirth. From a range of broad critiques of writings on the sociology of health and gender, they suggested that much of the literature has been sociologically naïve and uncritical of the role of female-dominated midwifery and the use of reproductive technology.

Specifically, they argued that much writing has been preoccupied with abnormalities in women's health; has universalized women's experiences regardless of ethnicity and class; equated reproductive technology with the medicalization of reproduction; assumed that an increased use of technology in childbirth is a 'bad' thing for women; and implied that women are powerless victims or dupes in this process. Furthermore, in juxtaposing midwifery and obstetrics, much writing has given uncritical support to the notion that midwifery is 'better' for women than male-dominated obstetrics; it assumes that midwifery has an underlying feminist viewpoint and it implies that midwives are 'with women', ignoring issues of power between women and their female caregivers.

Although feminist perspectives and political action in relation to women's health have been defended from a different epistemological basis, specifically in relation to critiques of reproductive interventions and midwifery, in general, such critiques hold and form the basis for some new directions for research in the sociology of reproduction. In particular, they have emphasized deconstructing notions of 'natural' and exploring the transformative possibilities of technology.

In summary, some sociological work in the area of human reproduction has played a key role in shaping policy and practice and has been grounded in women's concerns in a reflexive way. Early work that focused on pregnancy and birth has broadened out into an examination of reproductive technologies and the 'new' genetics and, increasingly, this work has been theoretically grounded within an anthropological perspective. Future work in the field of human reproduction that draws on sociological theories of risk and the sociology of the body would be fruitful, along with further work grounded in the sociology of science that critically examines the role of pharmaceutical and biomedical industries and the implications of the mapping of the human genome.

See also: *medicalization, medical model* and *medical technologies.*

REFERENCES

Annandale, E.C. and Clark, J. (1996) 'What is gender? Feminist theory and the sociology of human reproduction', *Sociology of Health and Illness*, 18 (1): 17–44.

Lock, M. and Kaufert, P.A. (1998) *Pragmatic Women and Body Politics.* Cambridge: Cambridge University Press.

Macintyre, S. (1977) 'The management of childbirth: a review of sociological research issues', *Social Science and Medicine*, 11: 447–84.

Oakley, A. (1980) *Women Confined: Towards a Sociology of Childbirth.* Oxford: Martin Robertson.

Riessman, C.K. (1983) 'Women and medicalisation: a new perspective', *Social Policy*, Summer: 3–17.

Rothman, B.K. (1986) *The Tentative Pregnancy: Amniocentesis and the Sexual Politics of Motherhood.* New York: Viking Penguin.

Stacey, M. (ed.) (1992) *Changing Human Reproduction: Social Science Perspectives.* London: Sage.

Zola, I.K. (1972) 'Medicine as an institution of social control', *Sociological Review*, 20 (4): 487–504.

JS

145

medical technologies

> **Definition:** *A useful working definition of what might be included under the term 'medical technologies' has been put forward by the US Office of Technology Assessment: 'the drugs, devices, and medical and surgical procedures used in medical care and the organizational and supportive systems within which such care is provided'.*

There are two significant aspects to note about the definition cited here. The first is the very existence of the Office of Technology Assessment (OTA), one of a number of official US government agencies which, between them, assess the effectiveness, economic value and safety of a wide range of medical technologies, mainly new ones pending their introduction into American health care. There are equivalent bodies in most other developed countries. For example, in the United Kingdom, there is a government-funded research and development programme of Health Technology Assessment and also the National Institute for Clinical Excellence, which is responsible for making recommendations about the adoption of new technologies within the National Health Service. Many of these organizations have been in operation since the 1980s, reflecting the growing significance of technology in modern health care: not least its economic significance. Medical technology is big business in two senses: its development, production and sales constitute a major area of economic activity, and the apparently inexorably expanding cost of health care services is often attributed to the pressures of technological innovation. Evaluating the value for money offered and the risks to health posed by new technologies has become an important part of the governance of modern health services at the national and international levels. This is one reason why sociological investigation of medical technology has been growing in recent years, as described in Elston (1997). And one strand in such research has been the study of the commercial medical technology industry and of national and international agencies established to regulate it. Such work has generally been informed by a political economy perspective and is critical of the commercial interests identified as being too influential, for example, in the regulation of the pharmaceutical industry.

The second feature of the definition is its inclusiveness with respect to what constitutes medical technology. The term is used to refer not only to complex machines, but also to procedures and hand-held instruments, and to the huge array of pharmaceutical products used in clinical and preventive treatments (and the associated industrial and research activity). In the past two decades, the 'new genetics' and developments in assisted reproduction have introduced new possibilities for and new concerns about technological intervention. New digital information and communication technologies are making possible new ways of organizing and accessing health care and health information. Examples include the exponentially increasing availability of health information on the Internet; the establishment of nurse-led telephone advice centres in many countries, such as NHS Direct in the United Kingdom; and the many forms of telemedicine whereby digitalized clinical information can be exchanged between remote settings. Sociologists have turned their attention to all these dramatic (and often expensive) innovations. However, it is also important not to overlook the routine and mundane technologies that are intrinsic to so much health care, whether it is in direct patient care or 'backstage', for example, medical record and administrative systems or the routine work of pathology and biochemistry laboratories, or even the equipment and substances in alternative medicine, such as acupuncture needles.

Timmermans and Berg (2003) have particularly stressed this point in a critical overview of medical sociological research on technologies. They suggest that the sociological literature on medical technologies can be divided into three main strands, each of which tends to focus on different kinds of technologies. The first strand they term 'technological determinism', a perspective that attributes great power to technologies, generally regarding technology *per se* as a 'driving political force in late modern societies' (2003: 99), or as a political tool in itself. They suggest, for example, that radical feminist writing that depicts new reproductive technologies as instruments for extending patriarchal control over women fits into this strand. So would much of the political economy tradition of research on the pharmaceutical industry mentioned above, and some literature on the 'new genetics' which emphasizes the actual or potential negative consequences for society and/or individuals of 'geneticization'. Indeed, this theoretical determinism strand within medical sociology tends to focus exclusively on controversial, new technologies that appear to extend medicalization to new areas of social life or to generate troubling new social and ethical dilemmas. The stance taken towards such technologies, and the political interests associated with them, is generally critical, if not strongly hostile. However, this negative judgement is not always supported by detailed empirical examination of whether, and if so, how, these technologies actually exercise their alleged negative power. For example, the introduction of high technology resuscitation and life-support machines has often been criticized as depriving the dying person of the possibility of a 'good' dignified death. However, in a detailed ethnographic study of the use of resuscitation technologies in 'sudden' dying episodes, Timmermans (1998) found that use of the technologies contributed to dignified dying, by allowing a brief respite during which relatives, friends and staff could prepare for what was almost certain to happen. Another example is Rapp's (2000) study of the pre-natal diagnostic technology of amniocentesis. Using observation and in-depth interviews, she shows

147

that decisions about whether to take pre-natal tests and how to act in the face of an adverse result are very complex. Outcomes are by no means simply determined by the availability of a technology which has the potential to identify chromosomal abnormalities before birth. The key point is not that controversial new technologies may have the negative effects that are feared, but that good sociological research is required to establish whether they actually do and, if so, in what circumstances.

Timmermans and Berg label the second strand of sociological research on medical technologies 'social essentialism'. Here, they suggest, technologies are viewed as 'blank slates to be interpreted and rendered meaningful by culture' (2003: 101). This strand of research tends to concentrate on technologies used directly in patient care, such as imaging equipment. Such studies are often of great sociological significance. For example, Strauss et al.'s (1985) important study of sentimental work is a powerful account of the social organization of work in high technology hospital settings, of the ways in which staff manage to work with patients using complex machinery and of the experience of patients undergoing invasive investigations and treatment. However, there is some validity to Timmermans and Berg's criticism that the actual technologies, how they operate and what they accomplish (or fail to) in interacting with staff and patients, make only fleeting appearances in the study. The technical properties of the technologies are clearly secondary and sometimes appear quite unrelated to the meanings given to them by human actors.

The third, and most recent to develop, strand of sociological work on medical technologies, and the one which Timmermans and Berg (2003) themselves advocate, is one that brings together concepts and methodological approaches from the interdisciplinary field of science studies and from medical sociology. From the former, sociologists have followed the maxim of Latour (1987), a leading French sociologist of science, to study science and technology 'in action'. Latour's recommendation underpins an approach often known as 'actor-network theory'. In this approach technologies are not regarded as isolated inanimate objects with fixed characteristics, but as, at least metaphorically, 'actors'. This does not mean that technologies are being regarded as having ideas, intentions or self-consciousness. What is being drawn attention to is the ways in which technologies may, because of their particular properties, exert influences on, for example, the rate of uptake of new therapeutic practices. At the same time, the technologies are themselves subject to being changed in the course of their interactions

medical technologies

with people and other objects. For Latour (1987), technologies are regarded as members of 'networks' in the sense that they can be involved, when in use, in relationships with a whole range of persons, other technologies, practices, and so on. Thus, rather than presuppose that technologies are necessarily powerful shapers of society, or that, in themselves, they are neutral bearers of externally derived cultural and social meanings, this 'technology in practice' approach treats these as questions to be answered empirically.

Exponents of the approach employ very detailed, usually observational methods in health care settings, of how technologies are actually used in practice and what the effects (intended and unintended) of their use actually are. This approach, they argue, has the advantage that it can be used to study mundane technologies, such as the taking of cervical smears or asthma inhalers, as well as dramatic ones. It has proved particularly useful for the study of information and communication technologies and for administrative technologies. For example, Berg (1997) has studied the use of protocols in clinical practice (standardized recommendations for action for given diagnoses), which are in increasing use in many sectors of health care. His work shows how such protocols are never absolutely determining of professionals' action, in that they always have to be interpreted in particular situations. Protocols are not simply encroachments on professional autonomy, as some have argued: they may simultaneously act as constraints on some professionals' activities and enhance the autonomy of others.

This third approach is not without its critics, partly because of its association with some controversies in the field of science studies (see Elston, 1997). For example, the so-called constructivist approach that it draws on has sometimes been accused of inappropriate relativism, and the apparent attribution of social agency to technologies in some work has been criticized. The emphasis on (usually) small-scale ethnographic studies of particular health care settings might be thought conducive to the neglect of wider political questions, for example, about inequitable access to valuable technologies (although Timmermans and Berg (2003) explicitly reject this criticism). Nevertheless, the move towards empirically grounded studies of the technologies themselves, stimulated by both insights from cognate academic fields and contemporary developments in health care, is undoubtedly rejuvenating medical sociology's interest in medical technologies.

See also: *medicines regulation, geneticization* and *medicalization.*

REFERENCES

Berg. M. (1997) 'Promises of the protocol', *Social Science and Medicine*, 44: 1081–8.

Elston, M.A. (1997) 'Introduction: the sociology of medical science and technology', in M.A. Elston (ed.), *The Sociology of Medical Science and Technology*. Oxford: Blackwell, pp. 1–27.

Latour, B. (1987) *Science in Action: How to Follow Scientists and Engineers through Society*. London: Open University Press.

Rapp, R. (2000) *Testing Women: Testing the Fetus*. London: Routledge.

Strauss, A., Fagerhaugh, S., Suczek, B. and Wiener, C. (1985) *Social Organization of Medical Work*. Chicago: University of Chicago Press.

Timmermans, S. (1998) 'Resuscitation technology in the emergency department: towards a dignified death', *Sociology of Health and Illness*, 20 (2): 144–67.

Timmermans, S. and Berg, M. (2003) 'The practice of medical technology', *Sociology of Health and Illness*, 25 (Silver Anniversary Edition): 97–114.

MAE

geneticization

> **Definition:** **Geneticization refers to the way in which diseases, conditions and behaviours may come to be regarded as being determined, wholly or in part, by genetic factors. Increasingly many of society's problems are being explained by genetic influences, upon which solutions may be based.**

Geneticization is a relatively new concept in medical sociology. It is associated with the rise of the 'new genetics': 'the body of knowledge and techniques arising since the invention of recombinant DNA technology in 1973' (Cunningham-Burley and Boulton, 2000: 174). This technology enables scientists to identify and possibly to manipulate a piece of DNA which would then carry a new genetic code. Thus individuals' genetic make-up comes to be seen as a determining factor in disease risk and, in theory, could then be altered in order to prevent or treat certain diseases or conditions.

The term 'geneticization' was first used by Lippman (1992) and Wertz (1992). They claimed that this process affects not only how we define, prevent and treat disease but also, increasingly, how we explain problems which may be more behavioural in character. Allen (1999) argues that the

150

concept of geneticization builds on that of medicalization. Through medicalization a problem or behaviour is given a clinical name, labelled and given scientific legitimacy. Such naming has the effect of making a problem appear as a single disease entity arising from a single cause and this encourages people to view it as a 'disorder'. At this point the cause of the disorder may be regarded as arising *outside of* the individual, for example, repetitive strain injury arising from repeated wrist movements while typing, or poliomyelitis being caused by exposure to a virus. With geneticization, however, a disorder is claimed to have a genetic component, thus laying the problem firmly *within* the individual and his or her family. Alcoholism, homosexuality and intelligence have all, at some point, been described by scientists as having a genetic component, although, as Conrad (1999) has pointed out, many such claims have not been confirmed in subsequent research. But the concern is that, just as new conditions have come to be identified and labelled through medicalization, so existing disorders and problematic behaviours may be additionally subject to geneticization, rather than being seen in psychological, social or cultural terms.

Many critics liken the new genetics to eugenic policies that began in the late nineteenth century and remained popular across Europe and the USA until the 1940s. Eugenics can be defined as the 'right to be well born' or 'the science of human improvement by better breeding' (Allen, 1999: 11). Eugenic beliefs were based on Mendelian genetics and studies of inheritance. Their proponents alleged that many social problems could be eradicated by using *negative eugenics* through the enforcement of sterilization laws, thereby preventing the reproduction of individuals deemed to be genetically unfit. A clear racial and class bias was evident in identifying socially undesirable traits, for example, 'feeblemindedness', 'low moral sense' and 'habitual criminality'. Using *positive eugenics*, the genetically fit were encouraged to reproduce in order to increase desirable social traits (ibid.). Although today's clinicians and researchers do not espouse a clear-cut eugenic position, the development of the 'new genetics' raises fears of its possible recurrence. This fear has been especially voiced by some sections of the disability movement who regard research to prevent impairments as devaluing the lives of existing disabled people.

The Human Genome Project (HGP), referred to by many scientists as the 'Holy Grail' of biology, is a multi-national project to map the whole human genome (approximately 80,000 genes). It began in October 1990 and a draft sequence of over 90 per cent of the human 'blueprint' was published in February 2001. The HGP attempts to map a 'baseline norm'

151

of the human genome, although what is considered 'normal' and abnormal is problematic, primarily because these states are not a dichotomy but poles of a continuum. Proponents of the new genetics argue that, whereas earlier eugenics was based on 'bad' science, genetic procedures arising from the HGP are based on 'good' science. However, modern determinist views of the role of genes have been challenged inside and outside biology, by emphasizing the developmental character of human life and its crucial interaction with the environment. Focusing on the overriding importance of genes runs the risk that society subsequently prioritizes research agendas and public policies orientated towards biological rather than social tenets. Although Wertz (1992) maintains that most societies have enough money for genetic research and for improving society and the environment, a more widely held view is that resources will be taken away from other research and social needs to fund genetic advances. Five per cent of the HGP budget was earmarked for examination of the social, ethical and legal issues arising from the project that affect the individual, family and wider society (Collins, 1999). It is to these issues that we now turn.

There has been much debate among scientists, medical sociologists, ethicists and the lay public on how genetic knowledge should be used. Indeed, that medical knowledge should be used responsibly by society is one of medicine's, as well as medical sociology's, central tenets. One issue concerning genetic knowledge is the ownership of information about individuals (and of individuals' DNA), as genetic databases and 'biobanks', based on data and samples from hundreds of thousands of individuals, are currently being created. The patenting of some genes, for example, BRCA1 and BRCA2 (implicated in some inheritable forms of breast cancer), has already taken place. This is partly so that industry can use this information on a financially viable basis for future research and to develop new products such as diagnostic and predictive tests, new medicines and therapies to treat or 'cure' conditions. (Cunningham-Burley and Boulton, 2000). Whether an individual's genetic profile should be disclosed to other family members is also fiercely contested. Some geneticists argue that this information should be shared by siblings and other close relatives, as their 'patient' is the family and not the individual. Others, paradoxically, would not give a child a definite genetic diagnosis, in order that the child can obtain health insurance in adulthood. Indeed, insurance companies in the USA have already tried to withhold payment for babies identified prenatally as having a genetic condition (Wertz, 1992).

Certain aspects of the new genetics can be seen as reductionist. In diagnosing some conditions as 'genetic', the complex and unpredictable ways that genes interact with other factors to produce health and disease can be overlooked. Although a single gene may be identified as causing a disease, the time of onset or intensity of the condition arising from the presence of that gene is unknown. For example, although the cystic fibrosis gene was identified in 1989, scientists are unable to predict with any certainty the severity of the disease or survival age for any individual. Knowledge that there are genetic factors involved is of even less predictive value in the management of multi-factorial conditions where the environmental influence is strong, such as heart disease.

Geneticization may also lead to diseases being defined by technical explanation rather than patients' own experiences (Cunningham-Burley and Boulton, 2000). Furthermore, narrowing the definition of disease may lead to a reduction in the range of interventions considered for treatment. If a disease is due to faulty genes then, the medical response is currently likely to take the form of screening for those genes, followed by prophylactic measures (such as mastectomies for those at high risk of inheritable forms of breast cancer) or treatments involving gene modification, rather than using other approaches. This can exaggerate individual responsibility for health, leaving collective solutions such as societal and environmental reforms unexplored. There is also a tendency for scientists to take for granted that an individual will be willing to modify certain behaviours if deemed genetically 'at risk' through predictive testing (Collins, 1999).

Collins predicts that, in the near future, 'genetic approaches to disease prevention and treatment will include an expanding array of gene products for use in developing tomorrow's drug therapies' (ibid.: 33). However, there are not, as yet, clinically effective treatments for most disorders thought to have a genetic component, raising the issue of what effect genetic knowledge has for people identified as having such a condition. The 'at risk' status of late-onset disorders identified in childhood will also have effects on many aspects of daily life, both for the individual and the family. It might be concluded that individuals should have the right not to know, as well as to know their genetic make-up.

Genetic screening is currently one of the most common applications of the new genetics. Screening programmes may be aimed at the individual who is deemed at high risk of a certain genetic disorder: or an entire population may be targeted, as seen in calls to test all foetuses for cystic fibrosis gene mutations. Whereas governments in the first part of the last century enforced eugenic policies through sterilization laws, the new genetics is premised on individual choice. However, Wertz (1992) observes that pressure to conform to societal expectations means that individual free choice may be constrained and that the burden of decision-making is likely to fall on women.

Often scientists charge the lay public with being ignorant of scientific matters in general and of genetics in particular, although how public knowledge and understanding are measured is contentious because of their sociological complexity (Cunningham-Burley and Boulton, 2000). Despite many social surveys indicating the lay public's support, in principle, for screening programmes for some conditions where there is a clear genetic cause, for example, Huntington's chorea, cystic fibrosis and inherited forms of breast cancer, in practice, a low uptake in screening for these diseases has been observed. Possible reasons for this include lay understandings of hereditary conditions and lay assessment that the costs of genetic information outweigh the benefits, especially where diseases can be identified but not effectively treated (Cunningham-Burley and Boulton, 2000). Furthermore, as Wertz (1992) observes, there is no societal consensus as to which (if any) pre-natally diagnosable genetic conditions are appropriately 'treated' by offering women abortions. Nonetheless, research has shown, for example, in the case of Duchenne muscular dystrophy, that lay people are able to reconcile genetic information with reproductive choices (Parsons and Atkinson, 1992). In Parsons and Atkinson's study, while the understanding of genetic-related risk was often imperfect, the women concerned were able to translate the statistical information they received into descriptive statements that provided a reasonable foundation for decision-making.

Although the stigma of some diseases may be reduced by lifting the 'blame' from individuals and their families and by a process of normalization, an area for concern is the possible stigma attached to or compounded by genetic labelling (Wertz, 1992). As noted, sections of the disability movement argue that many genetic interventions stigmatize certain sections of society. Indeed, at its worst, geneticization may lead to the creation of an underclass that is unemployable and uninsurable due to their genetic make-up. Genetic disability could itself become a mark of low social class, thus compounding existing inequalities. If the focus of preventive health policies narrows to genetic interventions such as population screening for defective genes, society may no longer discuss providing proper social support to those who need it.

Scientists themselves agree that genetic research will impact on many aspects of society over the coming century and that it is difficult to predict where the greatest challenges will lie. The new genetics clearly has an important place in sociology, both for how we define disease and use

geneticization

that knowledge. Many of the ethical issues arising from geneticization and the 'new' genetics are not completely new, but it is imperative that the debate is kept alive.

See also: *medicalization* and *stigma.*

REFERENCES

Allen, G.E. (1999) 'Genetics, eugenics and the medicalization of social behaviour: lessons from the past', *Endeavour*, 23 (1): 10–19.
Collins, F.S. (1999) 'Shattuck Lecture – Medical and societal consequences of the Human Genome Project', *New England Journal of Medicine*, 341 (1): 28–37.
Conrad, P. (1999) 'A mirage of genes', *Sociology of Health and Illness*, 21 (2): 228–39.
Cunningham-Burley, S. and Boulton, M. (2000) 'The social context of the new genetics', in G.L. Albrecht, R. Fitzpatrick and S.C. Scrimshaw (eds), *The Handbook of Social Studies in Health and Medicine*. London: Sage, pp. 173–87.
Lippman, A. (1992) 'Prenatal genetic testing and screening: constructing needs and reinforcing inequities', *American Journal of Law and Medicine*, 17: 15–50.
Parsons, E. and Atkinson, P. (1992) 'Lay constructions of genetic risk', *Sociology of Health and Illness*, 14 (4): 437–55.
Wertz, D.C. (1992) 'Ethical and legal implications of the new genetics: issues for discussion', *Social Science and Medicine*, 35 (4): 495–505.

KL

surveillance and health promotion

155

> *Definition:* **Within the context of health promotion, medical sociologists use the term 'surveillance' to refer to activities such as surveys, screening and public health campaigns, which are designed to monitor, regulate and induce good health practices in both individuals and the population in general.**

Health promotion refers to those planned activities that are designed to prevent illness and improve the health of the population. Such activities comprise: assessing health needs; developing and evaluating interventions which will facilitate the improvement of people's health status; and supporting health professionals and the public by providing information on the most effective means to achieve good health. The goal of health promotion is to effect change at both an individual level (by encouraging people to lead 'healthy' lives) and a societal level (by bringing about institutional changes which will make for a more healthy social and physical environment). Health promotion therefore is but one aspect of what has been called 'surveillance medicine', which emerged as a dominant form of health and medical care in the latter half of the twentieth century (Armstrong, 1995).

A number of writers have argued that the mechanisms of surveillance underpin modern health care. Armstrong (1995) states that: a 'cardinal feature of surveillance medicine . . . is its targeting of everyone' and that health care is concerned not just with those who are ill but with those who are well. It is not just orientated towards treating the symptoms of disease but also to identifying and monitoring risk factors, which 'point to' the possibility of a future illness. Writing in France, the philosopher Castel (1991) makes a similar observation but uses the term 'epidemiological clinic' instead of 'surveillance medicine'. He suggests that since the latter half of the twentieth century we have moved from a health care system that was premised upon 'dangerousness' to one based upon 'risk'. In the past, the dominant mode of working among health professionals was to err on the side of caution to prevent the development of disease. Consequently, the illnesses possessed by patients were treated as being potentially 'dangerous'. Today, however, health care focuses on the social and behavioural characteristics of the person, and this in turn involves a mode of surveillance which – with the aid of technological advances – makes the calculation and possibilities of 'systematic pre-detection' more and more sophisticated. These surveillance activities create a whole new range of risk factors. The mechanisms of health promotion surveillance therefore identify those individuals and groups who are 'at risk'. The concepts of surveillance and risk, within the context of health promotion, are mutually constitutive.

Having analysed the use of the term 'risk' in medical journals in Britain, the USA and Scandinavia, Skolbekken (1995) argued that the use of the term had reached 'epidemic proportions'. Skolbekken examined journals published between 1967 and 1991, for the first five years (1967–72) the number of 'risk articles' published was around 1,000 and for the last five years (1986–91) there were over 80,000. He argues that health promotion provides 'the ideological frame needed to explain the present emphasis on factors regarded as risks to our health . . .

156

Through the ideological frame of health promotion we get a glimpse of some of the functions served by the risk epidemic' (ibid.: 296). He cites these functions as: first, to predict disease and death, in other words, to gain control over disease which in turn confirms our faith in medical science. Second, it is sometimes assumed that the findings of this type of research may help to save money as people are less likely to require acute and therefore, expensive services. Third, it contributes to medicalization. Risk factors that are hypothesized to be linked to disease come to be treated as 'diseases to be cured' (ibid.: 299). Certainly, in the public health and health promotion documentation, health-related behaviours such as smoking or drinking alcohol come to be treated as variables that need to be explained. Whether or not the first function is legitimate, or the second function is likely, may be undermined by the third point, which draws attention to the 'unscientific' nature of much of this research. There is considerable controversy within the medical journals about the links between, say, diet and coronary heart disease and the merits and demerits of various interventions, for example, the lowering of cholesterol levels.

A number of sociologists have pointed to the fact that society today is characterized by a 'politics of anxiety', indeed, that it is a risk society. A point on which all these authors appear to agree is that the risks associated with modern-day living are person-made, they are a product of social organization and human actions. Armstrong contrasts the health risks of today with the health risks present in the nineteenth century. While in the nineteenth century health risks were associated with the 'natural' environment and dangers lurked within water, soil, air, food and climate, today the environmental factors that impinge on health, such as acid rain and radiation are the consequence of human actions. Of course, not all contemporary health risks are human products. AIDS, for example, is the consequence of a virus. Nevertheless the disease has come to be conceptualized within a social matrix; it exists within a wider context of social activities and is envisaged in terms of complex social interactions between gay men, intravenous drug users and those requiring and administering blood transfusions. In this respect, it has increasingly become articulated in the same terms as humanly created risks, which need to be monitored and regulated – or subjected to surveillance.

The techniques deployed in the scrutinization of these 'risk factors' within the context of public health and health promotion are primarily: screening for a range of diseases and symptoms; the collection of information on patients by health professionals; epidemiological studies;

157

social surveys; and qualitative studies. Once a 'factor' such as eating 'fatty foods' is found to be statistically associated with another indicator of ill health (or risk factor) such as cholesterol levels, it is deemed to be a risk. The social aspects of eating this type of food may then be explored by sociologists and anthropologists who aim to answer questions such as: Why do people eat fat? What does eating fatty foods means to them? What is the social and symbolic significance of eating fatty foods? This information is considered to be crucial to the development of effective health promotion. The findings of the epidemiologists and the social scientists are drawn upon by health promoters to encourage people to eat less fatty foods. The government will keep an eye on the population's fat consumption and set nutritional targets. Thus, surveillance techniques and risk go hand in hand. Mechanisms of surveillance that focus on individual risk factors may contribute to the formation of a new individual 'risk identity' (Armstrong, 1995).

Those medical sociologists who have developed and applied the concept of surveillance have based their ideas on the work of Foucault (1979), in particular, on his concept of disciplinary power, most vividly articulated in his book *Discipline and Punish*. Disciplinary power refers to the way in which bodies are regulated, trained, maintained and understood and is most evident in social institutions such as schools, prisons and hospitals. Foucault argues that it is within such institutions that knowledge of bodies is produced. For example, the observation of bodies in prisons yielded a body of knowledge that is now known as criminology and the observation of bodies in hospitals contributed to medical science. Foucault refers to this process as power/knowledge. Disciplinary power – a form of surveillance – works at two levels. First, individual bodies are trained and observed. Foucault refers to this as the anatomo-politics of the human body. Second, and concurrently, populations are monitored by regulatory controls – the 'bio-politics' of the population.

The sociological notion of surveillance, which has been informed by Foucault's work, is not without its critics. Arguably, the idea of disciplinary power itself is inappropriate as it under-estimates the impact of other forms of power which may be wielded by those groups who have greater resources and, thereby, the capacity to control and dominate others. Second, and relatedly, it is argued that to say the mechanisms of surveillance simply generate knowledge of people's health and illness excludes the possibility that certain interest groups might generate particular forms of knowledge about health, disease and illness, which may serve to enhance their commercial or professional status. Finally, it

surveillance and health promotion

is argued that the notion of surveillance is overly descriptive and fails to account for the origins and motivations of change, as well as underplaying the influence of human agency.

The concept of surveillance, however, provides a valuable analytic tool with which to make sense of contemporary developments within health care more generally and health promotion in particular (Lupton, 1995). Surveillance procedures can contribute to existing forms of repression, for example, they have negative consequences for the health experiences of women (Nettleton, 1996). The concept of surveillance is also useful in contributing to an appreciation of the ways in which collective, societal levels of intervention (for example, screening or education campaigns) can have an impact upon individuals in terms of the development of their 'risk identities' and upon the nature of their interactions with health professionals, see, for example, a study of two types of health surveillance in Sweden, by Lauritzen and Sachs (2001). Finally, the concept can enable health practitioners and health researchers to gain an analytic appreciation of some of the societal implications of the routine day-to-day practices of health promotion.

See also: *risk* and *the new public health.*

REFERENCES

Armstrong, D. (1995) 'The rise of surveillance medicine', *Sociology of Health and Illness,* 17 (3): 343–404.

Castel, R. (1991) 'From dangerousness to risk', in G. Burchell, C. Gordon and P. Miller (eds), *The Foucault Effect: Studies in Governmentality.* Brighton: Harvester Wheatsheaf.

Foucault, M. (1979) *Discipline and Punish: The Birth of the Prison.* Harmondsworth: Penguin Books.

Lauritzen, S.O. and Sachs, L. (2001) 'Normality, risk and the future: implicit communication of threat in health surveillance', *Sociology of Health and Illness,* 23 (4): 497–516.

Lupton, D. (1995) *The Imperative of Health: Public Health and the Regulated Body.* London: Sage.

Nettleton, S. (1996) 'Women and the new paradigm of health and medicine', *Critical Social Policy,* 16 (3): 33–53.

Skolbekken, J. (1995) 'The risk epidemic in medical journals', *Social Science and Medicine,* 40 (3): 291–305.

SN

PART 4

Health Work and the Division of Labour

professions and professionalization

Definition: *Within sociology the term 'profession' is usually used to denote a type of occupation accorded high status and a high degree of autonomy over its work; with medicine being regarded as an example. 'Professionalization' refers to the process of achieving the status of a profession.*

In everyday English usage, to describe an occupation as a 'profession' may be simply to identify it as a particular kind of occupation, typically one with high status and high rewards, requiring long formal training and delivering a personal service. Or, it might also be, particularly if it is one's own occupation being described, to make claims about the trustworthiness of members of that occupation. The implication of this is that it is safe for clients to leave their fate in professional hands, to trust in 'professional judgement' and to leave decisions to professional discretion. Here, 'professional' connotes expertise and probity simultaneously. Accordingly, for many decades, sociologists have examined two complex and inter-related issues: first, what (if anything) distinguishes those occupations that are generally accepted as being professions from those that are not, given that many occupations would apparently like to be regarded as professions? Second, can we trust these professionals' claims of trustworthiness and their connected demands for autonomy (freedom from external monitoring), and what are the consequences of accepting (or, indeed, of refusing to accept) professionals' claims?

Sociologists' answers to these questions have been varied. But, across the now substantial body of literature on the sociology of professions (see Macdonald, 1995, for an overview), there has been a general consensus that, if any occupation warrants being called a 'profession', it is medicine. Within sociology the medical profession has often been used as a paradigm case for theorizing about professions and professionalization in general. And, within medical sociology, there has been much analysis of the implications of medicine's professional status for patients and other providers of health care. There has been much less consensus among sociologists, and perhaps in society generally, about, for example, the validity of nursing's claims to be a profession.

One key starting point for sociological interest in professions was the work of one of the great founding fathers of the discipline, Emile Durkheim. Writing in the early twentieth century, he argued that professions were (or ought to be) an important integrative force in rapidly changing, industrializing societies. Professions, for Durkheim, were, above all, occupations organized as cohesive communities based on shared ethical values. Durkheim's focus on professional ethics and on professions' functional contribution to society was taken up within functionalist sociology in the 1930s and lasted through to the 1960s. Particularly relevant to medical sociology was Talcott Parsons' analysis of the medical profession's role as agents of social control, illness being regarded as a form of deviance, which, if unregulated, could threaten the stability of society. All societies have to cope with illness. In modern societies, with their specialized division of labour and emphasis on rational authority, this necessary task has been entrusted, according to Parsons, to a specialist occupation possessing a body of theoretical knowledge. Because of doctors' specialist expertise, patients are expected to defer to their authority, while the doctors themselves are accorded the right to regulate and evaluate their own conduct. Such powers, Parsons notes, could be dangerous, for example, patients could be exploited for financial gain. So he suggested that there had evolved strongly institutionalized expectations that professionals conduct themselves in ethical and altruistic ways. In exchange, doctors (or other professionals) are given high rewards, which further reduces any temptation to exploit patients financially. Parsons was not claiming that all individual doctors ought to have, or actually had, unselfishness as a psychological characteristic. Rather, it was that the profession's norms and codes of ethics were such that professional success depended on pursuing community-orientated rather than directly self-interested goals. This, for Parsons, was the difference between professions and business (Parsons, 1954).

Thus, in this functionalist approach, a number of characteristics or traits of professions were identified as particularly significant for their role in society: namely, the possession of a body of theoretical knowledge; self-regulating practice; authority over clients; and community rather than self-orientation. As a related development, some sociologists saw these core traits as a way of determining which occupations really were professions and, therefore, which ones were not, but which might, for example, be classified as 'semi-professions'. Nursing, for example, was often so described in the 1950s and 1960s, allegedly because it lacked sufficient theoretical knowledge or powers of self-regulation to warrant designation as a profession. The implication was that only by acquiring these could such occupations become professions.

By the end of the 1960s the functionalist and trait approaches in the sociology of professions were subject to major criticisms. Among these were the charge that professional rhetoric about altruism and adherence to professional ethics was being taken at face value and that insufficient attention was being paid to what professionals actually did. In common with emerging sociological criticisms of functionalism in general, the model of some occupations evolving into professions and others not was recognized as giving insufficient attention to issues of power and to the historical circumstances that shaped occupational development. The new, more critical direction of both the sociology of professions and medical sociology that developed was much more sceptical about professionals' claims of beneficence and community orientation and much more interested in professional power and how it was acquired and exercised. As Macdonald puts it, sociological interest shifted substantially from functionalists' concern with the part that professions played 'in the established order of society', to asking 'how do occupations manage to persuade society to grant them a privileged position?' (1995: xii). The implication in some sociologists' answers in the 1970s was that this persuasion was something of a con trick, in that faith in medicine's powers developed ahead of its actual ability to deliver effective services.

Particularly influential within medical sociology was the work of Freidson (1970) who developed an extended and critical account of medical power, its significance in society generally and its implications for health care. Freidson does identify one characteristic as crucial for professional status, that of legitimated autonomy; that is, occupational self-control over the terms and conditions of its work According to Freidson, medicine, at least in the 1970s, had this to a very high degree. However, for Freidson, what was of interest about medical autonomy was less its function in maintaining social order, than how the occupation of medicine had acquired it and how it was maintained. Thus, in Freidson's work and in much of what followed in the 1970s, attention turned to professionalization as comprising a specific historical and political process and to the strategies and tactics used by occupational groups to gain control over the market for their services, or to gain state support for occupational self-regulation.

One development of this approach was the concept of 'professional

165

project', as the more or less self-conscious efforts of members of an occupation to work collectively to improve their status and their economic prospects. For example, Larson (1977) argued that, in the case of medicine, two aspects of the professionalizing strategy pursued in the nineteenth century were particularly important. One was using educational credentials to effect social closure, to restrict entry to the occupation to those able to obtain formal training. The other was enhancing the credibility of the occupation's claims to offer valued services, through espousing a scientific basis to medical knowledge. Thus, for Larson, the development of university-based medical education was an important factor in medicine's successful professionalization. Other sociologists have focused more on the significance of the expansion of a middle class able to purchase medical services in nineteenth-century Britain or the United States, or on the involvement of the state in supporting, at least partially, medicine's bid for monopoly control over health care provision.

One criticism that has been made of sociological analyses that use such terms as 'project' and 'strategy' is that these suggest a degree of self-conscious and deliberate pursuit of goals that may not have been in the minds of actors at the time. Moreover, these terms imply that professionalization was a process of doctors pursuing their own ends. Some sociologists, adopting a Marxist perspective, argued that these approaches were flawed because they failed to locate professions and their activities within a broader analysis of capitalism. Put simply, the Marxist or political economy approach linked the socially powerful position of doctors to the role that medicine plays in capitalist accumulation, for example, in safeguarding the health of the labour force, present and future, and in controlling workers' access to the privileges of the sick role. A weakness of this type of Marxist analysis is that it often appeared to offer only a version of the functionalist explanation of the high status and authority of medicine under capitalism, as stemming from its role in maintaining the established social order. But, unlike functionalists, these Marxist sociologists regarded this social order as an unjust and ultimately unstable one.

Sociology's interest in professions has, then, been dominated by the study of medicine. Even within medical sociology there has been much less interest in nursing and the other occupations that, in the 1960s, were designated 'semi-professions'. This began to change through the influence of feminism from the 1970s. That professionalized medicine was overwhelmingly male, and many of the semi-professions predominantly female, was no longer taken for granted, but became a topic worthy of sociological enquiry. For example, Witz (1992) has extended the concepts that shaped analysis of medicine's professionalization, particularly that of social closure through credentialism or use of legislation, to develop a more general model of gendered professional projects. Using the development of medicine, nursing, midwifery and radiography in Britain as her examples, she examines the strategies adopted by these different groups to improve their status, by attempting to usurp privileges of a superior group or exclude any incursions from an inferior group, or both. Women health workers were active participants in all aspects of this process. So she describes the means by which medicine sought to exclude women from their ranks, but also how women battled to win their place within medicine. In the case of nursing, some women also sought to exclude lower status women, in seeking the market advantages afforded by legally sanctioned, restrictive registration arrangements.

An alternative framework has been employed by Davies (1995). She takes issue with sociologists for seeing the autonomous professional doctor through blinkers that obscure the incorporation of gender into the health division labour, and the ways in which the possibility of being an autonomous professional is, in reality, sustained by the activities of other, mostly female workers. Nursing's predicament, for Davies, is that the very notion of professional autonomy is a masculine one, rooted in a vision of rationality and technological mastery as the appropriate ways of organizing the most efficient form of authority in complex society. She suggests that this may be incompatible with many of the values that nursing espouses and that this is why nursing has such difficulties embracing and pursuing the medical path to professional status.

The concepts of profession and professionalization have, then, provided powerful if sometimes unfocused lenses through which sociologists have examined medicine as an occupation. The more historically grounded accounts of medical professionalization produced in the 1970s and 1980s have given a rich picture of how this one group gained power and status (although, with hindsight, the critical stance taken towards medicine may have been somewhat overdrawn). The concepts of profession and professionalization may have been less helpful in explaining why some other health care workers did not acquire the same status, but more recent theorizing has addressed this. But by the 1990s, sociologists' interest in the medical profession's power and autonomy had shifted again, from accounting for its acquisition to considering its possible decline.

See also: *medical autonomy and medical dominance* and *decline of medical autonomy.*

REFERENCES

Davies, C. (1995) *Gender and the Professional Predicament in Nursing.* Buckingham: Open University Press.

Freidson, E. (1970) *The Profession of Medicine.* New York: Dodds Mead.

Larson, M.S. (1977) *The Rise of Professionalism: A Sociological Analysis.* London: University of California Press.

Macdonald, K.M. (1995) *The Sociology of the Professions.* London: Sage.

Parsons, T. (1954) 'The professions and social structure', in T. Parsons, *Essays in Sociological Theory.* Glencoe, IL: Free Press.

Witz, A. (1992) *Professions and Patriarchy.* London: Routledge.

MAE

professional socialization

Definition: Professional socialization refers to the social processes through which individual students learn to become members of a professional occupation. These processes include formal and informal means of learning both codified knowledge and technical skills, and also more tacit knowledge and 'craft' skills, norms and values and 'professional' modes of conduct.

168

Much formal health care is currently provided by members of a range of distinctive occupations, all of which claim the designation 'profession'. This generally connotes such characteristics as members' commitment to an organized occupational community and possession of a strong sense of professional identity, linked to shared values and knowledge. In using the term 'socialization' to describe the processes through which new entrants acquire their professional identities, sociologists are making an explicit analogy with primary socialization, the social processes through which children develop an awareness of general social values and norms and a distinct sense of self through interaction with others. Fundamental to the sociological approach here is that much more is involved in professional socialization than book learning and gaining technical competence (although these are important aspects of the process).

Thus, among the questions explored in sociological studies of professional socialization are the following: what is the relationship between formal pedagogy and informal modes of influence in the making of professionals? What are the crucial steps and status passages in the formation of professional identity? How is theoretical, classroom-based learning related to the practical tasks of doing, for example, medicine, nursing, midwifery and chiropody? How do those who will have to work with the sick and the dying learn appropriate professional demeanours? Is there a single professional culture transmitted in professional training and what are the implications for this culture of any changes in entrants' social characteristics? What kind of educational preparation is considered appropriate for optimally performing professional practitioners and how and by whom are the forms of professional socialization and definitions of optimal performance determined? What is the relationship between the power and status of a health care occupation and its mode of professional socialization?

Answering these questions has produced a body of research that has been of considerable historical significance in the development of medical sociology. In particular, the publication of two studies of American medical students, conducted in the 1950s by different teams of distinguished sociologists, set the framework for research on health professional socialization for several decades. In fact, for both these teams, the choice of medical education as a research topic was because they considered it to be a good case study for examining their general (and different) sociological perspectives, rather than an end in itself.

Thus, in *The Student Physician*, published in 1957, Robert Merton and colleagues employed a functionalist perspective. Indeed, the concept of socialization, with its emphasis on transmission of norms and values, is one that is particularly important in functionalist theory. Merton's team's research suggested that, during their long years of study, medical students did not just learn formally codified medical knowledge but were progressively, and relatively harmoniously, socialized into sharing their teachers' professional norms and values. Medical students, it was argued, gradually learnt to tolerate working with uncertainty, both that arising from their own ignorance and that stemming from the limitations of medical knowledge, as they looked forward to taking on their professional role. Some critics have argued that, in this analysis, medical students appear as rather passive, empty vessels being filled up with new values by their teachers.

169

In apparent contrast, the *Boys in White* studied by Howard Becker and his colleagues (1961) were depicted as very active participants in their learning, and as being distant from, even in conflict with, medical school staff. In this symbolic interactionist perspective, medical socialization was depicted as a process of students constantly 'making out', making short-term, even cynical, situational adjustments to immediate pedagogic demands (for example, passing examinations), as they pursued their prime goal of getting through medical school. However, one form of situational adjustment that Becker's team did note was the re-emergence of a more idealistic attitude to medical work as students approached graduation. Nevertheless, their study has sometimes been criticized for focusing too much on student culture, and for paying relatively little attention to what medical school was preparing these students for: that is, to be doctors.

Many of the themes raised by these two studies have been developed in subsequent studies of professional socialization. Most of these have adopted approaches broadly sympathetic to symbolic interactionism, but with more attention to the relationship between neophytes' immediate experience and their future professional roles. In particular, sociologists have studied how, and at what stage, medical students acquire a sense of professional mastery and the ability to conduct themselves with 'detached concern': that 'supple balance' of equanimity and compassion, of concern about patients without excessive emotional involvement that is considered professionally appropriate. For example, Hafferty (2000) has suggested that medical students undergo a particularly intensive form of adult resocialization through a series of encounters ridden by tension between lay and medical norms and values, with the latter gradually (but not always smoothly) coming to be seen as 'superior' to the former. Dissecting bodies in anatomy is an early instance of such pivotal experiences. In anatomy classes, medical students learn, in interaction with peers and medical school staff, to follow the 'feeling rules' of their chosen profession, rather than reacting to corpses as lay people might. Other research has studied later stages in the longitudinal process of medical socialization, including the early years of post-qualification and specialist training. One recurrent finding of these studies has been that, during the often stressful and exhausting intern and residency (junior doctor) years, professional culture and social control processes appear to encourage ways of managing medical errors, or of treating socially powerless or medically unrewarding patients, which are at odds with the ideals enshrined in professional codes of ethics (for example, Bosk, 1979).

Prior to the late 1970s, these studies of medical socialization in the

United States were, inevitably, studies of an overwhelmingly white, male population (about 90 per cent of the US medical school intake in the 1950s and 1960s were men). At that time, gender and ethnicity were not seen as salient analytical dimensions for studies of medical socialization, even in the many European countries where women and minority ethnic students had been a much larger proportion of medical school intakes for decades. This has slowly changed, particularly with respect to gender, reflecting the fact that, by 2000, the majority of medical students were women in many developed countries (including the USA), as well as the influence of feminist critiques of male-dominated medicine and medical institutions. Research has indicated persistent gender differences in specialty choice after qualification, suggesting that medical schools are not wholly homogenizing institutions.

There has been much less sociological research on socialization for other health care occupations than for medicine, but similar themes and similar contrasts between different theoretical approaches are found in studies of nurse education. For example, a major American study in the 1960s also focused on student culture, depicting the nursing student as 'an active, choice-making factor' in (usually) her socialization (Olesen and Whittaker, 1968: 300). A recurrent finding of research on nurse training organized on the traditional apprenticeship model has been of a marked disjuncture in student experience between what was taught in the classroom and what was actually done on wards in order to get through the work. Students distinguished between the 'real' professional nursing work with patients that they considered they were being trained for and the (to them) mundane 'basic' patient care tasks that they spent much of their ward-based time doing. Such findings have raised questions about what nursing skills and knowledge are, or ought to be, transmitted in nursing education. That nurses are overwhelmingly women has long been seen as an important factor in shaping their professional socialization, but the analytic framework has altered with the growing influence of feminist ideas on sociology and, arguably, on nursing. From a concern, in the 1950s and 1960s, with the extent to which individual student nurses' experience and aspirations were shaped by considerations of marriage and motherhood, there has been a shift to exploring the ways in which nursing knowledge and practice, nursing culture and values contain deeply embedded assumptions about the femininity of entrants (Davies, 1995).

This shift of focus also illustrates how, particularly since the 1980s, studies of the experience of individuals being socialized have been increasingly complemented by studies of the formal institutions of socialization and of educational policies and programmes. This reflects the

171

ways in which the training of health workers has been affected by health care reforms and other social changes. For example, the form and location of midwifery education have changed in many countries since the 1970s, in response to both consumerist and occupational pressures for women-centred childbirth (Benoit et al., 2001).

Finally, it is important to note that most of the studies of professional socialization published to date were studies of single occupations, with formal training organized along discrete occupational lines, in institutionally separate mono-professional schools. Such settings were seen as important expressions of and institutional bases for shaping distinctive professional identities. In recent years, there have been moves to integrate education for many health care occupations more fully into universities and, in some countries such as the United Kingdom, to provide more inter-professional training from the outset, with the explicit aim of producing a more flexible division of health care labour. Such developments, if they become established, may prove to have profound implications for our future understanding of what it means to be socialized as a health professional.

See also: *medical autonomy and medical dominance, malpractice and uncertainty.*

REFERENCES

Becker, H.S., Geer, B., Hughes, E.C. and Strauss, A. (1961) *Boys in White: Student Culture in Medical School.* Chicago: University of Chicago Press.

Benoit, C., Davies-Floyd, R., van Teijlingen, E.R., Sandall, J. and Miller, J.F. (2001) 'Designing midwives: a comparison of educational models', in R. Devries, C. Benoit, E.R. van Teijlingen and S. Wrede (eds), *Birth by Design: Pregnancy, Maternity Care and Midwifery in North America and Europe.* London: Routledge, pp. 139–65.

Bosk, C.A. (1979) *Forgive and Remember: Managing Medical Failure.* Chicago: University of Chicago Press.

Davies, C. (1995) *Gender and the Professional Predicament in Nursing.* Buckingham: Open University Press.

Hafferty, F.W. (2000) 'Reconfiguring the sociology of medical education: emerging topics and pressing issues', in C.E. Bird, P. Conrad, and A.M. Fremont (eds), *Handbook of Medical Sociology.* 5th edn. Upper Saddle River, NJ: Prentice Hall, pp. 238–57.

Merton, R.K., Reader, G. and Kendall, P.L. (eds) (1957) *The Student Physician: Introductory Studies in the Sociology of Medical Education.* Cambridge, MA: Harvard University Press.

Olesen, V. and Whittaker, E. (1986) *The Silent Dialogue: a Study of the Social Psychology of Professional Socialisation.* San Francisco: Jossey-Bass.

MAE

medical autonomy and medical dominance

> *Definition: Medical autonomy is the legitimated (that is, publicly accepted) control that the medical profession exercises over the organization and terms of its work. Medical dominance is a relative concept, indicating the authority that the medical profession can exercise over others, for example, other occupations within the health care division of labour, patients or over society, through being cultural authorities in matters relating to health.*

The concepts of autonomy and dominance have been much used in discussions of professional power, especially in relation to the medical profession. Indeed, they have often been used as if they were interchangeable. Clearly, they are very closely related, logically and empirically. In a complex division of labour, only an occupation able to exercise dominance over others can have very high levels of legitimated autonomy and vice versa. But keeping an analytic distinction between the two is useful when analysing professional power – a recurrent theme within medical sociology in the past 40 years, particularly in the work of the American sociologist, Eliot Freidson. Although the theme has recurred, the emphasis has changed. From the 1960s to the 1980s, medical sociologists' primary interest was in the origins and persistence of medical autonomy and in its social consequences (which sociologists often regarded somewhat sceptically). By the 1990s, the questions medical sociologists were asking were more concerned with the possible decline of medical autonomy and dominance and, to some extent, with the possible negative consequences of this. Thus the two concepts have remained key ones throughout the period and this entry aims to explain their development by focusing particularly on Freidson's work.

Control over some terms and conditions of work and the ability to exercise some discretion in carrying out tasks are not, of course, the sole prerogative of professions. The members of virtually all occupations have these powers to some degree, and generally press, individually and

173

collectively, to maintain and extend them. Users of almost all services have to place a degree of trust in the suppliers of those services, at least some of the time. However, Freidson argued, in a landmark book on the American medical profession, that, unlike other occupations, only professions have been '*deliberately* granted autonomy, including the exclusive right to determine who can legitimately do its work and how the work should be done' (1970: 72, emphasis in the original). For Freidson, possession of a high level of state-sanctioned autonomy, and, by implication, institutionalized expectations of societal trust in the occupation's claims, are the defining characteristics of a true profession. And, he claimed, medicine, at least in the United States around 1970, was, in this sense, a clear example of a profession, although his attitude at the time towards medicine's claims to be exempt from external regulation was highly critical. Freidson was not suggesting that medical autonomy was absolute. Medicine has never been exempt from general legal frameworks regulating financial conduct or the obligation not to harm others in providing services. But Freidson's point was that medicine had, for example, a considerable degree of officially and publicly respected authority to determine what would (and what would not) constitute illegal or unjustified harm caused by medical treatment. This autonomy had been achieved, he argued, through an essentially political process of professionalization; through the profession having convinced, over time, the public, or at least socially powerful groups, that its services were of value and then obtained legal sanction for its autonomy. The latter was expressed in the establishment of statutorily defined, self-regulating professional licensing and disciplinary systems, such as the British General Medical Council, which, when first established, was an entirely medical institution.

A distinction needs to be made between professional autonomy as possessed by individuals by virtue of their membership of a profession and the autonomy vested in a profession as an organized, corporate body. An example of the former at local level within medicine is what is often termed by individual doctors' 'clinical freedom': that is, the right of doctors, at least when fully trained, to make their own judgements about what is best for a particular patient and to have that judgement accepted as authoritative by others both within and outside the profession. It is possible to imagine a situation in which individual doctors' clinical judgements are regularly subjected to evaluation by their professional peers, without those peers being themselves subject to external (that is, non-professional) judgement. Indeed, this is precisely the situation that, in his later work, Freidson (for example, 1986) suggested was emerging within medicine during the 1980s. Collegiate control over the behaviour of individual doctors was increasing, as a means of heading off challenges to the autonomy of the organized profession of medicine. For example, standardized protocols for treating particular types of cases have been increasingly adopted, following agreement among doctors in the relevant field, perhaps within local hospitals or nationally, about best practice. More recently still, Freidson (1994) has raised the possibility that this process will, through fostering stratification between the professional elite and the rank and file, weaken the internal coherence and hence the power of the medical profession.

Autonomy in clinical decision-making or standard setting is only one, although, arguably, the most significant aspect of medical autonomy. Various typologies of autonomy have been put forward in the sociological literature but three main categories are usually identified: (1) clinical or technical autonomy – the right of the medical profession (or individual members of it) to set standards and evaluate clinical performance; (2) political autonomy – the right to make policy decisions as the legitimate experts on health and medicine; and (3) economic autonomy – the right to determine levels of personal remuneration or the level of resources available for their work (Elston, 1991: 61). Historical and comparative analysis suggests that these different aspects of autonomy can, to some extent, vary independently of each other. For example, for much of the twentieth century, the medical profession in the United States enjoyed a very high level of economic autonomy, particularly through its fee-for-service-based payment system compared to their peers in the United Kingdom, especially after the establishment of the National Health Service in 1948. However, the experience of British doctors after 1948 shows that, contrary to what many doctors feared at the time, working for the state did not, in itself, bring about a marked diminution in other aspects of their autonomy (or, indeed, in financial rewards). Rather, state involvement simultaneously boosted some aspects of medical power and circumscribed others (Larkin, 1993). Although after 1948 the British medical profession could not directly determine the overall level of resources going in to the state-funded health care system, collectively and individually, they had substantial autonomy in spending those resources that were allocated. Working without the constraints imposed by patients' varying ability to pay directly may have enhanced British doctors' clinical autonomy relative to that exercised by their US counterparts, at least until relatively recently (Harrison and Schultz, 1989).

Thus, autonomy can be exercised (or gained, or lost) at different levels, and over different aspects of medical work. And not all segments of the medical profession within the same society may enjoy equal levels of autonomy. There may be differences between specialisms, positions in occupational structures, and these can be related to social group membership. In any discussion of whether medical autonomy is increasing or decreasing, these complexities need to be borne in mind.

Medical dominance is also a concept that has been applied in different contexts and to refer to different aspects of medical power. Three aspects have been particularly important within medical sociology: (1) medical dominance within society generally, that is, its cultural authority to determine, for example, what is to be counted as sickness; (2) medical dominance over patients; and (3) medical dominance over other occupations in the increasingly complex division of health care labour and in the process of policy-making. The first of these aspects can be subsumed, for present purposes, under the concept of medicalization and the second under 'the doctor–patient relationship'. It is the third aspect, medicine's state-sanctioned dominance over other health occupations that is closely associated with claims about medical autonomy, particularly in Freidson's work. Indeed, his early writings on professional power and autonomy have sometimes been termed 'the professional dominance' perspective. For Freidson (1970), a crucial part of the professionalization process for medicine (that is, its achievement of autonomy) was the gradual subordination of other occupations, such as nursing, to medical control. As a result, although nursing in the mid-twentieth century had considerable control over some aspects of its work, Freidson argued that it still lacked full professional status because the work of nurses was subject to 'doctors' orders'. Unless nursing could control a discrete area of work that was undertaken without dependence on medicine, he argued that it could never attain the status of a full profession. And, he claimed, medicine was likely to act in such a way as to preclude nursing achieving such independence. Having been first past the post, medicine would constantly seek to defend its autonomy from others' encroachment.

With the benefits of hindsight, it has been argued that Freidson's (1970) depiction of medical autonomy was overdrawn and his account of professional dominance over-simplified. For example, he neglected gender and the role of the state, and appeared to assume that clear distinctions could be drawn between professions and other would-be professions, solely by reference to autonomy and the competitive struggle over it. The distinctive historical development of other health care occupations is perhaps also underplayed in Freidson's account of professional dominance. For example, Larkin (1993) argues that, at least in the British case, the medical profession's apparently state-sanctioned autonomy was always more circumscribed by the state than Freidson's account suggests. Moreover, according to Larkin, rather than medicine deliberately establishing and seeking to maintain control over other occupations in the health division of labour, medical control over other occupations was much more indirect and best conceived of as a form of proxy management of health care by medicine on behalf of the state, rather than as direct medical dominance.

When first published, Freidson's theory of professional dominance and his account of professional autonomy as acquired through active political strategies had a great impact on medical sociology. That criticisms have been made subsequently of his work should not detract from recognition of the significance of his early work for the sociological analysis of medical power. Freidson's own account of professional power has been modified in the past 30 years. From the deeply sceptical view, expressed in *Profession of Medicine* (1970), of the value to society of accepting medical claims to be exempt from external evaluation, Freidson's later work accepts that at least some of the activities of medicine require the exercise of considerable levels of judgement, and that this constrains the extent to which non-medical, external regulation is possible or appropriate. How professional autonomy is best regulated is an enduring question for him, as for medical sociology generally.

See also: *decline of medical autonomy, medicalization* and *practitioner-client-relationships professions and professionalization.*

REFERENCES

Elston, M.A. (1991) 'The politics of professional power', in J. Gabe, M. Calnan and M. Bury (eds), *The Politics of Professional Power*. London: Routledge, pp. 58–98.

Freidson, E. (1970) *Profession of Medicine*. New York: Dodds Mead.

Freidson, E. (1986) 'The medical profession in transition', in L.H. Aiken and D. Mechanic (eds), *Applications of Social Science to Clinical Medicine and Health Policy*. New Brunswick, NJ: Rutgers University Press, pp. 63–79. Reprinted in Freidson, E. (1989) *Medical Work in America*. New Haven, CT: Yale University Press, pp. 206–25.

Freidson, E. (1994) *Professionalism Reborn: Theory, Prophecy and Policy*. Cambridge: Polity Press.

Harrison, S. and Schulz, R.I. (1989) 'Clinical autonomy in the United Kingdom and United States: contrasts and convergence', in G. Freddi and J.W. Bjorkman (eds), *Controlling Health Professionals: The Comparative Politics of Health Governance*. London: Sage, pp. 198–209.

Larkin, G.V. (1993) 'Continuity in change: medical dominance in the United Kingdom', in F.W. Hafferty and J.B. McKinlay (eds), *The Changing Medical Profession: An International Perspective*. Oxford: Oxford University Press, pp.81–91.

MAE

decline of medical autonomy

> **Definition:** *Medical autonomy is the legitimated control that the medical profession exercises over the terms and conditions of its work. Since the 1980s, many medical sociologists have suggested that this characteristic expression of professional power is being reduced by external challenges.*

The future of medical autonomy and, more generally, of professional power and authority has become a major issue in British and American medical sociology since the late 1980s. There is now a substantial literature (Gabe et al., 1994; Hafferty and McKinlay, 1993) addressing the question of the extent to which one of medical sociology's generally shared assumptions during the 1970s is being rendered obsolete and, if so, why. This assumption is that the medicine is a profession able to exercise a very high degree of autonomy, that is, legitimated control over many aspects of its work, and is *the* dominant occupation in the health care division of labour and the dominant voice on matters of health in society generally. As outlined below, contributors to this literature have employed a variety of concepts, drawn from different theoretical perspectives. However, some preliminary points about the issue will help to set the context in which these concepts have been put forward.

The first, self-evident point is that to speak of the decline of medical or professional autonomy implies that there is or was autonomy to lose. Intrinsic to the generally critical stance towards professional power that characterized medical sociology in the 1970s was an analysis of medicine's acquisition of autonomy, not simply as a functional societal response to the problems posed by managing ill health in industrial societies, but as the contingent outcome of a successful professionalization project undertaken by medicine. If the acquisition of professional autonomy is the product of specific historical and political circumstances, then it follows that changes in historical and political circumstances might have implications for the power of professions such as medicine. Some have argued that the extent of medical power and its imperialistic tendencies over society or other occupations may have been over-stated in the 1970s. However, few would dispute that, compared with most other occupations, the social and cultural authority exercised by the medical profession has been considerable and still is. Even those who are arguing that major change is taking place see this as a process underway, not a completed transformation. Moreover, in most cases, those who argue for a decline in medical autonomy link this to transformations that affect society generally and hence most, or even all, occupations. In this way, medical autonomy could decline while the relative dominance and advantage of medicine over other occupations remained unchanged. Moreover, as medical autonomy is a complex, multi-faceted phenomenon, changes in one aspect of professional power may not affect other aspects. Furthermore, there is relatively little agreement among contributors to these debates about what would count as firm evidence for or against decline, or how much decline would mark a significant change.

So, this is a very lively but somewhat speculative area of medical sociological activity at present. There is agreement that medicine at the start of the twenty-first century has been challenged on a number of fronts. The debate is over which, if any, of these are significant and how they can be explained theoretically. The challenges discussed in the literature can be categorized as arising from three main sources. The first is the growing and changing form of involvement of third parties in the funding, or organizing of health care. Thus, in the United Kingdom, the major reforms to the NHS that have been introduced since the 1980s, including the introduction of a more market-driven ethos and structure, have been seen by many as constituting an attack on producer dominance and professional exemption from external scrutiny. In the United States, the expansion of for-profit health care corporations, the move to managed care and associated new financial management of medical practice, have been widely hailed as representing an encroachment on professional prerogative, by those organized interests who increasingly buy medical services on behalf of patients.

A second type of challenge is seen as stemming more directly from the users of health care, the public. On the one hand, there is the apparent rise of consumerism with individual users rejecting, or being encouraged to reject, passive trust in medical expertise: a rejection expressed in increased complaints and malpractice allegations and in a more active involvement in clinical decision-making, or in increased resort to alternative medicines. There is also a more collective consumerist

179

challenge in the form of critical self-help groups and social movements, such as the women's health movement or gay rights activism in relation to HIV/AIDS.

The third form of challenge identified is that from other health care occupations. For example, there have been many recent developments in nursing education and practice, such as the move to incorporate nursing schools in universities or to expand nurses' roles into areas previously regarded as medical responsibilities. Similar developments have occurred in some of the other occupations characterized as 'professions allied to medicine', such as physiotherapy or pharmacy. These have been seen by some commentators as moves in a professionalizing strategy on the part of these occupations. That there are new areas of inter-professional boundary blurring in education and in delivering care involving medicine and nursing, and other fields, is clear. However, it is probably most helpful to follow Witz (1994) and see many of these changes as being themselves related to the first kind of challenge, that from third parties, such as the state in the United Kingdom.

Different concepts, drawing on different broad theoretical approaches, have been used to elaborate and explain these different types of challenge. Here, there is space to outline only the concepts particularly associated with third party and user/public consumer challenges, and two critical alternative positions.

According to some early American contributors to the debate (notably McKinlay and Arches, 1985), the effect of third party commercial purchasers of medical services on doctors' ability to determine their terms and conditions of work was tantamount to the incipient proletarianization of the medical profession. Drawing explicitly on Marxist theories of the logic of capitalist development, it was argued that the reduction in professional prerogatives such as the right to set remuneration was evidence that medicine was being incorporated into the class of those who produced surplus value for capital. Initial formulations of this position were controversial, not least because American doctors did not greatly resemble typical 'wage slaves' and because the underlying Marxist theory is itself highly contested. Subsequent formulations from a similar perspective have tended to use the concept of corporatization as less contentious and more indicative of the putative cause of the changes than proletarianization. Neither of these concepts can be unproblematically applied in societies where health care is mainly state-funded or provided but, arguably, some of the same rationalizing principles that underpin corporate managed care are in evidence here. Thus, in the United Kingdom, the concepts through which the changing fortune of medical autonomy in relation to the state has been considered include managerialism and privatization.

For those sociologists who see the challenge to medical autonomy as mainly arising from the public, either as individual users of services or collective groups, what is identified is a process of cultural change for which the term 'deprofessionalization' has been coined. On the one hand, exponents of this position argue that there is a more informed, critical public, less inclined to be deferent to experts, a process fostered by the extensive media coverage given to specific incidents of gross medical malpractice. One example is the Shipman case, in which a British general practitioner was convicted of murdering a large number of elderly patients. On the other hand, through increasing specialization and computerization, expert knowledge is itself regarded as becoming more controllable and accessible to outsiders. It is claimed, therefore, that there is a reduction in the knowledge gap between profession and public and in the areas of indeterminacy that support the exercise of professional discretion.

Both the corporatization and deprofessionalization theses have attracted considerable criticism (see, for example, Hafferty and McKinlay, 1993). For example, they have been seen as insufficiently historically grounded and as generalizing too much from specific, short-term American developments. Freidson, author of one of the most influential accounts of the rise of medical autonomy, has argued that both sets of claims tend to underplay the significance of the organized character of the medical profession. He suggested that, rather than external control of medicine being of growing significance, it was increasing internal stratification of the profession that sociologists should attend to. Through enhanced disciplinary procedures, promulgation of clinical guidelines and protocols and the emergence of new cadres of medical managers, a professional elite is, according to Freidson (1994), increasingly dominant over rank-and-file medical practitioners. This in itself may weaken the coherence and hence the autonomy of the profession over time.

Light (2000) has suggested an approach based on a more pluralist view of modern societies (or at least of the United States) than the neo-Marxism of the corporatization thesis. He suggests that rather than presume medical dominance as the starting point for analysis, the medical profession should be seen as only one of several major countervailing powers in society with interests in health care, with the other powers including the state, the health care industry, other provider groups and consumers. Light depicts a system in which these different interests compete for power, influence and resources and, if one

181

becomes predominant, a counter-movement will develop over time. The model has the merit of including more than buyers and sellers of medical services; and the rise and putative fall of medical autonomy can be set in the same explanatory framework. What is less clear is how adequately the theory explains which interests predominate at particular times.

There is general recognition among medical sociologists that the accounts of medical power and autonomy that seemed appropriate to the 1970s are no longer so clearly applicable 30 years later. There are undoubtedly new challenges to medicine's authority. What there is less consensus on is what their significance is for the future of medical autonomy. In the process of debate, what has become clearer is that while medical autonomy can be described as a 'conspiracy against the laity', to paraphrase the playwright George Bernard Shaw, it is also an institution from which the laity and other parties besides the medical profession may benefit. As Harrison (1999) points out in the context of the National Health Service, medical autonomy in the form of clinical freedom to provide the best for individual patients rather than act according to managerial rules may be of advantage to patients, at least to those individual ones. Clinical freedom in the form of doctors' taking responsibility for decisions about treatment may also be to the advantage of government and the state, or, in privatized health care systems, to corporate health care. It converts what might otherwise give rise to political or consumer protest, if taken in public into technical decisions, taken in the privacy of the consulting room. Thus, it cannot be assumed that third party buyers of medical services will always seek to erode medical autonomy.

See also: *professions and professionalization* and *medical autonomy and medical dominance.*

REFERENCES

Freidson, E. (1994) *Professionalism Reborn: Theory, Prophecy and Policy.* Cambridge: Polity Press.

Gabe, J., Kelleher, D. and Williams, G. (eds) (1994) *Challenging Medicine.* London: Routledge.

Hafferty, F.W. and McKinlay, J.B. (eds) (1993) *The Changing Medical Profession: An International Perspective.* Oxford: Oxford University Press. (Previously published as special issue of *The Milbank Quarterly,* 66 (Suppl. 2), 1988).

Harrison, S. (1999) 'Clinical autonomy and health policy', in M. Exworthy and S. Halford (eds), *Professionals and the New Managerialism in the Public Sector.* Buckingham: Open University Press, pp. 50–64.

Light, D.W. (2000) 'The medical profession and organizational change: from professional dominance to countervailing power', in C.E. Bird, P. Conrad and A.M. Fremont (eds), *Handbook of Medical Sociology*, 5th edn. Upper Saddle River, NJ: Prentice Hall, pp. 201–16.

McKinlay, J.B. and Arches, J. (1985) 'Toward the proletarianization of physicians', *International Journal of Health Services*, 15 (2): 161–95.

Witz, A. (1994) 'The challenge of nursing', in J. Gabe, D. Kelleher and G. Williams (eds), *Challenging Medicine*. London: Routledge, pp. 23–45.

MAE

medical pluralism

> **Definition:** *Medical pluralism refers to the co-existence in a society of differing medical traditions, grounded in different principles or based on different world-views.*

Pluralism is a concept that has been used in many different ways, most notably in relation to political phenomena. In contrast to monism or unity, the term acknowledges multiplicity and difference and that there are different ways of knowing and being. In political theorizing, the concept became popular in reaction to the monistic social theories of the nineteenth century (see Hegel, for instance) and was used to emphasize the existence of a range of social interests and interest groups. Pluralism is particularly associated with 'empirical democratic theory', which was popular from the 1950s to the 1970s, but has become a key concept for social scientists who wish to account for the existence of multiple selves, identities, sub-cultures and social relations (McLennan, 1995: 6). Importantly, some pluralist theorists have argued that pluralism only properly exists when socio-cultural differences are embedded in institutionalized social practices. Moreover, while the concept has enshrined 'the principle of equal but different' (ibid.: 3), more radical theorists have emphasized that 'structural pluralism' can accommodate an understanding of hierarchical power relations.

In the health care context the more specific concept of medical pluralism has been widely used. In particular, the idea of multiplicity has been drawn on to explain that while the content of health care systems

183

varies from society to society (dependent on social, cultural, historical and economic factors), a range of healing traditions is common to all. There are a number of ways of classifying pluralistic medical systems, for instance, by reference to the sphere of influence various healing modalities may command (such as cosmopolitan, regional or local, see Dunn, 1977) or by reference to the nature of the belief systems and the extent of convergence or divergence from biomedical conceptions of the body, health, illness and disease. Most of the work thus far has been concerned with the description of these various healing systems and the ways in which sick people and their kin make decisions about what kind of healer to use. This emphasis has produced very useful ethnographic studies but has largely failed to generate a critical analysis of the power relations that exist between the various healing systems or a critical evaluation of the use of the concept itself. For instance, it would be very hard, at the present time, to describe the co-existence of biomedicine and alternative medical systems as 'equal but different'. The twinning of work on medical dominance and medical pluralism to produce an understanding of 'hierarchical medical pluralism' would enable this oversight to be rectified.

Medical anthropologists were the first to use the concept of medical pluralism. Having always described different healing practices as part of their study of culture, the 1980s saw medical anthropologists give more specific attention to the collaboration between indigenous/traditional medicine and biomedicine in Latin America, Asia and Africa. Of particular importance is Leslie's (1980) edited collection in *Social Science and Medicine* which, in the face of population growth, unmet health need, the published efficacy of the 'barefoot doctor' programme and the World Health Organization's call for the integration of traditional medicine, brought together work that prioritized applied academic work on medical pluralism. Leslie pleaded for an end to the description of alternative or traditional medicines as merely anthropologically interesting in favour of work with a policy focus. Specifically, it was suggested that anthropology could help health planners to understand why indigenous peoples did not consult biomedical practitioners, and urged the development of ways in which other practitioners, normally excluded from state endorsed practice, could be trained and utilized.

Medical sociologists adopted the concept during the 1990s to describe the significant increase in the number and popularity of 'alternative medicines' in the West (Baer, 1995). This is not to say that medical pluralism in the West is a recent phenomenon. On the contrary, there has always been the possibility of choice between different practitioners, between consulting or self-prescribing, between using public or privately funded care and having multiple understandings of health and illness. Furthermore, historical evidence reveals that many therapies were popular in Western countries until biomedicine monopolized the market from the first quarter of the twentieth century. Nevertheless, in the late 1970s and 1980s, the importation of therapies to the health care market (for example, acupuncture) and the renaissance of older therapies have merited attention. Thus, Cant and Sharma (1999) prefer to call this the era of a '*new* medical pluralism'.

So far, most work on medical pluralism has tended to focus on describing the variety of medicines available to the general public and has neglected to utilize the concept to understand differences within individual medical systems. Indeed, most of the debate has centred on the central differences between alternative medicine and biomedicine and has, by implication, tended to portray biomedicine and the various alternative medicines as individually monolithic. Yet, it is generally accepted that biomedicine is far from unified, encompassing a variety of knowledges and healing practices, for example some biomedically qualified doctors choose to practise alternative medicine and do so very differently (see Dew, 2000). Similarly, there are huge discrepancies in the understanding and practice of individual therapies. For instance, homeopathy is provided by medically qualified and non-medically qualified practitioners, by untrained (Druidic) therapists and by a growing number of the lay public who choose to self-prescribe. Consequently, every healing tradition should be understood as a plural healing system in its own right.

In more recent years some anthropologists and sociologists have distanced themselves from applied policy studies and have concentrated instead on descriptive and theoretically driven work (Janes, 1999). For example, there is a wealth of literature that documents the socio-demographic characteristics of users of alternative medicine, the attractiveness of alternative medicine to users, the professionalizing project of alternative medicines and the ways in which different healing systems collaborate (see Cant and Sharma, 1999). Furthermore, there has been an interest in the ways in which biomedicine and other healing systems differ, the role of the state in the encouragement or discouragement of medical pluralism and an examination of the usefulness of contemporary theoretical concepts (such as globalization, risk and consumption) in understanding medical pluralism.

This re-orientation of the work on medical pluralism suffers from three major weaknesses. In the first place, there has been insufficient attention to the dominance of biomedicine in situations of medical pluralism. Weberian analysis has highlighted how biomedicine was able to exclude, limit and subordinate its competitors in the past. While there has been some examination of the ways in which biomedicine has attempted to protect its monopoly against the competition from traditional and alternative medicines, this work needs to be extended. Evidence shows that alternative medicines have had to de-radicalize their claims and limit their practice to gain legitimacy, status and state regulation (Cant and Sharma, 1999). There is a possibility that alternative medicine systems may become so like biomedicine that the understanding that pluralism signals difference may have to be re-evaluated. Yet the development of educational training programmes, the codification of knowledge and the establishment of professional organizations have given alternative medicine a stronger institutional base. Generally, pluralism has not challenged the cultural and social authority of biomedicine and, as such, the concept of medical pluralism cannot be fully comprehended without some appreciation of the concepts of medical dominance and professional self-interest. At the same time the study of medical pluralism presents an opportunity to examine the ways in which medical dominance is eroded as well as sustained (Dew, 2000).

Second, the issue of state regulation is important. While pluralism has always been part of everyday practice, the increased interest shown by national government and international organizations in the regulation of alternative medicines has changed the complexion of medical pluralism. There is now evidence of orchestrated medical pluralism, where governments have actively intervened to ratify which providers are legitimate (for instance, osteopathy and chiropractic have had most success in achieving state regulation). Not all practitioners and therapies attract the same degree of support or sponsorship and a hierarchy of success has been introduced into medical pluralism in the West. Much more conceptual work needs to be undertaken to understand the various ways in which pluralism is constructed. Lee (1982) has suggested that healing systems should be evaluated in terms of their structural (power, prestige, wealth, degree of state support) and functional (distribution and utilization) superiority to conceptualize the power relations that exist in situations of medical pluralism. Moreover, there has been reluctance by government to pay for alternative medicines; consequently, the availability of a plural health care market is dependent on a range of economic and geographical factors (for example, the distribution of therapists varies by locale). Questions about *why* the state should have taken an interest in medical pluralism also need to be addressed, referring perhaps to the role of alternative medicine in the capitalist production of health or as a new mechanism in the surveillance and governance of populations.

Finally, though theoretical questions have dominated recent work in medical pluralism, the massive increase in the range and number of therapies requires sociologists to turn their attention to questions that have a policy focus. In particular, there is a need to assess the various attempts to integrate different healing systems and the ways in which individual practitioners might successfully collaborate. There has been a tendency to adopt a non-reflective and non-critical stance towards alternative and indigenous healing systems and more attention must be given to the efficacy, evaluation and role of alternative medicine in the overall provision of health care.

The concept of medical pluralism has, through use, come to be associated with the co-existence of biomedicine and alternative medicine. However, its descriptive potential is much wider that this, encompassing the idea of differences within and across healing systems. The conceptual and applied development of this concept will mean that it continues to have strong and adaptive relevance for medical sociology.

See also: *medical autonomy and medical dominance* and *medical model.*

REFERENCES

Baer, H. (1995) 'Medical pluralism in the United States review', *Medical Anthropology Quarterly*, 9 (4): 493–502.

Cant, S.L. and Sharma, U. (1999) *A New Medical Pluralism? Alternative Medicine, Doctors, Patients and the State*. London: Routledge.

Dew, K. (2000) *'Deviant insiders: medical acupuncturists in New Zealand'*, *Social Science and Medicine*, 50: 1785–95.

Dunn, F.L. (1977) 'Traditional Asian medicine and cosmopolitan medicine as adaptive systems', in C. Leslie (ed.), *Asian Medical Systems: A Comparative Study*. Berkeley, CA: University of California Press.

Janes, C. (1999) 'The health transition, global modernity and the crisis of traditional medicine: the Tibetan Case', *Social Science and Medicine*, 48: 1803–20.

Lee, R. (1982) *'Comparative studies of health care systems'*, *Social Science and Medicine*, 16: 629–42.

Leslie, C. (1980) 'Medical pluralism in world perspective', *Social Science and Medicine*, 14B: 191–5.

McLennan, G. (1995) *Pluralism*. Buckingham: Open University Press.

SC

negotiated order

> **Definition:** *The concept of negotiated order derives from a symbolic interactionist perspective. It was intended to sensitize sociologists to the ways in which social order in complex social organizations is something that must be reconstituted or 'worked at' continually through, for example, negotiation and bargaining, rather than assumed to be set by pre-existing formal structures and bureaucratic rules.*

The conception of social order as negotiated was originally put forward in 1963 by a team of sociologists led by Anselm Strauss, in the course of their studies of American psychiatric hospitals. In a now-classic paper, published in a volume of sociological essays on the modern hospital, they drew attention to the complex division of labour involved in modern health care. As they expressed it, a hospital, or any other formal health care setting, can be 'visualized as a professional locale – a geographical site where persons drawn from different professions come together to carry out their respective purposes' (Strauss et al., 1963: 150). For example, in the psychiatric hospitals that they studied, there were different professionals (and, of course, non-professionals including patients) involved in the work, each group with different career tracks, goals and aspirations, training and values. Moreover, in this setting, there were also intra-professional differences in the form of the different psychiatric ideologies espoused by the individual members of the medical profession.

Strauss et al. therefore raised the question of how it was possible for this kind of complex division of labour to work at all, let alone more or less smoothly, most of the time, apparently able to adjust to the constant and inevitable changes that any complex organization has to face. Key to their answer was the view that studying the formal institutional rules of the hospitals alone was insufficient to explain how social order was possible. They argued that, within the hospitals they studied, the 'area of action governed by clearly enunciated rules [was] really very small' and administrators actively sought to keep the numbers of rules small (ibid.: 153). Moreover, most of the rules that did exist were tacit and implicit and, as it appeared to the researchers, could, in many cases, be stretched, ignored or breached in the course of work, with apparent impunity. For example, particularly in the large state psychiatric hospital that they studied, unqualified aides sought to control their conditions of work by withholding important information from professional staff. Nurses frequently undertook duties that were officially doctors' responsibility, without checking with doctors first, and without incurring sanctions or medical wrath when their doing so was apparent to others (Strauss et al., 1964).

This conception of social order as relatively fluid, and as constituted through social interaction, reflects Strauss et al.'s general symbolic interactionist approach to sociology. They were being explicitly critical of the then conventional emphasis in organizational sociology on organizations as stable, formally organized bureaucracies in which rule-following was the norm. In contrast, they argued that a hospital is a place where 'numerous agreements are continually being terminated or forgotten, but also as continually being established, renewed, reviewed, revoked, revised'. Social order is continually reconstituted through a complex relationship between a daily negotiative process and a periodic appraisal process (Strauss et al. 1963: 164–5). In their original formulation, Strauss et al. did explicitly point out that this did not mean that formal structures were irrelevant or that all aspects of activity were negotiable, as has sometimes been suggested by critics. Strauss et al. noted, for example, that, 'there is a patterned variability of negotiation in the hospital pertaining to who contracts with whom, about what, as well as when these agreements are made. Influencing this variability are hierarchical position and ideological commitments, as well as periodicities in the structure of ward relationships' (ibid.: 162–3). For example, the mobility of young doctors through the hospital, or the short visits to wards by specialists, was one reason why experienced nurses were, in practice, taking decisions that were beyond their formal responsibility. The absence of regular staff from a ward because of holidays might lead to suspension of normal negotiated ways of working and tacit understandings while new negotiations with temporary staff took place. In his later work, Strauss was even more emphatic about the need to consider the relationship between negotiation processes and extra-situational constraints (Allen, 1997; Strauss, 1978)

This model of social order as a negotiated one directed sociological attention, when studying hospitals, to the interplay of professionals and non-professionals, and to transactions among and between echelons, at the point at which multiple careers intersect. Strauss et al. suggested that the negotiated order model was not just relevant to hospitals or even to health care. Rather, it was proposed as a general model likely to be relevant in any organization marked by one or more of the following characteristics: the utilization of personnel trained in several different occupations; the presence of a key occupational group containing individuals trained in different traditions and with different occupational philosophies and values; and at least some professional personnel who are likely to be pursuing careers that carry them into and out of the organization.

Reflecting a general decline of interest in formal organizations in medical sociology, Strauss's suggestions about the general applicability of his model in analyzing organizations and their characteristics have not been explored very systematically by medical sociologists. However, the concept of negotiated order itself has been very influential since the 1960s, mainly through stimulating studies of interaction between professionals, or between professional and patients within work settings. In particular, the concept of negotiated order has been deployed in many studies of nurse–doctor interactions. In accordance with Strauss et al's original work, these interactions have been regularly identified as ones in which formally defined hierarchies and organizational rules, that is, that nurses follow doctors' orders, are not always strictly adhered to, although, in public, the etiquette of nurses deferring to doctors may be maintained (Hughes, 1988). Another feature of nurse–doctor interactions that makes Strauss's ideas relevant is the different temporal structure of the two kinds of work. In hospitals, nurses are on their wards for long periods, while doctors are generally intermittent visitors.

There are two main reasons why sociologists have been particularly interested in nurse–doctor relationships and how they may be changing in recent years. One is the changing expectations and behaviour of women in society generally, which may have affected how nurses (usually female) interact with their medical colleagues (who are also increasingly likely to be female (Svensson, 1996)). The second reason is policy development, specifically the moves to extend nursing duties to incorporate many tasks that were once officially the monopoly of doctors. In this situation of change, one might have expected negotiations about new divisions of labour to be readily apparent. However, Allen (1997) argues, on the basis of her observational study of nurse–doctor relationships on hospital wards, that, although tacitly accepted boundary blurring was widespread, it was very rarely the subject of explicit face-to-face negotiation. In interviews, there was uncertainty and disagreement about the proper division of labour, but on the wards this was not apparent. In the face of organizational pressures and staff shortages, tacit understandings and making situational judgements were much more significant in getting the work done than any overt negotiation. As she notes, the term 'negotiation' has often been used somewhat ambiguously and imprecisely in the sociological literature. Strauss et al. clearly did not see only explicit talking about work arrangements as constituting the interactions through which social order is 'negotiated'. In a formulation that accords with Strauss et al.'s original account, Allen proposes that explicit negotiation is only 'one of a number of possible processes through which social reality is routinely constituted' (1997: 515). Strauss (1993) himself went on to suggest that 'processual ordering' might be a better term, connoting the action involved, without necessarily implying that overt and explicit negotiation always occurs. His interest in the 'social worlds' that are created when different professionals work together, and which help order the ways in which they work together, was maintained.

What is central, therefore, to the approach to understanding organizational processes that is associated with the concept of negotiated order, is this view of social order within organizations as the product of social interaction rather than of bureaucratic rules and external constraints alone. However, it is not to be interpreted as implying that power and extra-situational factors and formal structures are irrelevant. To understand how, for example, the current increasing demands for formal accountability in the health care workplace are being interpreted and implemented, the interplay between interaction and formal structure needs to be studied.

See also: *hospitals and health care organizations* and *medical autonomy and medical dominance.*

REFERENCES

Allen, D. (1997) 'The nursing-medical boundary: a negotiated order', *Sociology of Health and Illness*, 19 (4): 498–520.
Hughes, D. (1988) 'When nurse knows best: some aspects of nurse-doctor interaction in a casualty department', *Sociology of Health and Illness*, 10 (1) 1–22.
Strauss, A. (1978) *Negotiations, Varieties, Contexts, Processes and Social Order*. London: Jossey-Bass.
Strauss, A. (1993) *Continual Permutations of Action*. New York: Aldine Gruyter.
Strauss, A., Schatzman, L., Bucher, R., Ehrlich, D. and Sabshin, M. (1964) *Psychiatric Ideologies and Institutions*. New York: Free Press.
Strauss, A., Schatzman, L., Ehrlich, D., Bucher, R. and Sabshin, M. (1963) 'The hospital and its negotiated order,' in E. Freidson (ed.), *The Hospital in Modern Society*. New York: Free Press, pp. 147–69.
Svensson, R. (1996) 'The interplay between doctors and nurses – a negotiated order approach', *Sociology of Health and Illness*, 18 (4): 379–98.

MAE

emotional labour

> **Definition:** *Emotional labour is the induction or suppression of feeling in individuals working in organizations, in order to sustain an outward appearance that produces an emotion in others; feelings therefore become a commodity.*

Hochschild (1983) popularized the concept of emotional labour, which is sold for a wage, and which she distinguishes from emotion work, which is undertaken in the private sphere. This entry briefly outlines the concept, which in medical sociology has been used particularly in relation to nursing; a gendered occupation, which is currently exploring the sometimes uneasy relationship between nursing skills and 'innate' female qualities.

Emotion is a relatively new substantive topic within sociology; theorists differ in the extent to which they consider that emotions are entirely socio-cultural products, or invariant responses to stimuli. It is only recently that the study of emotions has become part of research on culture and organizations (Putnam and Mumby, 1993), either because emotion has been seen as purely a physiological state and therefore not suitable for sociological study, or because organizations have been conceptualized as rational and instrumental, with no place for emotions. Putnam and Mumby argue that in organizations emotions are consistently devalued and marginalized; furthermore, rationality evokes a positive, masculine image whereas emotionality is seen as negative and feminine. Like many other writers on the subject, they take a feminist stance in arguing for the rehabilitation and revaluing of a previously devalued aspect of social life.

Elias, in his widely cited work on the civilizing process, argued that the display of feelings has become muted and that, increasingly, there are constraints upon what can be done in public. People should present themselves both as acceptable bodies and therefore as acceptable persons. However, it should be noted that Elias's argument was originally developed in the 1930s, and the actual data on which it is based are from a historical period ending in the eighteenth century. More recently, it has been proposed that the greater informality that developed during the twentieth century has increased demands upon our emotional management, as there are less ready-made scripts available and we need to create our own. Conversely, it could be argued that a greater exposure to the discussion of relationships and feelings on television and elsewhere gives people a wider repertoire of feeling rules, in that a greater number of personal situations are experienced vicariously. It is claimed that we are also controlled to a greater extent through our feelings and less through our externally observable behaviour. In Michel Foucault's terms, this could be seen as the growth of the panopticon, in which the need for external control is reduced because we monitor ourselves.

Another antecedent to the literature on emotional labour is Goffman, who argued that social interaction can be seen in terms of a performance (dramaturgy) with onstage and backstage areas. In the health field, a key concept that overlaps with that of emotional labour is Strauss et al.'s concept of sentimental work, which they contrast to instrumental work and define as 'an ingredient in any kind of work where the object being worked on is alive, sentient, reacting' (1982: 254). The roots of the concept of sentimental work go back to earlier research on nurses' strategies for maintaining composure in the face of difficult deaths.

Duncombe and Marsden (1993) explore the gendered division of labour, in which women do much of the domestic emotion work. They argue that further empirical research will be needed to map how emotional behaviour changes when individuals move between home and work, and how emotional behaviour corresponds to work and domestic activities, since there is a danger of a rigid Parsonian functionalism being reinvented, in which men are seen as having an instrumental function and women an expressive one. It should also not be assumed that emotional work in the home is either more 'natural' or potentially less stressful than paid emotional labour in the workplace.

Hochschild has published on the concepts of emotion work and feeling rules since the late 1970s. In *The Managed Heart*, her study of American flight attendants, Hochschild (1983) draws on Goffman and Marx to argue that in the United States the growth of service industries has largely replaced physical labour. In the latter, the worker's feelings towards the product of his or her labour are immaterial; in the former, they are a key feature. She considers that jobs that involve emotional labour have three characteristics. First, they involve face-to-face contact with the public. Second, they require the worker to produce an emotional state in the other (which may not necessarily be positive; debt collectors, for example, may be required to induce a sense of menace). And, third, the employer exerts a degree of control over the emotional activity of the employee, through training and supervision. Employees rarely question feeling rules.

193

Emotional labour, which is sold for a wage, is similar to the emotion work that is done in private settings such as the family and also reproduces gender stereotypes (including the stereotype of male flight attendants and male nurses as gay). In establishing a theory of emotions, Hochschild argues that social life is largely regulated by ideologies of feeling, guided by what she terms 'feeling rules', or scripts; emotional labour shapes our actions when there is a gap between what we feel and the script and enables us to bridge that gap. Hochschild suggests that there are two kinds of emotional labour: surface and deep acting. In the former, only the outward expression changes; in the latter, feelings are changed from the inside, using techniques such as imaging and verbal prompting, in a process that has been compared to method acting. It is debatable how damaging this is, in creating alienation from the self.

Wouters (1989) considers (among other criticisms) that Hochschild wrongly excludes 'the true professions' from her analysis because they supervise their own emotional labour; under this term are included doctors, lawyers, social workers, salespeople and people working for the media. Several of the occupations in this very mixed category have in fact been studied by other researchers. Putnam and Mumby (1993) review studies on emotional labour in debt collection, police detection, Disney employees, secretaries and medical social workers. Other research has included clergy officiating at funerals. A search of CINAHL, the database of research in nursing and other health professions, found several studies on emotional labour related to nursing; interestingly, a parallel search of Medline found no studies related to medicine.

Hochschild's work was applied to nursing by Smith (1992), who equates emotional labour with the concept of care, in her widely quoted observational study of how learner nurses are socialized into nursing. Caring, Smith found, did not come naturally. 'Nurses have to work emotionally on themselves in order to appear to care, irrespective of how they personally feel about themselves, individual patients, their conditions and circumstances' (1992: 136). She goes on to argue that care, which is currently ill-defined, should be recognized and valued, supported educationally and organizationally. Currently, she states, nurse leaders exhort nurses to care, but do not take into account its emotional complexity, the gendered division of labour, nor power relations between doctors and nurses.

James (1992), in her observational study of hospice care, argues that 'care = organisation + physical labour + emotional labour'. She compares domestic care-work with the work of hospice nurses. Family care has been a model for hospice care, but its implementation in a hospice setting is constrained by the hospital-based division of labour, such as the sheer number of staff needed to provide 24-hour care. Although Hochschild keeps emotional work (in the private sphere) and emotional labour (paid for, in the public sphere) separate, in a setting like a hospice they are blurred, since home-based care is felt to be the preferred model for the care of dying people. As in physical labour, the practitioners who are most closely involved with patients in undertaking emotional labour are of low status and are seen as unskilled or semi-skilled. Emotional labour remains largely informal and grafted on to the dominant biomedical system.

James argues that emotional labour is likely to be increasingly recognized as part of health care, but that the concept of 'total care', which was used in the hospice, needs to be questioned, since it may be unduly intrusive and may also set unattainable goals for staff. She considers that 'the real challenge is not just to recognize emotional labour and its significance as a component of care, but to build upon the emotional labour which is already part of our health care system without destroying or "commercialising" the social fabric upon which it depends' (James, 1992: 504).

Within the literature, there seem to be varying opinions (or ambiguity) as to whether emotional labour is heavily constrained by scripts, or requires spontaneity, flexibility and space. The degree of constraint over emotional labour may depend on the setting. For example, in the hospice, there is contact between patients and nursing staff (particularly the auxiliary nurses) over a period of time, a physical intimacy and also an unpredictability, which is lacking in activities such as airline travel. Caring for dying patients also raises emotional issues that would be rarely, if ever, encountered in other organizational settings and nurses may distance themselves for self-protection. It is notable that several of the studies of emotional labour in nursing are of settings involving death and dying, for example, James's study and also much of Smith's material. An illuminating comparison would be with the emotional labour of nursing in settings that lend themselves more to 'McDonaldization', such as outpatient clinics. Further purchase on the concept of emotional labour could also be gained by considering the changes in the settings where it has been studied, for example, the growth of air rage in the airline industry and of racism or violence by patients in the National Health Service.

There is also a need to differentiate more (as Hochschild does not) between commercial and public settings, although the growth of market ideologies in the British public sector may be blurring this distinction. Several authors have argued that care is being squeezed out as the disciplines of the market have invaded the public sector both in nursing and in care management. Emotional labour takes time and is not easily quantified; it is therefore often delegated to less highly trained (and cheaper) staff. Valuing 'feminine' skills such as caring may be a risky occupational strategy if technical skills thereby become submerged. Nevertheless, several of the nursing writers on emotional labour argue that caring, which they equate with emotional labour, is the central task of the nurse, is vital to the patient's well-being and should be valued and remunerated. Thus, emotional labour has moved from being solely an analytical device to being almost a slogan, part of the caring discourse which nursing uses to establish its separate identity from medicine.

See also: *dying trajectories* and *informal care.*

REFERENCES

Duncombe, J. and Marsden, D. (1993) 'Love and intimacy: the gender division of emotion and "emotion work"', *Sociology*, 27 (2): 221–41.

Hochschild, A.R. (1983) *The Managed Heart: Commercialization of Human Feeling.* Berkeley, CA: University of California Press.

James, V. (1992) 'Care = organisation + physical labour + emotional labour', *Sociology of Health and Illness*, 14 (4): 488–509.

Putnam, L.L. and Mumby, D.K. (1993) 'Organizations, emotion and the myth of rationality', in S. Fineman (ed.), *Emotion in Organizations*. London: Sage.

Smith, P. (1992) *The Emotional Labour of Nursing*. London: Macmillan.

Strauss, A., Fagerhaugh, S., Suzcek, B. and Wiener, C. (1982) 'Sentimental work in the technologized hospital', *Sociology of Health and Illness*, 4 (3): 254–78.

Wouters, C. (1989) 'The sociology of emotions and flight attendants: Hochschild's *Managed Heart*', *Theory, Culture and Society*, 6 (1): 95–123.

LM

196

informal care

Definition: *Informal care refers to unpaid care, both affective and instrumental, provided in the domestic or private arena, often by women and often for family members.*

The term informal care emerged from empirical work on community and institutional care in the 1960s. The following discussion outlines the evolution of the term and provides a basis for considering its present use(s). The term tends to be used more as an empirical category than a theoretical concept (Thomas, 1993). The sub-categories defined in much of the research on informal care include the type of care being provided (task-oriented and/or affective), the relationship of the person providing the care to the care recipient and the amount of care being provided. The informal carer is often fulfilling several roles. These include care provider, companion to the care recipient and advocate for the care recipient in the care decision-making arena. A methodological point, related to the different roles played by informal carers, is that a clear distinction should be made between the informal carer participating in research in their own right and the informal carer acting as a proxy for the dependent person (who is either too sick to be directly involved or who is dead). As an empirical category informal care is therefore prone to definitional difficulties. What is often missing from conceptualizations of informal care is a sense of the process and development of that care over a period of time and recognition of the 'emotional work' involved in being an informal carer.

Theoretical issues underpin the different empirical uses of the term informal care and these are considered here, alongside empirical and policy approaches. The initial research on informal care took the form of a series of qualitative and small-scale quantitative studies. By the late 1970s and early 1980s the initial ideas coming from social policy and community care were developed by feminist writers. Pioneering work sought to conceptualize caring as an integral aspect of domestic labour. A key paper at that time, by Finch and Groves, elaborated what they called a 'double equation': 'That in practice community care equals care by the family and in practice care by the family equals care by women' (1980: 494). Related to the concern to recognize informal care as an integral part of domestic labour was the move to calculate the costs of informal care, as the costs associated with such care were not always acknowledged. Calculations tended to be based on the public costs of care giving. This approach to the economic evaluation of the care given in the community increased the tendency to marginalize and devalue the role of informal care. As a response to this perceived under-valuation there was an acknowledgement of the informal caring role and organizations representing informal carers were started.

In 1985 the General Household Survey (GHS), a national survey of living conditions in the United Kingdom, included a series of questions that identified people looking after a sick, handicapped or elderly person (Green, 1988). This survey quantified who was providing what type of care. At that time one adult in seven (14 per cent) was providing informal care and one in five households (20 per cent) contained a carer. The publication of these survey findings stimulated a reconsideration of the picture of informal carers as middle-aged women, either single or married, looking after elderly dependants. Attention was drawn to older women caring for elderly spouses and the role that male carers were playing (Arber and Ginn, 1990). However, the GHS methodology and subsequent findings were criticized. The GHS asked about 'extra family responsibilities'. This assumed that everyone knew what constituted 'normal' family responsibilities. It was thought that, as a consequence of difficulties in interpretation, there was under-reporting, by women, of tasks they felt to be part of 'normalcy' (Green, 1988). Also, the different types of care being provided and the demanding and skilled nature of some of that care were lost in a global picture.

The GHS did serve to highlight the amount of care being provided by the informal sector. With the majority of care being provided by this sector, the health beliefs that informal carers have and implement in their role have an impact on the care being provided. The picture of the nature and extent of informal care provided by the GHS findings illustrated the particular juxtaposition of the professional–lay divide in the United Kingdom. This constructed divide is based on monetary remuneration and issues of professionalism. Debates within the feminist social science literature began to change, moving from a position of potentially reinforcing a dependency to questioning the overall division of labour between the public and private sectors. It was argued by some commentators that the earlier work by feminists on informal care served to entrench women within the caring role, rather than question the overall division of formal and informal work. Arguing for a recognition of the labour of informal care and for due recompense for the work in some ways could be interpreted as maintaining the status quo rather than seeking to change the overall balance between formal and informal work.

Alongside the empirical findings of the GHS and the papers it generated from secondary analysis, qualitative research, based on the 'caring biography' was carried out. This type of research placed the caring role within the context of the person's wider life world. One of its foci was the motivation to provide informal care. There was a view, which had been articulated in community care policy, that informal care was a 'natural role', based on an innate sense of reciprocity. The implicit assumption was that it was a 'natural role' for women. This view was contested by Finch and Mason (1993) in their work on the negotiated nature of the 'care bargain'. The 'care bargain' was seen to be struck in the context of normative views on familial duty and care. Their research provided a more socially constructed approach to the motivation to provide, or not to provide, informal care. It reflected the changing nature of the family and the different types of interpersonal relationships in which informal care was being provided. The acknowledgement of the diversity of interpersonal relationships between the informal carer and the care recipient was highlighted through work on HIV and AIDS. The possibility of disenfranchisement of the informal carer from the care decision-making process predominated by professional carers is further increased if the informal carer is provided from outside the direct family.

The influences on patterns of informal care and its relationship with formal care come not just from the micro-context of the private domestic world, but also from the broader structural forces operating in different societies. An example of this is King and Chamberlayne's (1996) research which used Balbo's work on the modernization of domestic roles in welfare societies to compare the informal care provided in what was then East and West Germany. They found that in West Germany carers tended to be 'pulled' into the home, whereas in East Germany carers were 'propelled' out into the public arena. The literature discussed so far has focused on patterns of informal care that reflect the dominant cultural traditions within society. The divide between the public arena for care, where care is provided by formal carers and the private arena of care where care is provided by informal carers, is less rigidly maintained in other cultures. By the 1990s a much more complex account of caring was being presented which began to recognize different caring relationships, as well as issues of ethnicity, race and culture.

In conclusion, it can be seen that theoretically the concept of informal care raises issues concerned with the social division of labour within society (Thomas, 1993). As Stacey argued over 20 years ago:

> We lack a conceptual framework, let alone a theory with any explanatory power, which will permit us to analyse paid and unpaid labour in a variety of social institutions and social settings within one notion of the division of labour, which can encompass the domestic arena of Adam and Eve as well as the industry of Adam Smith, which can articulate the home as well as the market place and the state and relate the class order to the gender order. (1981: 172)

Without this theoretical framework in place, social policy and research on informal care continue to run the risk of being piecemeal.

See also: *emotional labour* and *social support.*

199

REFERENCES

Arber, S. and Ginn, J. (1990) 'The meaning of informal care: gender and the contribution of elderly people', *Ageing and Society*, 10 (4): 429–54.

Finch, J. and Groves, D. (1980) 'Community Care and the family: a case for equal opportunities', *Journal of Social Policy*, 9 (4): 487–514.

Finch. J. and Mason J, (1993) *Negotiating Family Responsibilities*. London: Routledge.

Green, H. (1988) *Informal Carers: A Study Carried Out on Behalf of the Department of Health and Social Security as Part of the 1985 General Household Survey*. London: HMSO.

King, A. and Chamberlayne, P. (1996) 'Comparing the informal sphere: public and private relations of welfare in East and West Germany', *Sociology*, 30 (4): 741–61.

Stacey, M. (1981) 'The division of labour revisited or overcoming the two Adams', in P. Abrams, R. Deem, J. Finch and P. Rock (eds), *Practice and Progress: British Sociology 1950–1980*. London: Allen and Unwin.

Thomas, C. (1993) 'De-constructing concepts of care', *Sociology*, 27 (4): 649–69.

LY

200

PART 5

Health Care Organization and Policy

— hospitals and health care organizations —

> **Definition:** *Organizations are typically large groupings of people, usually structured on bureaucratic or impersonal lines, established to achieve specific objectives. Individual hospitals and entire national systems of health service provision, where there are co-ordinating authority relationships, as, for example, in the British National Health Service, can both be regarded as health care organizations.*

Professional health care today is generally provided through formal organizations. A patient's visit to a doctor in her or his office may involve booking an appointment, retrieving, updating and refiling personal medical records, issuing bills or prescriptions that have to be processed by other organizations and other administrative activities; all expected to be conducted according to established organizational procedures. Modern health care professionals deliver care that is embedded in complex networks of other workers: for example, receptionists, clerical workers, cleaners, technicians, accountants and especially managers who are formally responsible for co-ordinating all these activities. Moreover, individual health care institutions and locales for care may themselves be linked in networks and wider organizational structures, for example, a state health system such as the NHS or a multinational commercial company running a chain of hospitals. Studies of patients' interactions with professionals, inter-professional relations, the introduction of new medical technologies, inequalities in access to care, the role of the state in health care and professional regulation are all, at least in part, studies of organizational processes and structures. So, in one sense, the sociological study of formal health care *is* the study of health care organization. However, the concept of organization itself has not been especially prominent within medical sociology for much of the past three decades (Davies, 2003), in marked contrast to the situation in the 1960s.

In the 1960s, the hospital as a social organization was a major topic of enquiry within medical sociology, as demonstrated in an important

203

collection edited by Freidson (1963). This interest was not surprising. At the time, the hospital was almost universally regarded as being the central location for health care, with primary and community care relatively neglected in policy and in sociological analysis. Moreover, hospitals appeared to be particularly interesting organizations from a sociological perspective. A key concept in organizational sociology at the time was bureaucracy, as developed from the work of the leading early twentieth-century sociologist, Max Weber. Weber argued that, in industrialized societies, bureaucracy had become the dominant mode of formal organization, because it embodied the type of authority accorded greatest legitimacy in such societies. Weber termed this type of authority 'rational-legal authority', that is, socially accepted power based on rules and regulations enacted by law or equivalent formal processes. According to Weber, a model bureaucracy (what he termed an 'ideal type') had a number of key features, for example, a hierarchy of positions, with specified functions, organized into a single control and disciplinary system. The occupants of positions were recruited and promoted on merit, worked full-time and were paid by salary.

The formal structure of hospitals, in most parts of the Western world in the 1960s, diverged from this bureaucratic model in significant ways. Although there were hierarchies of positions, notably for nursing and administrative staff, there was not a single authority line: recruitment, promotion and disciplinary structures generally being organized by professional groups within the hospital, or even by external bodies. Moreover, the dominant occupational group in hospitals, the senior doctors, were not clearly part of any ordered hierarchy, being autonomous rather than subject to managerial control. Furthermore, depending on the particular national health care system, these doctors were often not full-time employees of the hospital where they worked, being paid on fee-for-service rather than salary, or sometimes doing both private and salaried work. For sociologists of the early 1960s, then, hospitals were, organizations characterized by formal structures, which gave rise to great scope for professional–bureaucratic conflict. A recurrent policy preoccupation in most health systems was, and still is, the incorporation of medical activity and its regulation into organizational frameworks and authority structures.

It has sometimes been claimed that one source of professional–bureaucratic conflict is a tension between professionals' goals which are concerned with individual patients' welfare and bureaucratic concerns with institutional efficiency and order. More generally, Goffman (1961) suggested that a tension between institutional efficiency and humane standards was endemic to people-processing organizations, particularly to those which he termed 'total institutions': that is, large, impersonal facilities in which individuals spent long periods of time as, sometimes involuntary, residents, for example, prisons and homes for those with physical or mental impairment. In *Asylums*, a now classic book based on research in a large American psychiatric asylum, Goffman presented a graphic picture of such organizations as ones where residents are stripped of their previous social identities on entry They are then subjected to institutional regulation of all aspects of their lives, or to attempted regulation, in that Goffman simultaneously described the active resistance of residents in the 'underlife' of the institution.

During the 1960s, Goffman's negative depiction of total institutions was one component in a developing critique, informed by social research, of large, long-stay psychiatric asylums as causing rather than curing mental illness. This critique of institutionalization helped bring about a marked shift, in most developed countries, towards community-based care for those with long-term dependency needs. And the gradual disappearance of one organizational form, in turn, was probably one factor in a shift of medical sociology's interest away from studying institutions and organizations as such after the 1960s. Although the emerging, geographically dispersed community care services also constituted organizations, they were not usually analysed as such by medical sociologists. Perhaps one reason for this was that at the time, 'organization' was considered as virtually synonymous with 'hospital' or, at least, with fixed, bounded locations of health care.

A further factor in medical sociology's declining interest, by the 1970s, in hospitals as organizations was the growing influence of symbolic interactionist ideas, as expressed in the seminal paper on negotiated order by Strauss and colleagues in Freidson's (1963) edited collection. Rather than regard hospitals as stable, albeit complicated, bureaucracies, in which actions were predictable and governed by formal rules, sociologists such as Bucher and Stelling (1969) argued that organizational forms and structures should be regarded as relatively fluid and the outcome of informal negotiation and bargaining. Although it is clear, especially with hindsight, that these arguments did not imply that there were no organizational constraints, or that formal rules and structures were irrelevant to those who worked in health care organizations, what they led to was a re-orientation of many medical sociologists' interest. Studies of health care provision were dominated by micro-sociological investigation of specific interactions between providers and users of care, or between different groups of professionals. Specific health care organizations came to be seen more as the 'backdrop' to these interactions rather than occupying centre stage (Davies, 2003). And, while medical sociology's interest in professions continued unabated through the 1970s and 1980s, interest in bureaucrats (in the form of health service managers) diminished somewhat.

In these two decades, there was considerable interest within medical sociology in the macro- or societal level of health care organization. Such work focused on the broad features of national (or international) systems of health care, and associated policy-making and regulatory institutions and their activities, generally relating these to wider social and cultural social processes and structural features of society. Much of this work was informed by theoretical concepts derived from Marxism: focusing, for example, on class conflict as a determinant of welfare regimes, or the changing role of the state in securing capitalist accumulation. Not surprisingly, studies of national health care systems and health care organization at the societal level have been particularly well developed in the United Kingdom and those European countries with relatively integrated, state-organized national health care systems, such as the UK's NHS. A major preoccupation of macro-level research on health care organization from the 1980s has been the changes to such systems, as captured by concepts such as privatization and consumerism.

However, because of its focus on official policies and government policy-making, and an inevitable reliance on official documents and public statements, this kind of macro-level analysis cannot show how policies are implemented in practice and what fate befalls government-initiated reforms within the local organizations that actually deliver health care. For this, what is required are sociological studies at the *meso* or mid-level, focusing on 'the intermediate layer where policy and organizational and managerial processes tend to be concentrated' (Hunter, 1990: 215) and micro-level studies of management as well as clinical activities. Yet, as Hunter and others noted, it was at this level that medical sociology was relatively inactive, leaving meso-level organizational research in health care mainly to the fields of health policy and organization theory.

However, where medical sociologists have undertaken research at the meso level of health care organization or undertaken micro level studies of organizational processes, what has been consistently shown is that, whatever the formal lines of authority and accountability, what happens at the local or peripheral level is not determined by central diktat. Through local interpretation, negotiation and bargaining, and the influence of local circumstances and history, the official goals of central government or corporate headquarters may be transformed in practice.

For example, this was shown in Strong and Robinson's (1990) ethnographic study of the implementation of major management reforms in the NHS in the 1980s in local health settings.

However, given the major changes in modes of health care delivery and the organization of care taking place in most Western countries, it is not surprising that medical sociology's interest in health care organization is reviving and the value of meso- and micro-level studies of organization and organizational processes is increasingly recognized. Developments within organization theory, such as the increasing attention to gender as an integral part of organizational life and moves to regard organizations as not necessarily defined by 'bricks and mortar' but as possibly highly permeable institutions and distributed networks, have been taken up by sociologists studying health care organization in the early twenty-first century. The rise of managerialism, particularly in public sector health care, has revived social science interest in the relationship between professionals and managers and in professionals who are also, increasingly, managers.

The health care organizations now emerging look very different in many respects from the hospitals studied by medical sociologists in the 1960s (Davies, 2003). There are new forms of service based on new digital technologies, with telemedicine linking participants separated by hundreds of miles. The individual hospital's centrality in health care is no longer so indisputable (Armstrong, 1998). The drive towards primary care-led services, the development of managed care systems and integrated services around the patients' pathway through care, are all trends which may further erode the boundaries between hospitals and other loci of care, and between public and private sectors of care. Inter-professional boundaries are being challenged or redrawn in clinical activity and in education. Professional autonomy and self-regulation are subject to greater external scrutiny. All these developments require managing and are giving rise to new organizational structures and processes. In the context of these, organization looks set to re-emerge as a key concept within medical sociology.

See also: *negotiated order, privatization* and *managerialism.*

REFERENCES

Armstrong, D. (1998) 'Decline of the hospital: reconstructing institutional dangers', *Sociology of Health and Illness*, 20 (4): 445–57.

Bucher, R. and Stelling, J. (1969) 'Characteristics of professional organisations', *Journal of Health and Social Behaviour*, 10: 2–13.

Davies, C. (2003) 'Some of our concepts are missing: reflections on the absence of a sociology of organisations', *Sociology of Health and Illness*, 25 (Silver Anniversary Issue): 172–190.

Freidson, E. (ed.) (1963) *The Hospital in Modern Society*. New York: Free Press.

Goffman, E. (1961) *Asylums*. Harmondsworth: Penguin Books.

Hunter, D. (1990) 'Organizing and managing health care: a challenge for medical sociology', in S. Cunningham-Burley and N.P. McKeganey (eds), *Readings in Medical Sociology*. London: Routledge, pp. 213–36.

Strong, P. and Robinson, J. (1990) *The NHS – Under New Management*. Buckingham: Open University Press.

MAE

privatization

> **Definition: Privatization refers to a set of policies that aim to limit the role of public sector health care, increase the role of the private sector, while improving the performance of the remaining public sector.**

The health service in Britain, like those of other developed countries, has long been pluralist in the sense that publicly funded (through taxation) and privately funded (through payment for a service in person or by private health insurance) health care has co-existed. However, the health care reforms of the 1980s and 1990s have shifted the balance profoundly in favour of greater private sector involvement. In this entry the strategies employed to achieve this and the reasons for doing so are considered, with particular reference to the private acute sector. The consequences of such restructuring for the National Health Service (NHS) and the principles on which it was founded will also be discussed.

One strategy for shifting the balance between the public and private sector has involved the development of policies to encourage the growth of the private sector. In the 1980s planning controls were relaxed on the development of private hospitals and the power of local authorities to object to such developments was curtailed. In addition, NHS consultants' contracts were revised to enable them to undertake more private practice in addition to their NHS commitments and tax changes were introduced to encourage higher levels of private health cover. Together these changes created the climate for private hospital development and provided opportunities that were fully exploited by the private sector. Between 1979 and 1989 the number of private hospitals increased by 30 per cent and the number of private beds by 58 per cent. At the same time the level of private health insurance increased from 5 per cent of the population in 1979 to a peak of 13 per cent in 1989, with company-purchased schemes being particularly popular (Calnan et al., 1993). Currently around 11 per cent of the population are covered by private health insurance (Humphrey and Russell, 2001), with coverage concentrated in London and the South-east of England. Unsurprisingly, those with policies tend to have professional and managerial jobs and to be male, though roughly equal numbers of both sexes are actually covered (Calnan, 2000).

A further strategy to shift the balance between the public and private sectors has involved the introduction of reforms that have facilitated greater collaboration between the two sectors. An early attempt was the Conservative government's policy of requiring NHS District Health Authorities to introduce competitive tendering for domestic, catering and laundry services in 1983. The intention was to challenge the monopoly of in-house providers of services on the assumption that costs would be reduced and greater 'value for money' would be achieved. In the event the financial benefits proved relatively modest, at least to start with, and the savings achieved were said to be at the expense of quality of service (Mohan, 1995). More recently, the NHS has been encouraged to contract out patient care to the private sector. These co-operative arrangements were initially undertaken on a voluntary basis by individual Health Authorities (HAs) that did not have in-house alternatives, for example, as a result of capacity constraints. Subsequently, HAs were directed by the Conservative government to use private hospitals as a way of reducing NHS waiting lists for non-urgent cases and those waiting more than a year. This policy has since been endorsed by the current Labour government who instituted a 'concordat' between the NHS and the private sector in 2000, following the publication of the NHS Plan earlier in that year to revitalize the health care system and raise it to wider, European Union standards. The concordat allows patients to be treated at NHS expense in the private sector when there is no spare room in NHS hospitals. The existing patchy arrangements between the sectors have thus been formalized, allowing NHS managers to plan ahead more effectively to reduce waiting lists.

Another example of collaboration has been the development of the Private Finance Initiative (PFI). The Conservatives launched this initiative in 1992 with the aim of encouraging private capital investment in the

NHS, especially with regard to the development of acute hospitals. Under PFI private companies design, construct, own and operate services over a period of 25–30 years, in return for an annual fee. From 1994 all planned capital development has had to be appraised as to its viability for PFI. The intention of the policy is to increase overall resources in the NHS while avoiding raising taxes or increasing public borrowing. It is also seen as a vehicle for bringing private sector skills into the NHS, as private sector managerial and commercial skills are employed to secure 'value for money'. Despite regular attacks on the PFI before its election victory in 1997, because of the economic risks and privatizing potential of the approach (Iliffe and Munro, 2000), New Labour has since embraced the policy enthusiastically on pragmatic rather than ideological grounds. While clinical services remain the responsibility of government, PFI is seen as permitting an element of risk to be transferred to the private sector, as building cost overruns are picked up by the private sector. Arguably it is a win-win situation as the NHS gets improved services while the private sector gets further opportunities to make a profit. Critics argue, however, that there are serious disadvantages associated with PFI-funded projects including reduced bed numbers (substantially in excess of what would be expected from long-term demand trends), the need for a quicker throughput of patients, a significant reduction in spending on clinical staff, especially nurses, and higher interest rate charges compared to the cost of government borrowing, thereby putting a severe strain on hospital Trust budgets (Mohan, 2002).

The third strategy has been to encourage competition between the NHS and the private sector. This is best illustrated by the Conservative government's willingness to encourage the NHS to expand its pay-bed provision, thereby sharpening competition for private patients and threatening the private providers' profit margins. Originally introduced when the NHS was established in 1948 as a concession to hospital consultants, pay-beds were in decline when the Conservatives came to power in 1979 and they continued to decline subsequently. In the late 1980s, however, the Conservatives decided to revitalize this provision in the face of increasingly severe financial constraints. The policy was also in line with their belief in generating competition between providers in order to enhance consumer choice and maximize efficiency. In 1988 it therefore used the Health and Medicines Act to relax the rules governing pay-bed charges so that hospitals could make a profit instead of simply covering costs. This propelled hospitals to upgrade their private wings or develop dedicated pay-bed units, as well as increasing the number of pay-beds on NHS wards. As a result, pay-bed income increased dramatically from just over £32 million in 1991–92 to £116 million two years later in 1993–94. The NHS now has 20 per cent of the private market and is an important provider of private health care in the UK.

These three strategies illustrate the shift to a new public–private mix of services, a mixed economy of health care. The policy has been driven in part by ideological considerations, especially those of the New Right with its emphasis on individuals exercising choice in the market. Economic and political considerations have also been important – especially the need to maximize efficiency and get value for money from existing tax revenues and the importance of being seen to act to reduce waiting lists. For New Labour these imperatives have led to the adoption of a pragmatic approach to health policy, in line with 'third way' thinking more generally, and a willingness to embrace those Conservative policies that have been deemed successful, such as PFI.

The British government may also have been encouraged to move towards a mixed economy of health care by segments of the medical profession and by some users of health care. Certain members of the medical profession have stood to gain financially from the expansion of the private sector, as a result of an increase in fees for private medical practice, paid out by insurance companies, and from ownership of new private hospitals. An increase in 'consumer' demand for private health care could be said to explain the growth in private health insurance in the 1980s although, as noted earlier, this increase was primarily a result of the expansion of company-paid schemes rather than individual-paid schemes. There is also evidence of growing dissatisfaction with the NHS in social attitude surveys, which might have encouraged a greater willingness to use private health care. Other evidence, however, suggests that there is still strong loyalty to the NHS, even among those who have private health insurance (Calnan et al., 1993), and that this loyalty has acted as a brake on those politicians who might otherwise have favoured a greater shift towards private health care on ideological grounds.

Whatever the reasons for the development of the public–private mix, it can be argued that the shift towards a greater role for private medicine has undermined the egalitarian principles associated with the founding of the NHS and created a two-tier system. It is certainly the case that those with private health insurance can 'jump the queue' for elective surgery and that these people tend to be better off. However, there is little evidence to suggest that the quality of care provided in the private sector is superior to that offered by the NHS. While private care might be more comfortable and convenient, the levels of medical and technical care are similar. More significant, perhaps, is the impact of the introduction of commercial imperatives in the NHS and the increasing emphasis on health care as a commodity and patients as consumers. This cultural change is arguably as transformative as any of the other alterations to the public–private mix and supports the claim that the NHS is being privatized from within.

See also: *managerialism* and *consumerism.*

REFERENCES

Calnan, M. (2000) 'The NHS and private health care', *Health Matrix* 10 (3): 3–19.

Calnan, M., Cant. S. and Gabe, J. (1993) *Going Private: Why People Pay for their Health Care*. Buckingham: Open University Press.

Humphrey, C. and Russell, J. (2001) 'Private medicine', in T. Heller et al. (eds), *Working for Health*. London: The Open University in association with Sage Publications.

Iliffe, S. and Munro, J. (2000) 'New Labour and Britain's National Health Service: an overview of current reforms', *International Journal of Health Services*, 30 (2): 309–34.

Mohan, J. (1995) *A National Health Service? The Restructuring of Health Care in Britain since 1979*. Basingstoke: Macmillan.

Mohan, J. (2002) *Planning, Markets and Hospitals*. London: Routledge.

JGA

managerialism

Definition: **Managerialism refers to an ideology that reframes healthcare using managerial symbols and language and encourages health care professionals to accept managerialist thinking.**

Since the 1970s many countries have recognized that they need to contain health care costs, improve performance and outcomes and make their services more user-sensitive and have turned to management as the solution (Hunter, 1996). In place of an administrative approach where managers 'oiled the wheels' in consultation with other health care workers, an industrial model of management has been introduced, regardless of its relevance or appropriateness for public services like health care. The emphasis now is on managers taking control, setting performance targets and imposing budgetary and workload ceilings. This approach has set managers on a collision course with other health care professionals such as doctors because of these professionals' claim to autonomy. In this entry the development of what has been called 'New Public Management' (NPM) in Britain is briefly described and the implications for social relations in health care and, in particular, for relations between managers and doctors, are considered.

It is possible to see the development of NPM in Britain as involving two elements: challenging professionals in the health service and incorporating them (Harrison and Pollitt, 1994). Each will be considered in turn. Challenging health service professionals involves subordinating professional autonomy to managerial will, an approach first adopted in 1983 with the introduction of general managers into the National Health Service (NHS) as recommended in the Griffiths Report. Prior to this report NHS managers, or as they were then called, administrators, acted as diplomats, helping to organize the facilities and resources for professionals to get on with their work and reacting to problems as they arose. Decisions were made consensually by multi-disciplinary teams that included doctors and nurses, as well as administrators. The Griffiths Report recommended altering the organizational culture of the service by introducing features of business management, along the lines suggested particularly by US management theorists (Ranade, 1994). General managers were to be appointed at each level of the service, in place of consensus teams, to take responsibility for shaping the NHS and control its direction. These new managers would take responsibility for developing management plans, ensure quality of care, achieve cost improvements and monitor and reward staff. At the same time managers would be paid by performance as a spur to good management, as happened in the private sector.

These proposals, which were accepted wholesale by the Conservative government of the time, were designed to alter the balance of power in favour of managers at the expense of other professionals, especially doctors. Before the Griffiths Report, doctors' clinical freedom to make decisions about patients regardless of cost had been seen as a major determinant of the level of expenditure. In the new system doctors were to be more accountable to managers, who had strict control over professional and labour costs through a system of management budgets that related workload objectives to the resources available. In practice, general managers were unable to challenge the medical domain, let alone make significant inroads into it. While they now found it easier to close hospital beds and make other changes to the service without long periods of consultation, in every other respect they were no more able to control doctors than their predecessors (Harrison and Pollitt, 1994). Consequently, doctors continued to exercise considerable autonomy and managers continued to lack real control over medical work.

In 1989 the Conservative government published a White Paper, *Working for Patients*, subsequently enacted through the 1990 NHS and Community Care Act, which attempted, among other things, to shift the balance of power more forcefully in the direction of managers. The White Paper recommended that managers should have greater involvement in the specification and policing of consultants' contracts, discussing consultants' job description with them on a yearly basis and helping to determine the merit awards which are awarded to some consultants to supplement their salaries.

At the same time a plethora of new techniques of managerial evaluation were developed. Quality assurance and performance indicators, made possible by advances in information technology, increased opportunities for the managerial determination of work content, productivity, resource use and quality standards (Flynn, 1992). Moreover, under New Labour, the introduction of 'clinical governance' as a mechanism to control the health professions, especially doctors, gave managers further powers to challenge clinical autonomy. Chief Executives of hospitals now became responsible for clinical as well as financial performance. From 1999, Chief Executives were expected to make sure that their clinicians were restricting themselves to treatments recommended on grounds of clinical and cost effectiveness by the National Institute for Clinical Evidence (NICE), and were complying with service guidelines for specified conditions under the National Service Frameworks (NSF). Furthermore, managers were also required to provide evidence to demonstrate that doctors in their Trusts were complying with these guidelines for the rolling programme of inspections to be conducted by the Commission for Health Improvement (Harrison and Ahmad, 2000) and its successor (the Commission for Healthcare Audit and Inspection).

These developments would seem to have given managers the opportunity to constrain British doctors as never before, along the lines identified by the proletarianization thesis. Advocates of this position argue that doctors are being deskilled, are losing their economic independence and are being required to work in bureaucratically organized institutions under the instruction of managers, in accordance with the requirements of advanced capitalism (McKinlay and Arches, 1985). However, as Freidson (1989) indicates, the widespread adoption of new techniques for monitoring the efficiency of performance and resource allocation does not, on its own, illustrate reduced professional autonomy. What really matters is whose criteria for evaluation and appraisal are adopted and who controls which actions are taken.

The more oblique approach to the management control of professionals involves the incorporation of professionals into management activity on managers' terms. This approach pre-dated the White Paper, *Working for Patients*, but was significantly enhanced by it. For example, under the Griffiths Report doctors were encouraged to become general managers and a few experiments were set up involving the delegation of budgetary responsibility to doctors. At the same time most doctors were reluctant to become managers and continued to exercise considerable autonomy. Following the 1989 White Paper, however, doctors were required to be involved in management at every level. They were forced to become part-time managers, integrated into the management structure, and could no longer ignore it. Thus doctors became part-time clinical directors who, while retaining their professional identity, became subordinate to managers and were expected to 'manage', using their position to control their medical colleagues. Although sometimes reluctant to take the role initially they generally came to see it subsequently as a way of retaining control over the service. Having learnt the language of management, their bilingual skills enabled them to reinterpret and reframe problems, to adopt a clinical perspective on managerial issues and a managerial perspective on clinical matters (Thorne, 2000). Through clinical directors the medical profession thus retained a central position in shaping services and work organization.

In contrast to arguments about proletarianization, mentioned earlier, attempts to incorporate the medical profession by turning them into managers have arguably been used by doctors to enable them to re-professionalize. Creating new forms of expertise by assimilating management skills has enabled clinical directors to extend their jurisdiction and domain. The resulting differentiation between these clinical directors and other doctors may, however, lead to greater internal stratification and hence the fragmentation of the medical profession (Thorne, 2002).

Whatever its impact on the medical profession, the growth of managers has been enhanced by a series of government policies, initiated first by the Conservatives and subsequently modified by New Labour. The introduction of an internal market in the 1990 NHS and Community Care Act, with the division of the NHS into providers and purchasers, has given managers a pivotal role. Likewise, the introduction of the Patient's

Charter in 1991, involving the setting of rights and service standards that consumers could expect, has helped to enhance the power of managers who have been responsible for monitoring and enforcing these service standards.

At the same time there are countervailing forces at work, which may restrain the advance of management (Harrison and Pollit, 1994). We have already seen that doctors (and nurses) have taken up management posts, bringing a different set of priorities and values with them. In addition to this 'colonization of management' by health care professionals, managerial power and authority may be curtailed by the fragmentation of management itself. Thus, those working for Hospital Trusts providing services may have different interests to those involved in purchasing these services. And top management who are concerned with controlling the overall system may prioritize things differently to middle managers who are more interested in maximizing service provision. Furthermore, managers may be constrained by consumer power, as reflected in surveys of consumer opinion that general managers are expected to undertake. Information about such preferences can be used by professionals seeking to defend their specialty as well as by middle managers seeking to convince top management that they need more resources. While such consumer power may be indirect as it is more a resource for others (doctors, nurses and managers) than for users themselves, the development of Patient and Public Involvement Forums for each Primary Care or Hospital Trust from 2003 (in place of Community Health Councils) may provide a more direct challenge to the power of managers. These Patient Forums will listen to people's concerns about local services, carry out inspections and generally represent the views of citizens to the relevant Trust. Managers will be expected to respond to these representations.

The march of New Public Management may therefore be constrained but its impact on professionalism has still been significant. While some have argued that doctors have been proletarianized, others have suggested that they have responded by employing management skills to extend their jurisdiction and thus re-professionalize. Either way the development of NPM has arguably transformed what used to be a high-trust relationship between managers and other health care workers, with all parties observing a diffuse pattern of mutual obligations, into a low-trust relationship with mutual suspicion replacing the mutual honouring of trust (Hunter, 1996). The longer-term impact of such a transformation is yet to be seen.

See also: *decline of medical autonomy* and *consumerism.*

216

REFERENCES

Flynn, R. (1992) *Structures of Control in Health Management*. London: Routledge.
Freidson. E. (1989) *Medical Work in America: Essays in Healthcare*. New Haven, CT: Yale University Press.
Harrison, S. and Ahmad, W. (2000) 'Medical autonomy and the UK state', *Sociology*, 34 (1): 129–46.
Harrison, S. and Pollitt, C. (1994) *Controlling Health Professionals: The Future of Work and Organization in the NHS*. Buckingham: Open University Press.
Hunter, D.J. (1996) 'The changing role of health care personnel in health and health care management', *Social Science and Medicine*, 43 (5): 799–808.
McKinlay, J. and Arches, J. (1985) 'Towards the proletarianization of physicians', *International Journal of Health Services*, 15: 161–95.
Ranade, W. (1994) *A Future for the NHS?* Harlow: Longman.
Thorne, M. (2002) 'Colonizing the new world of NHS management: the shifting power of professionals', *Health Services Management Research*, 15: 14–26.

JGA

consumerism

> **Definition:** **Consumerism, when applied to health care, suggests that users of health services should and do play an active role in making informed choices about health.**

The term 'consumer' has its origins in the world of private business and reflects recognition that producers should take account of the preferences of the purchasers of their goods in order to maximize their profits. Its use blossomed first in North America where market researchers were employed by manufacturers after the Second World War to establish consumer demand for their products and customer relations departments were set up to provide a service to customers and seek to meet their needs (Seale, 1993). In the UK context the rights of the consumer were recognized with the founding of the Consumers' Association in 1957. This organization aimed to provide readers of its magazine with information about the quality of high street products so that they could make an 'informed choice' when making purchasing decisions (ibid.).

The language of consumerism was first applied to users of UK public-sector services such as health care in the late 1970s and early 1980s. It was initially criticized on the grounds that the consumption of medical care is different from, say, the consumption of supermarket goods. For example, in the UK people do not pay directly for medical care provided by the National Health Service (NHS), but do so through taxation. And they can exercise more choice when buying from a shop, compared with deciding which doctor to see and which treatment to have. Furthermore, consumers of health care are at the same time producers of good health in that they are involved in the prevention of illness through health maintenance practices in the home. From this standpoint, the distinction between consumption and production is artificial (Stacey, 1976). Despite these concerns consumerism has become a leitmotif of health policy and practice in the past 30 years in the UK, as will be seen below.

The influence of consumerist principles can be seen, first and foremost, in a range of policies introduced by Conservative governments during the 1980s and 1990s. An early example was the decision by the Thatcher administration in 1983 to follow the advice of the Griffiths Report and introduce managerialism into the National Health Service. General managers were appointed at each level of the service who were to give pride of place to the preferences of patients when making health care decisions. Griffiths argued that managers should try to establish how well the service for which they were responsible was being delivered, by employing a range of research techniques and other methods to find out their customers' needs and their views about service standards and its quality. While the use of these techniques may have legitimated managers' claims to knowledge about their customers and what they wanted, the kind of information collected seems to have been of limited use to patients, as the focus appears to have been on their views of hotel aspects of care (for example, cleanliness and food) rather than their assessment of effectiveness (Calnan and Gabe, 2001).

A second policy development was the creation of an internal market for health care in which money was meant to follow the patient/consumer. Premised on the idea that competition enhances efficiency the 1990 NHS and Community Care Act, which introduced the internal market, divided the NHS into purchasers and providers of health care while reaffirming the principle of health care free at the point of use. To make the market work, supply side providers such as large hospitals and community units were given the opportunity to become self-governing trusts, with the promise of increased financial freedom and greater autonomy. On the demand side, general practitioners (GPs) were permitted to become fundholders, able to place contracts for non-emergency care for their patients. A justification for the development of this market for health care was that it would shift the culture of the NHS from one determined by the preferences and decisions of professionals to one shaped by the views and wishers of users. GPs were, however, purchasing services on their patients' behalf, and were thus acting as proxy or surrogate consumers, with patients having no purchasing rights of their own. It was assumed that these fundholders had the incentive to fulfil this role effectively as otherwise their patients would simply switch to a competing practice. Critics subsequently questioned patients' motivation to shop around and noted that they had limited choice as regards alternative GPs with which to register (Calnan and Gabe, 2001). However, it has been suggested that fundholding GPs did achieve certain benefits for their patients, in terms of shorter waiting times and quicker test results, although arguably this was at the expense of non-fundholding patients.

A further policy informed by the concept of consumerism was the introduction of the Patient's Charter in 1991, one of a number planned by the Conservatives to transform the management of the public services. The Patient's Charter was designed to make the health service more responsive to individual consumers and raise quality overall at nil cost, by setting rights and service standards that consumers could expect. New rights were established such as the right for detailed information about quality standards and waiting lists; guaranteed admission to hospital within two years of being put on the waiting list; and having any complaint investigated and dealt with promptly. Critics of the Patient's Charter have argued that while it may have increased individual users' right to information, it is premised on the dubious assumption that making such information available to the public will of itself change the practice of clinicians and managers. As such, it ignores the vested interests that different health care occupations have in the maintenance of the status quo (Crinson, 1998).

Since 1997, when the Labour government came to power in the UK, the emphasis has shifted from one of competition to partnership and co-operation. Primary Care Groups and now Trusts have replaced fund holding, with groups of general practices compulsorily federated with a cash-limited budget for providing primary care and purchasing hospital and community services. Central to these organizational arrangements has been the requirement that users and local people be involved in decision-making. The focus to date seems to have been mainly on communication and consultation rather than more participative or community-driven forms of involvement. However, the emphasis on consultation seems to be what lay people prefer, as there is little evidence that there is much enthusiasm for participating in health-related decision-making at service level. This may change with the establishment in 2003 of the Commission for Patient and Public Involvement in Health. The Commission's task is to get as many people as possible involved in decision-making about local health services. Its remit includes training local people in skills that will maximize the chance of their voice being heard, and encouraging Patient Forums (due to replace Community Health Councils) to use modern technologies and approaches other than meetings to generate as much interest as possible.

Alongside this concern with public participation at the collective level has been an emphasis on patient partnership at the level of doctor–patient interaction. Under New Labour's NHS Plan (2000) doctors are being encouraged to share information and decision-making with their patients. Indeed, patients are now being recognized as 'experts' in their own care. At present, however, it is unclear to what extent users want to be involved in decision-making about their care. Empirical research suggests that while many patients say they would like information about their condition, a much smaller number say they want to participate in treatment decisions, preferring doctors to decide on their behalf (Charles et al., 1997). It also seems that they may adopt both 'consumerist' and 'passive patient' roles at various times, depending on the context (Lupton, 1997). Nor is it clear that doctors will necessarily be willing to share information with patients, as the basis for joint decision-making. In some cases they may prefer to limit the nature of the information they impart to patients, thereby maintaining their professional dominance.

While the language of partnership may be the current British government's preferred discourse, consumerism has not been completely displaced. Two recent initiatives – the creation of NHS Direct and NHS walk-in centres – seem to be more in line with increasing individual consumer choice and personal responsibility for care than with shared decision-making. Thus the NHS Direct nurse-led telephone help line is designed to provide faster advice and information about health, illness and the NHS so that people are better able to care for themselves and their families. And NHS walk-in centres are designed to widen access to primary care services by offering no-appointment consultations in the evening and at weekends as well as during traditional office hours. In both cases the message seems to be that the NHS is accessible, convenient and customer-focused (Iliffe and Munro, 2000).

Finally, how is the popularity of consumerism and, more recently, partnership in policy circles to be explained? One explanation is that the different government initiatives have been driven by ideology. Certainly the policies of the Conservatives seem to have been heavily influenced by a neo-liberal ideology based on a belief in the value of self-reliance, individual responsibility and the rule of the market, with sovereign consumers expressing demand on the basis of knowledge about the choices available. Yet the Conservatives did not follow this ideology to the letter as the market they created was internal to the NHS and the service remained free at the point of use. The present Labour government seems to have accepted elements of neo-liberalism (increasing individual choice, and maximizing personal responsibility for health care), combined with a more collectivist approach, thus, reflecting a preference for pragmatism.

An alternative explanation is that the emphasis on consumerism reflects more general socio-economic changes, encapsulated in the phrase 'post-Fordism' (Nettleton and Harding, 1994). From this standpoint the health service reforms described above parallel a shift from Fordist principles (mass production, universalization of welfare, mass consumption) to those of post-Fordism (flexible production techniques designed to take account of rapid changes in consumer demand and fragmented market tastes). In a post-Fordist society it is the consumers rather than the producers that call the tune. While this approach has some value in placing the health policy changes mentioned above in a broader context, it fails to distinguish between surface changes in appearance and underlying social relations. While the rhetoric has been about enhanced consumer power or partnership, producers in the form of the medical profession and health service managers arguably continue to hold the upper hand over the users of services.

See also: *citizenship and health, managerialism* and *practitioner–client relationships.*

REFERENCES

Calnan, M. and Gabe, J. (2001) 'From consumerism to partnership? Britain's National Health Service at the turn of the century', *International Journal of Health Services,* 31 (1): 119–31.

Charles, C., Gafni, A. and Whelan, T. (1997) 'Shared decision-making in the medical encounter: what does it mean? (or it takes at least two to tango)', *Social Science and Medicine,* 44 (5): 681–92.

Crinson, I. (1998) 'Putting patients first: the continuity of the consumerist discourse in health policy: from radical right to New Labour', *Critical Social Policy,* 18: 227–39.

Iliffe, S. and Munro, J. (2000) 'New Labour and Britain's National Health Service: an overview of current reforms', *International Journal of Health Services,* 30 (2): 309–34.

Lupton, D. (1997) 'Consumerism, reflexivity and the medical encounter', *Social Science and Medicine,* 33 (5): 559–68.

Nettleton, S. and Harding, G. (1994) 'Protesting patients: a study of complaints submitted to a Family Health Service Authority', *Sociology of Health and Illness*, 16: 38–61.

Seale, C. (1993) 'The consumer voice', in B. Davey and J. Popay (eds), *Dilemmas in Health Care*. Buckingham: Open University Press.

Stacey, M. (1976) 'The health service consumer: a sociological misconception', in M. Stacey (ed.), *The Sociology of the National Health Service*. Sociological Review Monograph No 22. Keele: University of Keele.

JGA

—— social movements and health ——

> *Definition: **A social movement is a loose network of people, groups and sometimes organizations that actively seeks to bring about (or to resist) some social or cultural change. The desired change may be specific and limited, or may affect the whole of society. Many social movements have been concerned, directly or indirectly, with health issues.***

Large-scale contemporary social movements with which readers are likely to be familiar include the women's, green or environmentalist, disability and animal rights movements. Dramatic events, or media coverage of them, regularly bring national liberation, religious and revolutionary movements to our attention. Within developed, democratic societies today, there are a range of smaller-scale, intermittently visible campaigns, which seek to mobilize support for (or against) some contentious issue, often related to health, for example, gun control or the legalization of marijuana. Thus, the term 'social movement' has been applied to a very diverse range of phenomena, typically characterized by: having mass mobilization (for example, consumer boycotts, demonstrations, petitions) or the threat of it as their main source of power; and acting, at least some of the time, outside formal structured organizations, such as bureaucratized pressure groups. Social movements

222

may include organizations and their goals might include gaining support from political parties, but they are not themselves organizations. Medical sociologists have become interested in social movements in recent years because many broad social movements have health-related issues among their concerns and because of the increasing impact of directly health-related movements on health care.

The 1960s saw the emergence or revival of a number of broad social movements in Western societies. For example, the Civil Rights Movement in the USA and the nuclear disarmament campaign in the United Kingdom were followed by student protest and anti-war movements and the women's movement. These new movements differed in some respects from many older social movements studied by sociologists. For example, participants were not, on the whole, obviously materially deprived or socially excluded. Rather, they were disproportionately young, well-educated students or members of welfare and 'people-orientated' professions, including health care. The issues at the heart of campaigns were often moral rather than economic ones, requiring personal and cultural change as well as, or rather than, political changes. Formal organizations and reliance on experts were often explicitly rejected in favour of non-hierarchical groupings and the adoption of lifestyles that adhered to movement values.

These new movements had a profound effect on sociology generally. Many young sociologists were themselves participants and, therefore, sought to relate movement ideas to their academic activities. Not surprisingly, the study of social movements gained new impetus. In North America, much of the new scholarship sought to develop general theories explaining why some contentious issues were associated with successful movement formation and others were not. In the light of evidence from the movements around them, it was argued that scale of grievance was not a sufficient explanation of movement development. In what became known as 'resource mobilization theory', sociological attention turned to examining the resources (both tangible ones such as money and less tangible ones such as expertise and media contacts) that could be mobilized by those concerned about particular issues, rather than the issues alone. More recently, cultural aspects of social movements have come more to the fore in American sociology and there has been some convergence with the more macro-sociological approaches that were dominant in European sociology in the post-1960s' era.

Reflecting the greater influence of Marxist and post-Marxist theory there, European sociology of social movements has been much concerned with the relationship between the labour movement (and class conflict) and other social movements. Social theorists such as Touraine, Habermas and Offe have identified the so-called 'New Social Movements' (NSMs) that emerged from the 1960s, as harbingers of a new societal and political order, sometimes termed 'post-industrial' society. NSMs are regarded as pioneers of a new, non-institutionalized form of politics, which tends to 'bypass the state', acting through cultural and lifestyle shifts or direct action rather than through conventional parliamentary politics and legislation (Offe, 1985). Class identification as the basis for political action is, according to NSM theorists, declining in favour of other aspects of identity (for example, gender or sexuality) as bases for political action. This new politics is primarily concerned with questions of morality and personal autonomy, rather than with the distribution of economic rewards, the issue seen as dominating institutionalized, that is class-based, politics.

There has been much debate over exactly what, if anything, is specifically 'new' about NSMs. After all, most pre-1960s' social movements began as very loose, non-hierarchical networks and some were mainly about moral issues. Nor has political activity concerned with questions of distributive justice and economic reward disappeared in Europe or elsewhere. However, one does not have to accept all the theoretical claims made about NSMs to recognize that, for example, feminism and environmentalism have had an impact on the culture and social institutions of many contemporary societies (and on their institutionalized politics). Conventional political parties and voting are less class-based than at the start of the 1960s and 'political' activity now extends far beyond political parties and parliaments. The notion of 'politically correct' language or imagery is but one manifestation of the latter development.

Access to health care, inequalities in health and public health risks have long been significant concerns in institutionalized, parliamentary politics. Moreover, concerns and claims about health have been prominent aspects of many social movements, both NSMs and those of the past. In part, this reflects the potential for mobilizing support by appealing to the public's self-interest, through claims about the health benefits of desired changes (or the health risks of inaction). For example, environmentalists' arguments against genetically modified crops are often couched in these terms. But the 'politics of health' has long been broader than this. For example, health issues were an important aspect of the Victorian women's movement in the United Kingdom, with vigorous feminist protest around 1870 against legislation that empowered authorities in some localities to forcibly inspect and detain women prostitutes suspected of having venereal diseases. At issue here, as in some other Victorian social movements, were questions of personal autonomy versus state and medical control over women in the name of public health. Such questions were to recur a century later, as a central part of what is often termed 'second-wave' feminism, so central that it is possible to identify a 'women's health movement' (WHM) from this period, in Europe, North America and elsewhere.

The core activities of the WHM were challenging medicine's claims to be *the* cultural authority on women's health needs and critiquing patriarchal ideas and practices in medicine; creating and promoting women's own knowledge about their bodies; establishing new health care facilities organized along feminist lines; and securing women's rights to choose in matters of reproduction, that is, in the management of childbirth, contraception and abortion and, somewhat later, conceptive and prenatal interventions. The impact of these activities on medical sociology was profound, not least because of the involvement of many medical sociologists in the WHM. The feminist critique of patriarchal medicine, and the emphasis on women's knowledge and self-determination, brought new concepts and ideas to sociological research on women's health and reproduction and new topics for study. These latter included the movement itself (for example, Ruzek, 1978) and the controversy and counter-mobilization that were generated, especially in relation to abortion rights. Thus, in the WHM and its parent, the women's movement, many of the values and principles identified as central to NSMs and their salience to health are readily apparent. These include repudiation of 'victim' or 'passive patient' status (for example, in questions of childbirth management). Medical science and technology were treated with suspicion, and personal experience was valued as a source of knowledge to rival doctors' professional expertise.

Other NSMs that grew out of the social and cultural changes of the 1960s also had a strong health dimension. Two recurrent features are particularly relevant to medical sociology: (1) challenging medical experts' knowledge claims; and (2) the emergence of 'politics' based on identities deriving from disability or illness. Questioning the presumed beneficence and the truth claims of institutionalized medical science, and the positing of other sources of authoritative knowledge have, as noted above, been prominent in environmentalist campaigning. Brown and Mikklesen (1990) have shown how personal experience and 'popular epidemiology' were pitted against officialdom in US community activists' campaigns over toxic waste dumping.

225

Rejection of medical authority in favour of self-representation and the authority of personal experience is at the core of the disability rights movement that has emerged in many countries in the past 30 years. Directly inspired by the civil rights and women's movement and, especially in the USA, by the experience of young men injured in the Vietnam War, what began as a movement for independent living and self-support by disabled people developed into the vigorous assertion of an alternative, 'social' model of disability (Shakespeare, 1993). By analogy with racist or sexist oppression, it was argued that disabled people were oppressed by the institutions and practices of the able-bodied and should embark on collective action for change. This 'social' model rejected any elision between disability and chronic illness. As a result, medical sociologists found themselves criticized as allegedly colluding with medical experts.

If disability activists have tended to reject medical intervention as a source of oppression, another group of 'sufferers' has campaigned collectively against medical science's insufficient engagement with their illness. Epstein (1996) has shown how HIV/AIDS activists in the USA marshalled their own knowledge as a resource in their campaigning for more and faster research into possible treatments. This was possible because many of those infected, at least in the early phase of the HIV/AIDS epidemic in the USA, were relatively well-educated, affluent people who could draw on their own experience in, and the wider support of, the gay and lesbian movement. Scepticism of medical claims-making, and refusal to accept the right of doctors to speak for those with HIV/AIDS led initially to high-profile direct protest action, often involving imaginative use of the media, for example, the disruption of prestigious scientific meetings. However, over time, many activists learnt enough medical science to be able to debate credibly with scientists, and to exert influence on the conduct of drug trials and the course of research. Epstein's study documents a major milestone in user involvement in medical research.

As well as these areas of non-institutionalized health politics for which the term 'social movement' seems clearly apposite, many smaller-scale user and self-help groups and campaigns have developed in the past 30 years. Some (although not all) of these are characterized by rejection of medical paternalism in favour of alternative services and an emphasis on personal autonomy and experiential knowledge. One example would be the mental health users' movement studied by Rogers and Pilgrim (1991). As Kelleher (1994) has suggested, self-help groups are part of the culture of new social movements, without necessarily being themselves full social movements: not least because mobilizing resources is likely to be difficult for the seriously ill.

Social movements are significant for medical sociology in two ways. First, understanding how contemporary health campaigns connect with the broader social, political and economic changes analysed by NSM theorists has underlined how studying health can provide insights into more general social processes, particularly in periods of rapid social change. Second, ideas such as patient and user involvement in research, service planning and in treatment decisions and seeking to combat disability as a matter of right have now become widely accepted as health policy goals, if not always fully achieved in practice. Medical sociologists have shown that these ideas originated, in part, in social movement activity. They represent, albeit generally in diluted ways, the aspirations of these health movements and they illustrate how social movements can achieve their aims: by changing how we think about issues as well as through conventional political action.

See also: *chronic illness* and *disability* and *lay knowledge.*

REFERENCES

Brown, P. and Mikkelsen, E.J. (1990) *No Safe Place: Toxic Waste, Leukaemia and Community Action.* Berkeley, CA: University of California Press.

Epstein, S. (1996) *Impure Science: AIDS, Activism and the Politics of Knowledge.* Berkeley, CA: University of California Press.

Kelleher, D. (1994) 'Self-help groups and their relationship to medicine', in J. Gabe, D. Kelleher and G. Williams (eds), *Challenging Medicine.* London: Routledge, pp. 104–17.

Offe, C. (1985) 'New social movements: challenging the boundaries of institutional politics', *Social Research,* 59 (4): 817–68.

Rogers, A. and Pilgrim, D. (1991) '"Pulling down churches": accounting for the British mental health users' movement', *Sociology of Health and Illness,* 13 (2): 129–48.

Ruzek, S.B. (1978) *The Women's Health Movement: Feminist Alternatives to Medical Control.* New York: Praeger.

Shakespeare, T. (1993) 'Disabled people's self-organisation: a new social movement?' *Disability, Handicap and Society,* 8 (3): 249–64.

MAE

227

—social problems and— health

> **Definition: In the health field a social problem is a health-related condition or behaviour that is regarded in some way as 'undesirable' by society or by some sections of society, in that it represents a 'threat' of some kind.**

There are many sociological perspectives on social problems that can be applied to understanding the social significance of health-related conditions or behaviour. In this entry three broad approaches will be considered: functionalist, conflict and interactionist/constructionist. Each will be exemplified, for illustrative purposes, by referring to benzodiazepine tranquillizers – legally prescribed drugs whose use has been of social concern in recent years. Other health-related issues might be configured somewhat differently. Of course, this classification of approaches does not encompass all that has been written about social problems nor should it be taken as implying that these approaches are internally homogeneous and coherent. They simply represent the most frequently mentioned conceptual models that have been drawn upon in this area.

228

Functionalist approaches dominated the social problems field for more than half the last century, especially in the United States where they originated. Included under this rubric are 'social pathology' and 'social disorganization'. Social pathology focuses on the effects of rapid social change on individuals and suggests that social problems such as poverty or drug dependency are a consequence of individual failure to adapt to changed conditions. In contrast, social disorganization shifts the focus from the individual to the social and economic environment and how, for example, the rapid growth of cities in the early twentieth century gave rise to social disorganization in the form of homelessness and rising crime rates (Jamrozik and Nocella, 1998). Despite these differences of emphasis, social pathology and social disorganization share a common core: a belief that a social problem can be defined in functional terms as a form of behaviour or condition that impedes the fulfilment of societal goals, interferes with the smooth running of society and throws society into disequilibrium (Spector and Kitsuse, 1987).

Functionalists believe that sociologists are well placed to define what is or is not a social problem, on the grounds of their own expert knowledge of the structure of society. They accept that lay people may share this definition but also that they may not. If the problem is identified as one of individual failing, often due to ineffective socialization, the solution offered is moral education. If the problem is seen as systemic, perhaps because of a breakdown of the usually dynamic parts of the system due to social change, the solution is to bring back into equilibrium those parts of the system that are out of phase.

When applied to minor tranquillizers, functionalism attributes the large-scale use of these drugs to the inability of individuals to adapt to changed conditions or to the lack of social support from family, friends and neighbours in an increasingly socially disorganized (urban) environment.

Over the years functionalist approaches have come in for considerable criticism. In particular they have been blamed for failing to take seriously societal members' subjective definitions of social problems (Blumer, 1971). They have also been criticized for taking as their starting point social problems defined from the viewpoint of the existing social order and for suggesting that these problems are best dealt with through education. As a result, it is claimed, functionalists uncritically support the maintenance of the status quo.

Turning to the conflict approach, this is most often identified with Marxism, although it also subsumes non-Marxists interested in alienation. Sociologists associated with this approach, which became popular in the late 1960s and early 1970s, see society in terms of diverse groups with unequal access to wealth and economic and political power, and recognize those with the least wealth and power as alienated and discontented. It is this alienation that is viewed as the catalyst for social problems. Marxists go further, however, by relating this discontent to the underlying contradictions of the capitalist social system. They are also more likely to see social problems as disguised political issues and claim that the most powerful often have a vested interest in not solving social problems. Or they may suggest that attempts to ameliorate social problems can be seen as a form of social control (Scull, 1984). From this perspective social problems can only be resolved if the structure of capitalist society is radically changed (Jamrozik and Nocella, 1998).

When the conflict approach is applied to tranquillizer use at the micro level, it encourages attention to be focused on whether the prescribing of these drugs represents a medical solution to a social problem that does little to help patients to help themselves. Doctors are said to prescribe these drugs primarily to women and working-class patients and that, in so doing, they legitimize existing hierarchical social relations. They do this by suggesting to women patients that their symptoms of distress are a consequence of their sex's inherently unstable physiology and personality. Likewise, it is claimed they inform working-class patients that they need these drugs because of a failure to look after themselves adequately. From this perspective tranquillizer prescribing can be seen as a form of social control in that it minimizes the likelihood of people attempting by collective action to change the way in which their society is organized.

At the macro-level, attention is focused on the political economy of the pharmaceutical industry. Tranquillizers are seen as commodities produced for profit by drug companies that can be ruthlessly competitive in defending their interests against other companies and against consumer groups concerned about the dependence-forming properties and side-effects of their products. In order to maximize demand, drug companies are said to promote tranquillizers as the solution to individual problems of stress and anxiety, even though these problems are social in origin. In this context the state's role is seen as contradictory, attempting to guarantee the conditions for capital accumulation while at the same time acting in the 'public interest' and regulating the pharmaceutical industry as regards product safety and efficacy.

The advantage of the conflict approach over functionalism is that it emphasizes both the role of structural factors in the generation of social problems and stresses the significance of conflicts of interest between collectivities with differing amounts of power. However, to the extent that advocates of the conflict approach fail to take seriously the role of social processes in the development of social problems and treat cultural and symbolic aspects as marginal, they are said to weaken the explanatory potential of their arguments.

The third group of approaches that now dominates the social problems field – interactionism and constructionism – share a willingness to take the actor's perspective rather than 'objective' conditions as the starting point for their analysis of social problems. They focus on how actors define situations, persons and events as problematic and assume that social problems emerge through social interaction, making the history of such problems uncertain and contingent (Blumer, 1971). They are thus concerned with process rather than structure and meaning rather than causality.

Despite these similarities there are also significant differences between the two approaches, which should be noted. First, there is the matter of scale. Symbolic interactionists tend to focus on small-scale settings (for example, neighbourhoods) and interaction between individuals, whereas constructionists take a broader view and consider the relationship between expert definitions and bureaucratic institutions. Second, interactionists tend to operate with a more explicit notion of objective reality whereas constructionists set the existence of such a reality aside and focus solely on the claims-making of those alleging that a particular behaviour is problematic (Spector and Kitsuse, 1987).

A recent development of constructionism has been its intersection with post-structuralist approaches to discourse (Clarke, 2001). Attention has been focused on the ways in which forms of knowledge about social problems are socially produced and organized through language. From this standpoint, knowledge determines who is allowed to 'know' and 'say' things, with expert knowledge about social problems being privileged over lay knowledge. Power, in this view, is thus produced and distributed through knowledge.

When applied to tranquillizers, the interactionist approach is illustrated in attempts to describe the social meaning that taking the drugs has for users, accepting as given that those who use these tablets are experiencing real distress. To what extent, for example, do tranquillizer users feel that taking these drugs has made their status equivocal, on the margins between deviance and normality? A constructionist approach concentrates on the more macro-level and looks at the natural history of tranquillizers as a social problem. From this standpoint the focus is on the claims or discourse of scientific experts, for example, that tranquillizers have been over-used and have the potential to cause physical dependence at normal therapeutic dose. The extent to which the mass media legitimate these claims and mobilize public opinion against the use of these drugs is also seen as relevant in understanding the extent to which tranquillizers come to be seen as a social problem.

The value of the interactionist and constructionist approaches is that they draw attention to the emergent and changeable nature of social problems and the role of social interaction in such a process. Both approaches have been criticized, however. Interactionism's contribution to the study of social problems is said to have been limited by its failure to take account of the broader setting and the role of different social groups in the generation of social problems; whereas the impact of constructionism is said to have been reduced as a result of an unwillingness to tackle the question of relativism and to take seriously the experience of social problems.

key concepts

The charge of relativism stems from the claim of constructionists that social problems are nothing more than definitional activities. To make such a statement, however, arguably begs the question about the status of these analysts' own claims about claims-making activities. For if there is no role for independent evidence, identifying the conditions for the development of social problems becomes a never-ending and circular argument.

The second criticism that constructionists ignore the experiential dimension (such as suffering experienced through illness) seems to stem from the view that definitional processes are largely arbitrary in character, with meaning only located in relation to the power of interest groups. This is said to lead to an 'aloof' form of social analysis, with the analyst appearing to want to maintain a considerable social distance from the social relations of which he or she is a part (Gusfield, 1984).

There is, then, a range of approaches to the study of social problem as they apply to health. Functionalist and conflict approaches have generally been superseded by interactionism and, more recently, variants of constructionism. However, the latter is, as we have seen, not without its critics and some of those influenced by it have responded by seeking to make links with more structuralist concerns about power, inequalities and social divisions. Whatever the theoretical stance taken, however, perhaps the key message to take from recent debates is the need for a critical approach to studying health conditions and behaviours that are claimed to be social problems.

See also: *social constructionism, medicalization* and *medicines regulation.*

232

REFERENCES

Blumer, H. (1971) 'Social problems as collective behaviour', *Social Problems*, 18: 298–306.

Clarke, J. (2001) 'Social problems: sociological perspectives', in M. May, R. Page, and E. Brunsdon (eds), *Understanding Social Problems*. Oxford: Blackwell Publishers.

Gusfield, J.R. (1984) 'On the side: practical action and social constructivism in social problems theory', in J.W. Schneider and J.I. Kitsuse (eds), *Studies in the Sociology of Social Problems*. Norwood, NJ: Ablex Publishing Company.

Jamrozik, A. and Nocella, L. (1998) *The Sociology of Social Problems: Theoretical Perspectives and Methods of Intervention*. Cambridge: Cambridge University Press.

Scull, A. (1984) *Decarceration: Community, Treatment and the Deviant: A Radical View*. Cambridge: Polity Press.

Spector, M. and Kitsuse, J. (1987) *Constructing Social Problems*. New York: De Gruyter.

JGA

> **Definition:** *The New Public Health is a term popularized in the 1980s to describe the resurgence of interest in the social, economic and environmental determinants of a health and the advocacy of healthy public policy, rather than health services, to improve the health of populations.*

Medical sociology has had a close relationship with public health, or 'Community Medicine' as it was known in the UK until 1989. There is considerable overlap between the core concerns of the two disciplines, particularly regarding the social determinants of disease, inequalities in health and the structural barriers to improving health and health care. By the 1980s, public health practitioners and academics began heralding the 'New Public Health' (NPH), which was in part an explicit acknowledgement of these 'social' aspects of public health, and a desire to move away from what was perceived as a narrow and Victorian concern with 'drains and infection'. In the Preface to their book, *The New Public Health*, based on their experiences in Liverpool, John Ashton and Howard Seymour (1988) quote what is perhaps the defining model of the New Public Health, that of the 'fast flowing river'. 'Downstream' by the fast flowing river are health workers so busy pulling out drowning people that they have no time to look 'upstream' at whatever is causing so many to fall in. The NPH was about a shift towards 'upstream' thinking, to the social, economic and environmental causes of ill health. It also, perhaps, marked the culmination of a gradual shift of public health practitioners firmly into the medical academy from a background, in the UK, in local authorities (Green and Thorogood, 1998).

There has been considerable debate as to how far the theory and practice of the NPH were indeed a break from the old, with most writers identifying both evolution and more radical departures. For Ashton and Seymour (1988), the NPH within the UK followed on from three historical phases of activity. The first was the early nineteenth-century movement to improve housing and sanitation to control the epidemics of tuberculosis, whooping cough, measles and cholera that flourished in over-crowded urban populations. By the 1870s, the second phase was

233

built on emerging germ theories of disease, which suggested individual measures that could be taken to control infection, including immunization, and a growing social role, involving family planning and the development of school and community health services. The third phase was one of decline, as infectious disease was brought under control by the 1930s, resulting in a growing faith in the possibilities of hospital-based, therapeutic medicine. For Ashton and Seymour, the NPH emerged from challenges to the dominance of therapeutic, high technology medical interventions.

Within medicine, the turn towards the social causes of disease rather than medical intervention was based on work such as Thomas McKeown's (1979) analysis of the nineteenth-century decline in mortality in England and Wales. He argued that medical interventions such as drug therapies and vaccinations had made, historically, little contribution to the decline in mortality from infectious disease. Rather, increasing life expectancy was the result of improving social conditions, smaller family sizes, better nutrition and a healthier environment. Another challenge to the focus on health services, and an opportunity for public health, came from a number of influential national and international policy initiatives. First, the Canadian Minister of Health and Welfare, Marc Lalonde, published a report on the health of Canadians in 1974, which highlighted the preventability of much morbidity and mortality from chronic disease, and the need for a public health orientation to improve the health of the population. In 1986 the World Health Organization's (WHO) Ottawa Charter for Health Promotion (subtitled 'Towards a New Public Health') addressed health as a goal, rather than a reduction in disease. The Ottawa Charter stressed inter-sectoral healthy public policy, the importance of social, economic and physical environments for health and the necessity of re-orientating health services away from hospital-based provision to community-based systems.

Fran Baum (1998), in tracing the emergence of the NPH in Australia, outlines six eras of dominant policy and ideology: (1) indigenous control over health in the pre-colonial era; (2) the colonial era (with its focus on sanitary measures and quarantine); (3) nation-building (1890 to the 1940s); (4) affluence (with a growing role for state intervention from the 1950s to the 1970s); (5) lifestyle (with the emergence of programmes based on individual health promotion to reduce chronic disease); and (6) from the mid-1980s, the NPH. If the 'development' of the NPH was the post-McKeown rediscovery of the social determinants of ill-health, for Baum, the 'departure' was the emphasis on social justice and healthy public policy. Her vision of public health is not only inclusive and inter-sectoral, but also global in its reach, addressing international inequalities and the effects of globalization.

The NPH was bound to a new vision of health promotion, no longer a narrow 'education' function, but rather a participatory, community-oriented activity which involved citizens having a role in setting the health agenda, and developing broad-based health improvement initiatives within their own communities. The NPH may have marked the resurgence of public health practice as a medical discipline, but its rhetoric is firmly inter-disciplinary and collaborative. Given that the determinants of health lie largely outside the health service, 'healthy alliances' are needed to develop public policy that addresses the health of the population at the most 'upstream' point possible. The focus on alliances has tied the NPH to initiatives such as the WHO's Healthy Cities project, designed as a practical implementation of the policy principles enshrined in the Ottawa Charter (Petersen and Lupton, 1996: 127-9). The Healthy Cities project perhaps encapsulates the contradictions, as well as the achievements of the NPH (Ashton and Seymour, 1988). First, though stressing community action and participation, it relies on 'top-down' leadership. Second, to develop healthy public policy around issues such as road safety or hazardous waste removal requires the collaboration of public statutory organizations, voluntary organizations and the private sector; yet public health is still delivered within 'modernist' organizations, obsessed with 'scientific explanations and techno-rational 'fixes''(Petersen and Lupton, 1996: 144). Third, the emphasis on community participation elides the difficulties and social inequalities of the multiple communities and social identities that exist within the city.

Medical sociology's relationship to public health has been, in part, as an uncritical contributor of 'social epidemiology' to the public health project, particularly on topics such as health beliefs and behaviour of the public (Petersen and Lupton, 1996: x). However, there has also been a sociology 'of' the new public health. Sociological accounts have often, like those from within the profession, located a series of historical discursive shifts, but have focused more on their cultural implications rather than the medical objects addressed. David Armstrong (1993), for instance, utilizes Mary Douglas' arguments about the importance of 'hygienic rules' in maintaining the boundaries between elements in a classificatory system to outline the ways in which public health discourses have produced particular identities. Sanitary science introduced the physical body to the geographies of earlier periods of quarantine, and the writings of public health concerned the regulation of substances, which had to pass between

235

the anatomical space of the body and the external environment. Elaborate hygienic rules emerged to govern care of the mouth and teeth, the removal of excreta from the body and dwellings and, finally, the disposal of dead bodies, which became a problem of public health rather than religious practice. At the beginning of the twentieth century, argues Armstrong, the undifferentiated bodies of sanitary science were replaced by individual bodies, with their own particular constellations of habits and constitutions. Thus, a new regime of public health, personal hygiene, located danger not in the passage of substances from the environment to the body, but within the body itself and, more significantly, in the spaces between people. This space was only in part the physical space across which pathogens and other pollutants passed – it was also a specifically social space, across which relationships could be mapped and addressed by the science of 'social medicine'. For Armstrong, the innovation of the NPH was the delineation of a new space. This new space was a facet of the 'inversion of the nineteenth-century focus on the non-corporeal environment' (Armstrong, 1993: 404), resulting in a concern not with the impact of nature on bodies, but with the impact of human bodies on nature. The NPH addressed the dangers of the social and economic environment for the natural, and located itself in an ecological space, in which individuals are constructed as reflective subjects, recruited into the public health project as collaborators in the surveillance of hazards.

Petersen and Lupton (1996) expand on this argument in their post-structuralist analysis of the NPH as 'a new morality', with its exercise of a particular form of power. Their critique of both the epistemological base of the NPH and its implementation, in initiatives such as Healthy Cities, addresses the ways in which its discursive practices construct particular kinds of subjective individuals. Despite the emancipatory and egalitarian rhetoric, the NPH still delineates the normal and abnormal, the healthy and unhealthy. Community participation and empowerment become obligations on citizens to conduct themselves as self-caring individuals, orientated towards their own health rather than the social network. For Petersen and Lupton the key contradiction within the NPH is the reliance on modernist notions of the privileged status of science, progress and expertise within a post-modernist rationale of pluralism, difference and multiple identities.

This contradiction is perhaps most visible in the practice of contemporary public health professionals, especially physicians, whose contribution has, in theory, been marginalized within the rhetoric of multi-disciplinary collaborative, community-driven action. Caught between the global reach of the NPH and the everyday 'downstream' concerns of population health, the role of practitioners has been ambivalent. Most academic and service departments and courses are labelled not NPH, but Public Health, defined by the UK's Faculty of Public Health Medicine as 'the science and art of preventing disease, prolonging life and promoting health through the organised efforts of society' (http://www.fphm.org.uk). There is little in this definition that reflects the vision of NPH proponents such as Ashton and Seymour or Baum, and the activities of public health professionals are increasingly orientated towards such archetypal modernist projects as evidence-based medicine. As Green and Thorogood (1998: 37) have noted, the NPH occupies a 'virtual space', caught between local government and health, existing organizational structures and partnership working, and constituted by public policy provision (or lack of it) in other domains, including housing, road safety, employment, law and order.

See also: *citizenship and health, place* and *social constructionism.*

REFERENCES

Armstrong, D. (1993) 'Public health spaces and the fabrication of identity', *Sociology*, 27 (3): 393–410.
Ashton, J. and Seymour, H. (1988) *The New Public Health*. Milton Keynes: Open University Press.
Baum, F. (1998) *The New Public Health: An Australian Perspective*. Oxford: Oxford University Press.
Green, J. and Thorogood, N. (1998) *Analysing Health Policy: A Sociological Approach*. Harlow: Longman.
Lalonde, M. (1974) *A New Perspective on the Health of Canadians*. Ottawa: Information Canada.
McKeown, T. (1979) *The Role of Medicine: Dream, Mirage or Nemesis?* Oxford: Blackwell.
Petersen, A. and Lupton, D. (1996) *The New Public Health: Health and Self in the Age of Risk*. London: Sage.

JG

medicines regulation

> **Definition:** ***Medicines regulation refers to the role of the state in regulating the safety and efficacy of medicines.***

Until relatively recently medical sociology has paid little attention to medicines and their production by the pharmaceutical industry or how the state controls which medicines are available for consumption. This is now changing with work being undertaken on the political economy of medicines, focusing on the way in which the interests of the state and pharmaceutical industry may play out to the disadvantage of consumers. Particular attention is being given to the possibility of 'regulatory capture', where the government agency responsible for regulating the pharmaceutical industry comes to represent that industry rather than the 'public interest' (Abraham, 1995). The extent to which the relationship between government regulators and drug companies can be characterized in terms of 'corporatism' is also receiving attention. Here the focus is on whether drug companies have been granted semi-official status and then assist government to implement policies that directly affect them. Corporatism is usually applied to bargaining between organized interests and agencies of the nation-state but, in the case of the pharmaceutical industry, regulatory relationships also need to be analysed at the transnational level, because this industry and its science operate across national boundaries (Abraham, 1997).

In order to explore these issues a brief history of medicines regulation in the UK and the USA will be provided. This account will illustrate differences in the degree of corporatism and regulatory capture in the two countries and the possible reasons for these differences. Reference will also be made to the Europeanization of medicine's regulation and the extent to which the agency established to harmonize standards of regulatory evaluation across Europe has adopted the UK approach to regulation with its attendant consequences.

In the UK, before the 1960s, the safety and efficacy of medicines were, for the most part, not regulated by the state. Pharmaceutical companies could sell drugs as remedies, as long as they were unadulterated, at prices that the market could bear. Regulation was thus by the market, with drugs usually only falling out of favour if it became clear that they were toxic or ineffective (Davis, 1997). The government trusted the pharmaceutical industry to test their products for safety and efficacy before bringing them to market. In the early 1960s this trust was breached when reports started to be published about the disastrous side-effects of the sedative, Thalidomide. It seemed that drugs could destroy lives as well as save them (Abraham and Lewis, 2002). To restore public confidence in medicines, the UK government introduced regulatory mechanisms to check that new medicines were safe and effective before they were introduced. From the start, however, the government agreed that information submitted by the manufacturers would be treated as confidential, thereby sealing off the regulators from public scrutiny. It was also accepted that the review process should be rapid, so as not to delay the introduction of possibly valuable drugs. Producer interests thus remained dominant, with citizens' rights of security in healthy medications being circumscribed (ibid.).

In 1968 the Medicines Act was passed which provides the basis for contemporary British medicines regulation. This Act required the Department of Health, advised by a new Committee on Safety of Medicines (CSM), to become legally responsible for assessing drug safety and efficacy. Members of the CSM were permitted to hold consultancies and shares in pharmaceutical companies, allowing a low level of differentiation between the regulators and these companies (Abraham, 1997). Under the Act, pharmaceutical companies were required for the first time to obtain approval from the government for the marketing of new medicines. As before, however, it was agreed that all information about new drug applications should be treated as confidential. Moreover, information on adverse drug reactions was withheld from citizens, including lawyers and journalists, on the grounds that they lacked the medical expertise to interpret such information. Citizens' rights to health thus remained limited in the face of producer interests and medical power.

Since the 1970s the pharmaceutical industry has attempted to maintain its influence over the regulatory authorities through close consultation about regulations on data requirements for product licences. It has also complained regularly about the length of time taken to get decisions from regulators. In the 1980s, these concerns were heeded by the Conservative government who was keen to reduce state intervention in the economy, in line with its neo-liberal agenda. In 1981 the government reduced the amount of toxicological data drug companies were required to submit to the regulators before getting approval to conduct clinical trials; and, in 1989, it set up the Medicines Control Agency (MCA) in response to industry claims that regulators were inefficient and reluctant to approve drugs quickly. The MCA was to be funded by the industry through the licence fee charged and run as a business, selling its regulatory services to the industry and promoting itself as the fastest licensing authority in the world (Abraham, 1997). In effect, then, the British government had decided to reform the regulatory authorities as a new neo-liberal, corporatist partnership between industry and regulators. Consumers continued to be excluded despite attempts over the period to extend their rights through legal action against certain pharmaceutical companies, in the face of drug disasters such as Opren (prescribed for arthritis sufferers) and Ativan (for anxiety) (Medawar, 1992). Consumer organizations also tried to challenge the secrecy involved in medicines regulation by supporting a Medicines Information Bill in Parliament to establish public access rights to regulatory information about the safety and efficacy of medicines. The government refused to support the Bill and indicated that it was more concerned to protect the commercially sensitive information divulged by the pharmaceutical industry to the regulators in order to ensure that the industry continued to invest in the UK (Abraham and Lewis, 2002).

This corporatist partnership between industry and regulators has also shaped the process of Europeanization of medicines regulation. This process dates back to 1965 when the European Community, now the European Union (EU), made provision for regulating medicines in the Community. It acquired greater urgency in the 1990s when European governments and industrialists realized that an integrated EU-wide pharmaceutical market was needed if European drug companies were to be competitive on the world stage (Abraham, 1997). Common technical standards were agreed and a committee of European experts – the Committee for Proprietary Medicinal Products (CPMP) – was established, with representatives from each of the national regulatory bodies. Under this system pharmaceutical companies are encouraged to seek simultaneous approval for their products in more than one Member State. Once a drug had been approved by one Member State, other Member States were encouraged to accept this decision. However, the fact that decisions of the CPMP were not binding created uncertainty for the drug companies so, in 1995, the Committee's opinions became binding on Member States. The EU also agreed, under pressure from the drug companies, to introduce strict timescales for coming to approval decisions. National regulatory agencies now compete for licensing fees from the industry by presenting themselves as the fastest in approving drugs. Acting primarily on the basis of this economic imperative increases the chances that scientific checks needed to provide adequate levels of drug safety will be undermined (Abraham and Lewis, 2002). Under this neo-liberal model the regulatory science on which decisions are based remains secret, despite challenges from transnational consumer organizations for greater openness. As in the UK the same arguments are used about the need for secrecy in order to protect valuable intellectual property from commercial competitors. Thus it can be argued that the corporate bias towards the drugs industry at the national level has been reproduced supranationally.

Medicines regulation is rather different in the United States, mainly as a result of a different political environment. Regulation started much earlier in the USA than in Britain and the rest of Europe. Since 1938 drug manufacturers have been required to obtain permission to market a new drug from the American drug regulatory authority, the Food and Drug Administration (FDA). In the late 1950s the industry was exposed to embarrassing criticism during Congressional hearings conducted by Senator Kefauver. The result was the 1962 Drug Amendments to the 1938 Act. From then on manufacturers had to provide substantial evidence of effectiveness as well as safety and the FDA was required to withdraw approval already granted for a drug if it lacked evidence of efficacy (Medawar, 1992). The FDA was thus specifically required by Congress to protect the public from ineffective as well as unsafe drugs. In addition, as a result of the passing of the 1967 US Freedom of Information Act, members of the public now had the right to information about the FDA's grounds for approving a new drug and records of its meetings with particular drug companies. Drug regulators in the USA therefore operate in a political climate in which consumers have much greater opportunity to examine the extent to which regulators are protecting their interests instead of operating primarily in the interests of the drug industry. Moreover, the litigious nature of US society means that the relationship between the regulators, the drug industry and consumers is much more adversarial than is the case in the UK (Abraham, 1997).

Opportunities for regulatory capture still exist, however, as was recognized by Congress in the 1970s. It acknowledged that the FDA, during the Nixon administration, had become more 'industry-friendly' and had sought to neutralize medical scientists within the organization who were felt to be adversarial towards the pharmaceutical industry. In response, it prohibited FDA scientists from joining the industry for two years after leaving the Administration. In the 1980s, in the face of the neo-liberal political agenda of the Reagan and Bush administrations, the FDA was pressurized to limit its regulatory activities in order to avoid harming the drug industry's competitiveness. However, Congressional Committees reminded the FDA that it could be called to account and required to demonstrate that it was acting in the 'public interest' by subsequently investigating some of its regulatory decisions. These procedural checks, combined with the ability of consumer groups to use the Freedom of Information Act to examine the basis for regulatory decisions, have generally made the FDA much more cautious about embracing the values of the drugs industry than has been the case in Britain.

In sum, it seems that there are contrasting approaches to medicines regulation on the two sides of the Atlantic. In the United States regulators operate in a more adversarial climate and the political checks and balances reduce opportunities for regulatory capture and corporatism. In the UK and other EU countries a culture of secrecy prevails and corporatism and industrial capture are more apparent. There is, however, increasing pressure from consumer organizations in Europe which may, in time, threaten the stability of the relationship between the regulators and the pharmaceutical industry. Time will tell how successful this more active citizenship is in making regulators in Europe more accountable.

See also: *citizenship and health* and *consumerism.*

REFERENCES

Abraham, J. (1995) *Science, Politics and the Pharmaceutical Industry.* London: UCL Press.
Abraham, J. (1997) 'The science and politics of medicines regulation', in M. Elston (ed.), *The Sociology of Medical Science and Technology.* Oxford: Blackwell Publishers, pp.153–82.
Abraham, J. and Lewis, G. (2002) 'Citizenship, medical expertise and the capitalist regulatory state in Europe', *Sociology*, 36 (1): 67–88.
Davis, P. (1997) *Managing Medicines: Public Policy and Therapeutic Drugs.* Buckingham: Open University Press.
Medawar, P. (1992) *Power and Dependence: Social Audit on the Safety of Medicines.* London: Social Audit.

JGA

242

citizenship and health

> **Definition: Citizenship and health refers to those aspects of health affected by the changing nature of the state, and the relationships between the state, health care organizations and the people they serve, under varying social and economic conditions.**

The concept of 'citizenship' has a long history and a complex set of connections to 'democracy', 'rights', and modern concepts such as 'welfare' and 'consumerism'. During the course of the twentieth century health services and latterly health itself have become the focus for arguments about the proper relationship between the modern state and its citizens.

'Equality among citizens', along with liberty and respect for law and justice, was one of the building blocks of classical democracy in Athens and other Greek city-states from the sixth century BC onwards and became a central, evolving motif in western traditions of political theory from the seventeenth century onwards. The idea of the 'citizen' – for the French philosopher Rousseau, the highest role to which an individual could aspire – has been at the heart of the struggles of workers, women, and oppressed and disenfranchised people throughout the modern world. However, there is nothing intrinsically left or centre-left about the concept of citizenship. In the UK, where the people are constitutionally the subjects of a monarch, not the citizens of a state, Conservatives have employed it as a way of emphasizing the need for community vigilance on crime, disorder and other signs of moral degeneration and decay (Marquand, 1997).

Citizenship is an evolving concept. In the post-war period the debate can be traced back to T.H. Marshall's celebrated essay on the relationship between citizenship and social class (Marshall, 1950). Marshall argued that citizenship had three elements: (1) civil, emphasizing freedom of speech, thought and belief; (2) political, stressing the right to participate in the exercise of political power through voting and representation; and (3) social, by which he meant the right to welfare, social security and a general share in the benefits of economic and cultural development. In Marshall's work these three elements were placed within a developmental theory moving from civil through political to fully social citizenship. Although Marshall's theory has been criticized for oversimplifying the developmental process, and understating the importance of gender, it remains a useful conceptual starting point (Walby, 1994).

During the twentieth century health became an increasingly important signifier of citizenship, and universal access to health care became one of the great expectations of modern electorates. In the UK, in a series of bold political moves, Lloyd George, William Beveridge and Aneurin Bevan moved health services progressively to the centre of the political stage, alongside housing, social security and education. When the National Health Service (NHS) came into existence on 5 July 1948, it had been designed, as Bevan put it, 'to universalize the best', and was the first health system to offer free care to the entire population. Similar developments with different funding mechanisms emerged in other European countries in subsequent decades. These arrangements for health care in times of sickness were an important part of an enduring social compact between the state and the people, which provided the foundations for the 'welfare state', as it came to be called from the 1940s,

243

where basic provision and security 'from the cradle to the grave' were assured for the whole population.

These developments are now viewed as being the defining mark of a political consensus that emerged in response to the catastrophes of the twentieth century: the horrors and deprivations of war, economic slump, fascism, and the anxiety created in the ruling elites by the enduring threat of a disenchanted and radicalized working class. There was a strong belief that progress in science, politics and society was possible and that reconstruction was necessary. Although it was undoubtedly a political compromise, the NHS in the UK came to embody the hopes and values of post-war Britain. It was built on the belief that the whole population should have access to health care and that this care would be built on the best available scientific expertise and professional organization.

The inter- and post-war discussions about health care and welfare provided a context in which social scientists working in social medicine and social administration could make a contribution to political thinking and policy development. During this time there was nothing that might be characterized as a critical perspective on medicine or health care. In terms of policy analysis, Fabianism was the dominant approach to intellectual engagement and, within this framework, health services were simply the vehicle through which medicine and care could be more effectively delivered to the whole population. The approach was implicitly if not explicitly rooted in a Parsonian sociology of the sick role: illness was dysfunctional and medical care and health services represented the knowledge and social organization available to deal with illness and restabilize the individual and their social relationships. The social scientist's brief was largely restricted to doing the political arithmetic on health, illness and health services in order to support the work in which policy-makers and health professionals were engaged and improve the care to which people – whether subjects or citizens – had access.

Modern health care systems were the beneficiaries of what are now seen as the 'Golden Years' of the twentieth century, stretching from the start of the 1950s to the OPEC oil crisis and economic turbulence of 1973 and after. Increasingly, the only certainty in health care was that it was going to cost more. Much of the sociological analysis that emerged during the 1970s was ostensibly a critique of medicine as a form of social control. However, it was actually the beginnings of an extended examination of the relationship between citizens and professionally controlled health services in the light of growing evidence of the limited effectiveness of much modern medicine, persisting health inequalities in an era of globalization, the perception that patients are disenfranchised in the organization and delivery of health care systems and, latterly, the unfolding consequences of new genetic knowledge and medical technologies.

From the 1980s onwards the issue of the relationship between citizens and their health became increasingly sharp as the UK and other western societies engaged in severe economic restructuring, moving away from the corporatist compact on which they had hitherto been based towards market-style expectations and relationships. Management systems and budgets were introduced to control health professionals' expenditure, and quasi-markets were employed to stimulate competition between providers and, so it was argued, expand consumer choice. Health services, along with the rest of the welfare state, were increasingly framed in terms of value for money, and 'cradle to the grave' security was seen as a vice rather than a virtuous safety net for the casualties of economic dislocation. At the same time, evidence accumulated of widening inequalities in health status that were closely related to growing disparities in income and wealth.

In spite of, or perhaps because of, the severe squeeze on public services that took place during the late 1980s and early 1990s, debate about the roles and rights of patients, consumers, users and citizens in the planning and delivery of health services became much more high profile (Calnan and Gabe, 2001). Knowledgeable and informed consumers making rational choices about treatment became the leitmotif of reform across Europe and North America. Developments during the 1990s such as the Patient's Charter in the UK – a list of rights (not legally binding) to certain standards of care – were designed to make services more responsive to consumers and thereby improve quality at no extra cost, though such improvements are hard to detect in the evidence available (Calnan and Gabe, 2001).

During a period when health services came under increasing pressure from anti-public sector, anti-monopolistic governments enthusiastic about free markets, space was created for debate about the place of consumers within professionally dominated health care systems. Within this space critics were able to argue for the limitations of a consumer model of patient or community involvement in health services, and the need for a more radical citizenship approach to involving the public in decisions affecting their health. However, there has been little sign of a movement of power away from professionals to their patients or clients, and little evidence of any decline in the 'medical model' as the epistemological underpinning of health care planning and delivery (Suschnigg, 2001).

In the UK the Labour government, elected in 1997, abandoned

markets and toned down the language of consumerism. However, in their first term of office the government tied itself to the previous Conservative government's spending plans in an attempt to display the kind fiscal prudence which would please business and the middle-class vote. As a consequence the Labour government spent most of its first term battling against a growing sense of crisis and disappointment, created by the rising tide of waiting lists, waiting times, and high profile cases of medical malpractice. Increasing patient, citizen and community involvement, hinted at in a series of documents, never had the opportunity to reach the top of the agenda. Nonetheless, health service analysts argue that many of the changes now taking place will 'bring patients and citizens into decision-making at every level of service' (Lewis and Gillam, 2001: 113). Potentially more significant to healthy citizenship than greater patient involvement in health services is the growing attention given to the determinants of health, and the need for partnership between agencies and communities in fighting the root causes of ill health in the populations of which they are a part.

What implications do these developments have for citizenship and health? In some ways what we have seen is a backlash against professional society, and a critique of the assumption that the social provision embodied by the welfare state is the last word on citizenship. Indeed, arguments for a less professionally dominated health care system, and the demand for greater lay (consumer, community or citizen) representation on primary care boards or local regeneration partnerships, may signal a rediscovery of the political element in Marshall's theory of citizenship within the late-modern welfare state. Moreover, the renewed emphasis on the social determinants of health and the implications of developments in pharmaco-genetics take the issue of citizenship and health beyond simple consumer demands for better quality health services back to fundamental and enduring questions about civil and political rights.

Whether or not new forms of 'civic republicanism' (Marquand, 1997) or 'democratic experimentalism' (Unger, 1998) will lead to the kind of citizen involvement seen in the pre-NHS days of the Tredegar Medical Aid Society in South Wales, for example, where 1,500 people would turn out for the Annual General Meeting, and whether this is what modern citizenship is about, is something that will fire continuing debate in health policy and medical sociology.

See also: *consumerism, managerialism,* and *the new public health.*

REFERENCES

Calnan, M. and Gabe, J. (2001) 'From consumerism to partnership? Britain's National Health Service at the turn of the century', *International Journal of Health Services*, 31 (1): 119–31.

Lewis, R. and Gillam, S. (2001) 'The National Health Service Plan: further reform of British health care', *International Journal of Health Services*, 31 (1): 111–18.

Marquand, D. (1997) *The New Reckoning: Capitalism, States and Citizens*. Cambridge: Polity Press.

Marshall, T.H. (1950) *Citizenship and Social Class and Other Essays*. Cambridge: Cambridge University Press.

Suschnigg, C. (2001) 'Reforming Ontario's primary health care system: one step forward, two steps back?' *International Journal of Health Services*, 31 (1): 91–103.

Unger, R.M. (1998) *Democracy Realized: The Progressive Alternative*. London: Verso.

Walby, S. (1994) 'Is citizenship gendered?' *Sociology*, 28 (2): 379–95.

GW

evaluation

> *Definition:* **Evaluation refers to the independent assessment of the extent to which a service achieves its goals.**

Developed countries devote very large and growing proportions of their total wealth to health care. In the United States nearly 15 per cent of gross domestic product is spent on health care. It is not surprising that the question should be asked as to whether the enormous levels of societal resources dedicated to health care are worthwhile. The most obvious but deceptively simple question is whether such expenditures contribute to health. The task of evaluation involves assessing, in a structured and rigorous way, whether health care resources and activities achieve their intended goals in terms of improving health. Evaluation is a generic term that can equally be applied to assess the value of any area of modern society such as education, welfare benefits, transport or penal systems. However, the high costs and complexities of modern health care have made evaluation a particularly important feature of developed countries' health care systems.

The need to evaluate health care can be demonstrated at an aggregate or system level or at a more micro-level of individual therapies and

247

interventions. At a system level, it has always proved difficult to identify positive relationships between the amounts of resources that different countries devote to health care and the health status they enjoy. This is partly due to methodological limitations in available evidence. Mortality is frequently used as the sole indicator of health available to assess the health of different countries when it is clear that health care is just as concerned with sickness, disability and health-related quality of life; constructs that are far more difficult to measure. However, the lack of relationship between countries' expenditures on health and their levels of achieved health also provides powerful evidence for the need to evaluate what is achieved by modern health services.

At a micro-level the need to evaluate specific health care interventions is now universally accepted. In an enormously influential book, *Effectiveness and Efficiency*, the epidemiologist Archie Cochrane argued that there was very little evidence available to assess the value of all the medical, surgical and other interventions provided by the UK National Health Service (Cochrane, 1972). Very few of the services provided had ever been properly evaluated. Since that time the need for robust evidence of whether treatments and services are effective has been increasingly accepted. The National Institute for Clinical Excellence (NICE) in the UK and equivalent bodies in other countries have a central role in providing authoritative evidence regarding effectiveness of interventions; evidence that is intended to inform and influence whether interventions are publicly paid for. Considerable controversy has been aroused by decisions not to recommend public funding of interventions for which evaluative research provides insufficient evidence of effectiveness.

A valuable framework for the evaluation of health services was developed by Avedis Donabedian (1966). He argued that a fundamental distinction needs to be made between structure, process and outcome when evaluating health services. An evaluation of the structures of a health service would focus upon the adequacy of facilities, equipment, staffing volume and qualifications, funding and organization of a health care system. A simple example might involve examining the number of general practitioners available per capita throughout a health care system or between health care systems. Such evidence might help to assess geographical equity in availability of doctors between different parts of a country. However, it would ultimately not be possible to determine what the optimal number of doctors should be without asking questions about what services general practitioners provide. This leads to Donabedian's second type of evaluation: examination of process. Processes are the activities in terms of history taking, examination, use of diagnostic facilities, treatments, follow-up and coordination of care performed within the structures of services.

The final dimension of Donabedian's framework for evaluation is the most important; outcomes are the effects in terms of health gain that result from the structures and processes of health services. Because of the relative ease with which it can be assessed, outcomes of health care are often assessed, as noted, in terms of mortality. However, outcomes more appropriate to the actual role performed by modern health services need to include assessment of the impact of services upon pain, disability, health-related quality of life, reassurance and patients' ability to cope with health problems; all outcomes that are more complex to measure. The assessment of outcomes is complex because of the need to take account of the varying levels of need with which the health service is confronted. For example, hospitals in more deprived areas may face levels of sickness and background disadvantage in the patients that they treat that make it harder to achieve outcomes equivalent to hospitals in more affluent areas.

The method that has proved most reliable in evaluating health care interventions is the randomized controlled trial. With their informed consent to participate, patients are randomly allocated by investigators to receive either the novel treatment under investigation or either a placebo or the best available alternative treatment. The purpose of randomization is to minimize the possible influence on outcomes of factors other than the treatments under study. Randomization makes it very likely that such factors are equally present in the groups of patients receiving alternative treatments. One of the commonest of such effects is that severity of illness prior to treatment differs between patient groups.

The randomized controlled trial has proved to be the most successful method of evaluation in relation to drugs. A particularly valuable feature of many drug trials is that both patient and doctor are unaware of which treatment the patient is receiving. This so-called 'double-blind' trial substantially reduces risks of biased results. However, many of the interventions in modern health services that need to be evaluated cannot be subject to the double-blind trial. It may be desirable to evaluate the advantages of the nurse prescribing drugs instead of the general practitioner, compare hospital- with home-based rehabilitation for recovery from surgery, or compare self-help groups with health professionals in their ability to provide counselling, support and advice. In these and in a myriad of other situations in which evaluative research is required to inform the improvement of services, the randomized controlled trial cannot be truly double-blind. More importantly, the

249

options being compared are not like drugs. Drugs are now delivered in formats that completely standardize the active ingredient for each dose. The 'active ingredient' that makes a nurse practitioner, hospital, at-home scheme or self-help group effective in improving health outcomes may be quite complex and may vary enormously from one setting to another. For this reason, evaluative research on almost all other interventions than drugs is more challenging in that standard study designs such as randomized controlled trials need to be supplemented by other methods such as qualitative research that can unravel how or why novel interventions improve outcomes (Campbell et al., 2000). Only when 'the active ingredients' (for example, specific skills or ways of organizing services) of a new way of providing care are uncovered by more detailed ethnographic study is it possible to reproduce such effects outside the original evaluative study. The experimental approach to the evaluation of behavioural, social and population-based ways to improving health has been neglected until recently by sociology but is a potentially powerful approach (Oakley, 1998).

The social sciences have a central role in the evaluation of health services. First, social survey methods are increasingly important as patients are increasingly made the judge of outcomes through responses to questionnaires about pain, disability and other aspects of health status. Second, the social acceptability of modern health care requires social scientific methods to assess how health care is valued, for example, through measures of patient satisfaction (Coulter and Fitzpatrick, 2000). Social acceptability also needs to address unintended or unexpected consequences of health services such as medicalization – inappropriate use of medical language and resources to solve social problems.

A third role for the social sciences is to examine costs in relation to effectiveness of health care interventions. A basic principle of health economics is to consider whether alternative forms of service differ in terms of the efficiency with which they use economic resources to achieve improved health outcomes. Costs here do not just refer to direct monetary costs of healthcare. An essential aspect of the evaluation of the cost-effectiveness of health care involves assessment of indirect or hidden costs, for example the impact on carers, the family and community of alternative ways of providing health care. A community-based rehabilitation programme may appear to produce outcomes more cheaply than a hospital-based service but a full assessment of cost-effectiveness would need to consider if this was achieved at the expense of a major additional burden upon carers and family.

A fourth role for the social scientist arises from a key feature of any kind of evaluation research. Evaluation must first of all identify the goals of a service or intervention and then use its various methods to establish whether such goals are achieved. As Illsley argues (1980: 112), health provides an interesting challenge to the sociologist because so often the goals of health services are not clearly articulated and it may require sociological inquiry to raise fundamental questions of purpose.

A final role for the social scientist in the context of evaluation is to step back from the details of methodology and to consider evaluation as itself a social force shaping the direction of health care (Harrison, 1998). Advocates of evaluation and of related emphases in health care such as 'evidence-based medicine' (the need for health care to be based on the highest quality evidence of effectiveness) may be considered as a force challenging the traditional approach to health care that has always emphasized the importance of the autonomy and independence of the professional to judge what is best for each patient. Critics of 'evidence-based medicine' see a more sinister role of this movement being to reduce professional judgement to rules, protocols and guidelines but also ultimately to subject professional autonomy to greater external, managerial control, whether to improve the profitability of medicine as a business or to control its claims on the resources of the welfare state. The defence against such arguments is that patients, managers and health professionals all benefit from improved evidence of the effectiveness of health care interventions. Such evidence is at worst neutral in its significance for the power of these different partners in health care, and at best can increase the understanding and control over the health of patients as it becomes more widely available.

See also: *managerialism, the new public health* and *quality of life.*

REFERENCES

Campbell, M., Fitzpatrick, R., Haines, A., Kinmonth, A., Sandercock, P., Spiegelhalter, D. and Tyrer, P. (2000) 'Framework for design and evaluation of complex interventions to improve health', *British Medical Journal*, 321: 694–6.

Cochrane, A. (1972) *Effectiveness and Efficiency: Random Reflections on the Health Service.* London: Nuffield Provincial Hospitals Trust.

Coulter, A. and Fitzpatrick, R. (2000) 'The patient's perspective regarding appropriate health care', in G. Albrecht, R. Fitzpatrick and S. Scrimshaw (eds), *The Handbook of Social Studies in Health and Medicine.* London: Sage, pp. 454–64.

Donabedian, A. (1966) 'Evaluating the quality of medical care', *Milbank Memorial Fund Quarterly*, 44: 169–79.

Harrison, S. (1998) 'The politics of evidence-based medicine in the United Kingdom', *Policy and Politics*, 26: 15–31.

Illsley, R. (1980) *Professional or Public Health?* London: Nuffield Provincial Hospitals Trust.

Oakley, A. (1998) 'Experimentation and social interventions: a forgotten but important history', *British Medical Journal*, 317: 1239–42.

RF

malpractice

> *Definition:* **Malpractice refers to improper treatment or culpable neglect of a patient by a health service professional.**

Malpractice is often discussed in the context of regulating the behaviour of doctors and, in particular, the ways in which doctors are held accountable for their mistakes or errors. Various types of regulatory control have been introduced. These range from self-regulation through the General Medical Council (which is responsible for adjudicating on allegations of professional misconduct and revalidating doctors' licence to practise) and medical audit (continuous peer review of practice) to regulation as a result of individual patients making complaints or seeking legal redress through the courts. The focus here will be on the last form of regulation – malpractice litigation.

Malpractice litigation is based on common law, particularly torts of negligence. The term 'tort' is derived from Norman French and means a wrong or wrongdoing (Dingwall, 1994). Tort law is based on the view that people owe a duty of care to others and should avoid harming or injuring those they come into contact with. In the case of medicine, this means that a doctor has caused harm to a patient as a result of failing to act in accordance with their profession's customary standards. In bringing a case of malpractice a plaintiff needs to prove that there was negligence and that this negligence caused or contributed to damage or injury (Annandale, 1989).

Medical negligence claims have grown considerably in Britain in recent years. There was a sharp increase in claims in the 1980s, with a fivefold increase in frequency and a threefold increase in severity between 1980 and 1987 (Dingwall, 1994). The number of claims increased further in the 1990s with a parallel increase in the cost of awards. In 1990–91 the cost of medical negligence awards was estimated to be £60 million. By 1994–95 it had increased to £155 million. The latest figures show that provisions to meet the cost of medical negligence claims have doubled from £1.3 billion in 1996–97 to £2.6 billion in 1999–2000 (National Audit Office, 2001).

Most negligence claims are for small sums of up to £5,000, with amounts in excess of £150,000 being claimed by only 4.5 per cent of plaintiffs (Allsop and Mulcahy, 1996). Hospital specialties most likely to be claimed against are Obstetrics and Gynaecology, Orthopaedics and Accident and Emergency. Doctors working in these specialties tend to be sued for negligence as a result of misdiagnosis, often leading to a delay in treatment or inappropriate treatment. The other main cause of negligence relates to technical or surgical mistakes made before, during or after an operation (National Audit Office, 2001). Doctors working in Obstetrics and Gynaecology are particularly prone to large claims because damage at birth (for example, brain damage) carries with it lifetime costs in terms of health care. A single claim in this area can now run into millions of pounds.

In the past, hospital doctors in Britain subscribed to a medical defence organization (MDO) to cover possible liability for damages. As membership fees escalated in the 1980s Health Authorities found themselves subsidising their staff. The situation was compounded when MDOs announced that they intended to charge differential subscription rates, with high-risk specialities having to pay most. In 1990, the British government responded by requiring Health Authorities and Trusts to meet the full cost of negligence actions instead of contributing to the cost of MDO subscriptions. As a result, Trust managers acquired the financial incentive to handle negligence clams in the most cost-efficient way, encouraging the settlement of claims to minimize the cost, even when the doctors involved denied negligence and wanted to defend themselves (Allsop and Mulcahy, 1996). For many of these doctors such a managerialist approach was considered to represent an infringement of clinical autonomy. Since 1995 the NHS Litigation Authority has taken over an increasing number of claims against Trusts. Trusts, including Primary Care Trusts, have been encouraged to join the Clinical Negligence Scheme for Trusts, administered by the NHS Litigation Authority. Trusts pay the equivalent of premiums to be members of the scheme and receive assistance with the cost of cases in return. Premiums are related to Trusts' performance against a set of risk management standards.

It has been suggested that the medical profession has responded to this state of affairs by being more defensive in their medical practice. This defensive medicine has involved hospital doctors ordering treatments, tests and procedures (or on occasion withholding them) primarily to protect themselves from criticism or potential litigation. An often quoted example is the rise in the rates of caesarean section, which are said to be driven by the fear of litigation (Allsop and Mulcahy, 1996). Fears about being sued are also said to have encouraged GPs to make practise changes such as deciding not to treat certain conditions, increasing diagnostic testing, engaging in more detailed note taking and giving patients more detailed explanations (Summerton, 1995). In the United States there is also evidence of physicians attempting to recognize 'suit-prone' patients in the consultation, in order to reduce the likelihood of litigation. Patients who appear to be 'dependent', 'demanding', 'self-styled experts' or 'subservient' are all seen as potentially malpractice-prone. As Annandale (1989) notes, there is an inconsistency in such perceptions. Patients who are deferential and those who are consumerist and want to take responsibility for decisions about their health seem to be perceived as equally problematic. In her view, this seeming ambivalence among physicians actually reveals a reluctance to accept a reduction in authority, standing and control. Consequently, exhortations for doctors to provide more information and share decisions with patients in order to minimize the threat of litigation may fall on deaf ears.

The rapid increase in medical negligence claims in recent decades has led many commentators to talk about a medical litigation 'crisis'. Reference is regularly made to the United States where the total cost of malpractice claims has risen faster than inflation. Doctors in Britain (and the United States) tend to blame the growth of consumerism for encouraging patients to complain and take legal action if they feel their rights and expectations have not been met. Reference is also made to the greed of lawyers who have benefited financially from the rapid increase in claims. Such lawyers are said to have sought out patients and touted for business. Certainly there is evidence of lawyers in Britain advertising in local newspapers for prospective litigants to seek their advice to participate in class actions, for example, over the prescribing of benzodiazepine tranquillizers. In the USA physicians also criticize lawyers for their ignorance of medicine and the application of a confrontational, argumentative approach to solve what they perceive as medical disputes (Hupert et al., 1996)

In so far as there is a crisis, it is necessary to ask 'crisis for whom'? For doctors the crisis is one of increasing negligence claims, proactive lawyers and assertive patients. For patients, on the other hand, the crisis may be one of loss of confidence in the medical profession and a lack of sufficient resources to take negligent doctors to court (Allsop and Mulcahy, 1996). Certainly there is evidence that when patients (and their relatives) do take legal action, intense emotions are aroused that continue to be felt long after the original injury. For these patients the decision to seek legal redress is determined not just by the original injury but also by a desire to hold doctors to account and to make sure that lessons are learnt so that others do not experience similar incidents in future (Vincent et al., 1994).

Some commentators have nonetheless questioned the extent to which increased medical negligence represents a crisis. Dingwall, writing in 1994, has argued that we should not take the claims of doctors that they are facing a crisis at face value. Instead he suggests that the increase in malpractice claims should be seen as part of a wider cultural shift, which is affecting the professions in general, not just medicine. Accountants, architects, engineers and veterinary surgeons have all seen their liability claims increase in frequency and severity in recent times. The medical profession's response is therefore best seen as a moral panic and a symbolic expression of discontent with wider social and cultural changes that are affecting all professions.

Regardless of whether other professions are facing increased litigation, it can nonetheless be argued that the increase in medical negligence claims does represent a challenge to medical authority that has real consequences for the doctor–patient relationship. While malpractice as a regulatory tool may empower some patients and lead some doctors to make more considered decisions, it may also have the unintended consequence of encouraging doctors to undertake unnecessary tests and of undermining the trust necessary for the shared decision-making and patient partnership advocated by policy-makers. Despite this, medical negligence action does have a role as a regulatory tool in that it encourages at least some public discussion of standards. Any changes to the tort system, such as no-fault compensation (where the emphasis is on proof of causation rather than proof of fault), will need to demonstrate that they make doctors more accountable as well as being less costly (in terms of legal fees) and providing quicker redress.

See also: *consumerism* and *decline of medical autonomy.*

REFERENCES

Allsop, J. and Mulcahy, L. (1996) *Regulating Medical Work.* Buckingham: Open University Press.

Annandale, E. (1989) 'The malpractice crisis and the doctor–patient relationship', *Sociology of Health and Illness,* 11 (1): 1–23.

Dingwall, R. (1994) 'Litigation and the threat to medicine', in J. Gabe, D. Kelleher and G. Williams (eds), *Challenging Medicine*. London: Routledge, pp. 46–64.

Hupert, N., Lawthers, A.G., Brennan, T.A. and Peterson, L.M. (1996) 'Processing the tort deterrent signal: a qualitative study', *Social Science and Medicine*, 43 (1): 1–11.

National Audit Office (2001) *Handling Clinical Negligence Claims in England*. London: The Stationery Office.

Summerton, N. (1995) 'Positive and negative factors in defensive medicine: a questionnaire study of general practitioners', *British Medical Journal*, 310: 27–9.

Vincent, C., Young, M. and Phillips, A. (1994) 'Why do people sue doctors? A study of patients and relatives taking legal action', *The Lancet*, 343: 1609–13.

JGA